STUDIES IN VICTORIAN LIFE AND LITERATURE

Toward a Working-Class Canon

Literary Criticism in British Working-Class Periodicals, 1816–1858

Paul Thomas Murphy

Ohio State University Press
Columbus

Chapter 3 appeared in different form as "'Imagination Flaps Its Sportive Wings':
Views of Fiction in British Working-Class Periodicals, 1816–1858," *Victorian Studies* 32 (1988–89): 340–64. Reprinted by permission of the Trustees of Indiana
University.

Library of Congress Cataloging-in-Publication Data

Murphy, Paul Thomas, 1957–
    Toward a working-class canon : literary criticism in British
    working-class periodicals, 1816–1858 / Paul Thomas Murphy.
        p.   cm. — (Studies in Victorian life and literature)
    Includes bibliographical references (p.) and index.
    ISBN 0–8142–0654–9
    1. English literature—19th century—History and criticism—
Theory, etc.   2. Working class—Great Britain—Books and reading—
History—19th century.   3. Working class writings, English—History
and criticism.   4. Criticism—Great Britain—History—19th century.
5. Canon (Literature)   I. Title.   II. Series.
PR451.M87   1994
820.9'008—dc20   94-25458
                                                                                      CIP
Text design by Victoria Althoff.
Jacket design by Gore Design.
Type set in Baskerville.
Printed by McNaughton & Gunn, Inc. Saline, Michigan.
The paper in this book meets the guidelines for permanence and durability of
the Committee on Production Guidelines for Book Longevity of the Council on
Library Resources.

9 8 7 6 5 4 3 2 1

For

Thomas Dominic Murphy

and

Miranda Elizabeth Murphy

Contents

Acknowledgments

I am extremely grateful for the help of many librarians, in both the United States and the United Kingdom, for their efforts in digging up stacks of working-class periodicals, often at short notice. I would particularly like to thank the staffs of the British Library, the British Newspaper Library at Colindale, the Public Record Office, London, the Bodleian and Nuffield College Libraries at Oxford, the Mitchell Library in Glasgow, the National Library of Scotland, the Edinburgh Public Library, the Boston College Library, the Boston Public Library, and the Harvard University Library. Most of my research I conducted at the Norlin Library at the University of Colorado, Boulder, an undertaking not as insane as it might at first sound, thanks in large part to the extremely efficient staffs of the microforms department and the interlibrary loan service.

I have been extremely fortunate in having strong advice and superb readers at every stage of this project. Thanks are due to David Simpson and John Graham, who offered a number of valuable suggestions in the beginning. Thanks, too, to Keith Thomas, Kelley Hurley, Michael Preston, and Lee Chambers-Schiller, all of whom read early drafts. Patrick Brantlinger, then editor of *Victorian Studies*, read and commented on the fiction chapter, which appeared in modified form in that periodical. Richard Altick helped with that chapter as well, and was a reader of the full draft for the Ohio State University Press, along with R. K. Webb. I can't thank both of them enough for their suggestions. My wife, Victoria Tuttle, put up with me heroically, proofread this work tirelessly, and made many good suggestions. Some of these I may have crankily resisted, then accepted—but she was right each time, and I believe this work is far better than it would have been without her help.

I'm especially grateful for the moral and intellectual support of James Kincaid, who was helpful in reading and advising from the earliest stages of this project until its end.

I wish to thank as well family, friends, and colleagues, whose kindnesses are far too many to list. I do particularly want to thank Stephen Button and Linda Gough, who put me up for the weeks I was researching in London, and who provided me with therapeutic diversion from that research. Thank you all.

Introduction

IN 1828 politician Henry Brougham addressed the House of Commons on the rising tide of working-class literacy: "There have been periods when the country heard with dismay that the soldier is abroad. That is not the case now. Let the soldier be ever so much abroad, in the present age he can do nothing. There is another person abroad. . . . The schoolmaster is abroad, and I trust to the schoolmaster armed with his primer more than I do to the soldier in full military array for upholding and extending the liberties of their country."[1] By comparing educators with soldiers, Brougham showed himself strongly aware that a growing group of working-class readers entailed a growing working-class power, power that might be controlled by controlling what that class read. To that end, Brougham helped found the Society for the Diffusion of Useful Knowledge (SDUK) in 1826. The purpose of that organization was to provide inexpensive knowledge to the working class. Its best-known product was the *Penny Magazine,* which on the first page of its first number made clear that its attempt to enlighten the working class was in no way an attempt to empower them politically: the editors promised to steer absolutely clear of "the violence of party discussion" (31 March 1832: 1).

But Brougham and his colleagues were far from alone in offering the working class inexpensive knowledge. Between 1816, when William Cobbett lowered the price of his *Political Register* from 1s. ½d. to 2d. (a difference of 10½d.), and 1858, when the last of the Chartist periodicals with a mass readership, *People's Paper,* stopped publishing, hundreds of periodicals written both by and for the working class existed to voice what the SDUK would not: exclusively and self-consciously working-class views of politics, culture, and religion. If there was to be a schoolmaster abroad, working-class editors and writers were intent upon making that schoolmaster one of the working class, speaking working-class values.

1

Just as E. P. Thompson has shown in *The Making of the English Working Class* that the working class had much to do with creating their own political values, I argue in this study that the working class had much to do with the making of their own *literary* values, values clearly distinct from those of other classes.[2] While several studies have focused upon works of literature written by or for the working class, deriving literary values implicit in the works themselves,[3] no study has focused upon the explicitly stated literary values found in the hundreds of periodicals written by and for the working class. In this study I look at those periodicals and discuss the several ways in which the working class created its own literary aesthetic.

Working-class writers and editors actively sought to define for themselves the spiritual and political role literature played for an emerging working class. It would be foolish to argue that in the first half of the nineteenth century there was a uniform working-class "line" on literature. Instead, throughout the period working-class journalists conducted a lively and continuing debate about literature. Their disagreements, as well as their agreements, show a thriving and evolving aesthetic. Central to that debate was the question of whether literature should only serve political ends or have a function apart from the strictly political. Journalists early in the period generally distrusted the apolitical in literature; those writing later generally agreed that literature served the working class both aesthetically and politically.

Even the later journalists, however, never lost sight of the fact that in criticizing and promoting any work as "literature" they were further establishing an ideology for their class. I define "ideology" in this sense as Terry Eagleton does in *Literary Theory: An Introduction:* "the ways in which what we say and believe connects with the power-structure and power-relations of the society we live in" (14). Every act of evaluating what was and was not literature for their audience was an act of defining and promoting a working-class value system. In that sense, every work they criticized was political, and every evaluation was in effect an attempt to empower their class. Working-class views did not evolve from an appreciation of the political to an appreciation of the nonpolitical. These journalists never valued literature for the sake of beauty alone. Rather, their views generally broadened from an appreciation of overtly political works of writers such as Thomas Paine to a recognition that writers such as Alfred

Tennyson could also promote values important to the working class as a whole. This difference—between valuing overtly political literature and seeing the political implicit in all literature—is, I believe, an important shift in awareness, one that lies at the heart of this study.

Working-class periodicals provided hundreds, even thousands, of working-class writers with what was often their only access to an audience, and in doing so, helped show the working class that its own written expression not only could be literature as valuable as any other but could, in its own distinctive way, add to a working-class canon of "great" literature.

At the same time, editors and reviewers were very concerned with literary works of other classes and ages. For want of a better term, I refer in this study to such works and writers as "established"—that is, having a strong and reasonably steady reputation among other classes, particularly among the middle class—or, to put it another way, writers and works considered "canonical" by the middle class. I do not mean to imply by that term that established writers were in some way better, or more universally valuable, than unestablished writers (a group, of course, that includes most of the working-class writers of the day). Nor do I mean to imply that established works were necessarily incorporated into a working-class canon simply because they held a secure place in the middle-class pantheon. Quite the opposite. Most working-class journalists rarely accepted without question the established, traditional readings of these writers. Nor did they reject them out of hand. Rather, through a careful selection of certain writers and works and by offering new readings of both the lives and works of established writers, they made these writers serve working-class ends and speak working-class values. This study is, for the most part, a record of working-class journalists disestablishing and recanonizing established writers, or sanctioning new, unestablished writers, to fit the values of their own class. Thus, for example, to some Milton's republicanism reflected their own; Shakespeare became "one of the People"; and the Chartist poet Ernest Jones earned a secure place in a new, working-class canon.[4]

My analysis employs working-class periodicals in a number of ways. Obviously, I have paid close attention to essays and statements about specific literary genres—essays and statements that appear with surprising frequency even in what might at first seem exclusively political periodicals. I am also concerned with the literary and stylistic values adopted by the writers and editors of these periodicals and with those figures they saw as their models, as well as those they rejected. Besides these factors, I take into account the writers, established and unestablished, working-class and otherwise, that the editors of working-class periodicals chose to publish. Also, I have noted the reviews, notices, and even brief mentions of writers and works—again, both working-class and otherwise. These reviews and notices offer serious appraisals of now-forgotten writers and novel, important, and (to most modern readers) fresh views of well-known writers.

This work is not in itself a study of working-class literature but is instead a study of the perceptions of literature by working-class writers and editors. When I look at specific poems, stories, or essays in these periodicals, therefore, I am not as concerned with how the modern reader might evaluate them as literature as I am with how the working-class thinkers of the time criticized them, and, in turn, what they took literature to be.

Also, this is not in itself a study of the politics or political values of the working class or of working-class periodicals, which E. P. Thompson and others have thoroughly investigated. I do not ignore those values, however; I cannot. They are crucial to this study when they are inseparable from literary values; and, in the broadest sense, the two are always linked.

Neither is this primarily a study of the publishers, printers, editors, and writers of working-class periodicals.[5] Most of the successful working-class periodicals, however, owed much of their success to the individual energy, philosophy, or even eccentricities of their conductors. As I said, the views of those involved with working-class periodicals are far from uniform; in the ongoing debate in those periodicals over the forms and functions of literature, many and various voices offer much insight into collective views.

Finally, although the periodicals I look at constantly tested the sedition, blasphemy, and tax laws of the time, this study is not about the struggle for freedom of the press, except when that issue clearly involves literary questions.

The five chapters that follow divide roughly into two sections. Chapters 1 and 2 are contextual; chapters 3, 4, and 5 are generic.

In chapter 1 I provide a sense of working-class literacy. Although I do give some numbers and percentages, I go on to point out the many limitations to such a quantitative evaluation of literacy. I then look at working-class autobiographies to give a sense of how early reading experiences shaped working-class journalism. Further, in that chapter I discuss exactly what a working-class periodical is, a task that is not as simple as it may first seem, since there are several important distinctions between working-class periodicals and other "cheap" periodicals. I also sort periodicals that attempt to include all classes in their audience from those that are exclusively aimed at the working class. Finally, I deal with the problem of the class standing of editors, publishers, and writers of the periodicals; I argue that while in many (but not most) cases such men and women were not, for political or economic reasons, typical of the working class, they still generally strove to represent the views of that class.

In chapter 2 I provide a brief history of the working-class press between 1816 and 1858, paying careful attention to the literary aspects of these periodicals and to the evolving sense of a working-class canon on the part of the journalists. After showing the influence of Thomas Paine on these writers and editors, I look at the evolution of a working-class sense of literature through three readily distinguishable subperiods: 1816–29 (the years of the earliest working-class journalists), 1830–36 (the years of the "War of the Unstamped"), and 1837–58 (the years of the Chartist press).

Chapter 3 focuses on views of fiction in working-class periodicals, views that progressed and broadened through time. In the earlier periodicals editors and writers generally distrusted the genre as a whole, believing simply that what was fiction was not truth. This suspicion can be seen most clearly in working-class views of Sir Walter Scott and in the almost complete absence of fiction in early working-class periodicals. In time, however, working-class journalists accepted fiction as a valuable and positive genre for their class. They began to review certain works of fiction favorably, and later working-class periodicals even began to publish fiction themselves.

Chapter 4 concerns views of poetry in working-class periodicals. Unlike fiction, poems—lyric, dramatic, and even epic—were integral to working-class periodicals from the start. Paradoxically, however, many editors attacked poetry as a genre while publishing poems. Much of this conflict stems from the early view that poetry need not be beautiful but had better be explicitly political. Gradually, however, those involved with working-class periodicals generally accepted the view that poetry could serve their class both politically and aesthetically—or, rather, they politicized the aesthetic.

Finally, in chapter 5, I look at working-class views of the drama and at the relative lack of an evolution of views toward performance drama (as opposed to closet drama, written primarily for reading). I investigate the reasons why working-class journalists rarely felt that staged drama could serve the working class in the ways that fiction or poetry could. I then attempt to demonstrate that despite this pessimism toward the stage, the working class of the time had an obvious and deep thirst for the dramatic in their lives, and that in many ways the working-class press sought to provide for that thirst.

1

Schoolmasters Abroad

The Working-Class Press, 1816–1858

Working-Class Literacy and the Working-Class Press

WORKING-CLASS LITERACY in the first half of the nineteenth century was high. Most scholars of nineteenth-century British working-class literacy, basing their assessments upon evidence found in court records, marriage registers, regional and occupational surveys, and a number of other sources, place the figure at somewhere between two-thirds to three-quarters of the laboring population of Great Britain during this period.[1]

These figures cannot tell us much at all about a working-class audience for working-class periodicals or much about specific individuals or groups within that audience, any more than a knowledge of middle-class literacy can tell us about the readership of the *Westminster Review*. Estimates about a national rate of working-class literacy cannot take into account the enormous and ever-changing regional, occupational, and gender-based variations in literacy among this class at this time or among socioeconomic substrata within the class, variations largely attributable to widely differing social pressures and widely differing educational institutions and opportunities. Such estimates tell us nothing, to take only one example, about the differences between Scottish and English working-class literacy. Scotland, which unlike England had a national system of education at this time, apparently had an even higher rate of literacy than did England or Wales.[2]

Moreover, bare numbers give us no sense of the *quality* of working-class literacy; in many modern and nineteenth-century studies "literacy" is defined in its broadest sense—as the ability to read at any level at all. The most commonly cited evidence of literacy, for example—signatures in marriage registers—testifies at best to every form of literacy from the most rudimentary upward. Many readers considered literate in this sense cannot be considered "periodical literate," as it were; many would find reading and comprehending Cobbett's *Political Register* or *Northern Star* impossible.

Nor, of course, can conventional literacy rates offer any indication about working-class tastes. Certainly there were many readers capable of reading working-class periodicals who did not do so. Periodicals written by and for the working class competed, often unsuccessfully, with other periodicals, as well as with other media and other forms of entertainment, for the attention and generally limited free time of working-class readers.

What these sweeping literacy rates do show, and show impressively, is that the British working class was at this time what R. K. Webb calls a "*potential* reading public" (*British Working-Class Reader* 23).[3] Simply put, most members of the working class who wanted to read working-class periodicals did so. While education was not yet systematized or universally available in England and Wales, most of the working class had the opportunity to attend dame and other day schools, Sunday schools, mechanics' institutes, and other adult schools.[4] Also, many could learn basic reading skills at home, from a parent, child, or sibling. Through such opportunities most men and women of this class could and, as the statistics show, most *did* garner the basics of reading. But the activity of reading involved physical and economic costs, costs that must have seemed prohibitive to many. In many cases working women, men, and children did not see the point in spending their few free hours in the self-improving industry of reading. Nor could many parents afford the luxury of allowing their children time to study instead of work. Moreover, the activity of reading was often prohibitively expensive, owing to the high cost of some reading materials and of light by which to read them (Altick 93). Acquiring basic reading skills, as well as using them to read the Bible, *Robinson Crusoe*, or the *Poor Man's Guardian*, was at least as much a matter of sheer willpower as one of opportunity.

Olivia Smith, in describing the impact of that early working-class best-seller, Thomas Paine's *Rights of Man*, raises a point that can be applied equally to working-class periodicals in general. Noting the huge sales of that work, Smith writes: "The intriguing question behind such figures is the unknown numbers of those who began to read or write specifically because of the *Rights of Man* or because of the continuing political debate. There is sufficient evidence to demonstrate that such a phenomenon occurred" (58). In other words, insofar as Paine's work is concerned, interest preceded literacy. Similarly, many of later generations were most likely compelled by commentary on events by William Cobbett, Richard Carlile, John Doherty, Henry Hetherington, Ernest Jones, and others—the Paines of their day—to read and write themselves.

Working-class publishers and others were well aware of a working-class mass market that was always potential and at times actual. In order to break into that market, publishers of any class had to produce a product the value of which in some way overrode the high costs of working-class reading. Many targeted this market with their publications during this period, and several reached it. That there was, on occasion, an actual working-class mass market for reading matter is demonstrated in the huge sales of such works as James Catnach's often lurid chapbooks, ballads, and broadsides, some of which had sales of over half a million copies (Altick 287, 382). That there was, further, a working-class market clearly interested in self-improvement and factual knowledge is demonstrated by the large sales of two "useful knowledge" periodicals, *Penny Magazine* and *Chambers' Edinburgh Journal*, which in 1832 achieved circulations of at the very least 100,000 and 50,000, respectively (Altick 393). That there had been, and was still, a working-class market for literature devoted to working-class interests is demonstrated by the huge sales of the second part of Paine's *Rights of Man* between 1792 and 1793, variously estimated at between 50,000 and 200,000 copies, and the first twopenny issue of Cobbett's *Political Register*, "Address to the Journeymen and Labourers," which sold around 200,000 copies in 1816 (Altick 70–71, 325, 381; E. P. Thompson, *Making* 117).[5]

The above circulation figures are some of the largest of the period (and, in the case of *Rights of Man*, before this period). Such mass sales bear no discernible connection with the documented rise in the rate of literacy from 1820 on, a rise that continued throughout the century and culminated in something approaching national literacy.[6] The periodic appearances and disappearances of a working-class mass market did not reflect this gradual rise at all but indicated instead issues and events—political, criminal, and otherwise—that caught the interest of the working class.

Similarly, overall readership of working-class periodicals did not rise gradually between 1816 and 1858. Rather, it rose or declined in close correspondence with fluctuations in working-class political activity. It is no coincidence that there were three peak periods for the circulation of working-class periodicals: 1816–29, the years of postwar depression, of Castlereagh and Sidmouth, Jeremiah Brandreth and the Cato Street Conspiracy; Henry "Orator" Hunt and the Peterloo massacre; 1830–36, the years of the First Reform Bill, factory agitation, the "War of the Unstamped," and the new poor laws; and 1838–48, the years when Chartism attracted its greatest following. Certainly, working-class periodicals were published continually from 1816 on, but those published outside the peak years generally targeted a smaller audience. Events, not reading ability, were responsible for the varying size of the audience for working-class periodicals. It may be true that the sharp decline in circulation of the working-class press in the 1820s was due in large part to the Six Acts of 1819, which increased the prices of all the major working-class newspapers to amounts prohibitive to many readers, but it is equally true that a relatively calm political climate in the 1820s was the main reason why concerted working-class opposition to the newspaper tax did not flare up until the 1830s. And while the working-class newspaper with by far the largest circulation of the late 1830s and 1840s, the *Northern Star*, ran from 1837 until 1852, its circulation was much greater between 1838 and 1842 and again in 1848 than at any other time: annual stamp returns show that its circulation, on average, in 1838 was 11,000; 1839, 36,000; 1840, 18,700; 1841, 18,700; 1842, 12,500; and in 1848, 12,000 (Epstein 86 n). In no other year did the average weekly circulation top 8,700. James Epstein notes that during the few weeks of intense Chartist activity after the Bull Ring riots in Birmingham (July 1839), "sales perhaps reached 50,000 copies a week" (68). These peak periods, of course, were the times of the greatest Chartist activity.

It is worth pointing out in a discussion of circulation that the circulation and readership of working-class periodicals are two very different things. Circulation figures offer at best a sense of the proportion of readers who read any one periodical in relation to others. Many issues had more than one reader. Working-class periodicals were generally available at coffeehouses, reading rooms, and even some pubs, where, for a small price or for the cost of a drink, one could read several. Doherty, William Lovett, John Cleave, and many other working-class figures owned such establishments. Webb notes that there were 888 coffeehouses in London alone by the end of the forties (Kirby and Musson 340; Aspinall 24–29; Webb 33). Many working-class readers clubbed together to buy their papers; many bought used papers; and many passed old papers on to others. Some of these periodicals are estimated to have had an average of twenty or thirty readers per issue (Aspinall 24–25; Hollis 119; Webb 33).

I do not mean, in arguing that there was a huge potential audience for working-class periodicals, to suggest that literacy precedes literary understanding. The illiterate one-fourth or one-third of the working class were not barred completely from political or literary discourse published in or engendered by working-class periodicals. They, too, were capable of taking in and acting on the views of literature in these periodicals. As Webb writes of the working class at this time:

> There was also a hearing public. [Francis] Place pointed out that it was not uncommon for the men in a workshop engaged in quiet employment, such as tailoring, to commission one man to read aloud, while the others worked, doing his work as compensation. A letter in *Chambers' Journal* describes a similar procedure in hackling shops in Dundee and elsewhere. . . . Methodist, radical, Chartist, and self-improvement classes and meetings often included reading aloud as a feature; it was certainly done in homes where perhaps only one member of the family could read; and Tremenheere was alarmed by a Primitive Methodist preacher's reading the *Northern Star* weekly at a miners' meeting. And this too was a feature of public house life. (34)

Many of the illiterate were thus aware of working-class publications—and working-class journalists were aware of the illiterate in their publications. Writers such as Cobbett and Feargus O'Connor obviously adopted a colloquial and conversational voice in their writings; they wanted to be heard as well as read. Cobbett's writings, then as now, take on a greater energy when read out loud: Epstein, writing of O'Connor, notes that "it is obvious from the highly rhetorical style of the [*Northern*] *Star*'s lead articles that the paper was designed to be read aloud" (68). Reprinted speeches were a staple of the working-class press. And as with the strictly political, so with the literary. The various literary entertainments of the working-class press—poems, short literary varieties, and reviews with excerpts, such as the long review/summary of Dickens's *The Chimes* in *Northern Star* (1844)—for many must have been heard instead of read.

Such experiences of "reading" by the illiterate or the semiliterate are as important in their own way to this study as are the experiences and writings of the highly literate among the working class. Both types of readers made their own contributions to a developing sense of a working-class canon. Among those who considered Percy Bysshe Shelley to be a working-class hero—those, for example, who thought Shelley's *Queen Mab* to be the "Chartist's Bible"[7]—there must have been many who only knew about the work and its political agenda by hearing it or hearing about it. There must have been many who held Shelley's "Song to the Men of England" to be one of their anthems without actually being able to read it. Such men and women had notions about Shelley and his significance in their lives; their beliefs contributed to a working-class consensus about Shelley; and that consensus in turn was reflected or questioned in the working-class press. A comparison can easily be drawn between this group and the illiterate and unlatined of the Middle Ages; while the latter by necessity had to learn about the Bible and other important texts secondhand, their ideas about those works contributed importantly to the religious ethos of the day.

All this emphasis on numbers—how many could read and what those who could, did read—assumes, of course, that the size of the audience for working-class periodicals is somehow crucial to this study. Such an assumption is only partly true. Insofar as these periodicals were disseminators of working-class ideas and ideals, numbers of readers are very important as a measure of dissemination. If Carlile's distinctive views about literature reached an audience of ten instead of tens of thousands, his declarations would have, in a way, less value to the historian of literary criticism and, in particular, of literary influence. His at times immense working-class readership suggests that Carlile's literary ideas had a wide-ranging influence upon that class; in this way, numbers give him authority.

But there were other working-class writers who expressed their literary ideas in less-popular periodicals, some of which lasted only a week or two, and yet others who only appeared in print once, in the form, for example, of a letter to the editor. Their expressions, too, are important, though they may not have reached many readers at all. The task of this study is not simply to note the most influential pronouncements about literature in working-class periodicals. If such were the case I could have contented myself with studying the handful of working-class periodicals published between 1816 and 1858 that attained a circulation over 5,000 or 10,000. Literary discourse in every working-class periodical is both an attempt to influence and the product of influence. Only by studying a great number of subjective statements by many working-class writers and a great number of literary decisions by many working-class editors can we come to any sense of a working-class feel for poetry or fiction at this time, or of a working-class canon. In this way, the opinions of an anonymous "Lancashire Weaver" about poetry, or those of writers in the most ephemeral of the working-class periodicals of the "War of the Un-stamped," are as worthy of consideration as the literary ideas of such influential critics as George Julian Harney and Gerald Massey.[8]

Autodidacticism and Early Reading Experiences

With few exceptions, those who would become working-class journalists and critics were autodidacts. Certainly their self-education shaped their values and critical beliefs. An investigation of working-class biographies of the last part of the eighteenth century and the first half of the nineteenth suggests that the reading material of working-class children was widely divergent.

That divergence is not surprising if one considers the variety of sources of reading material and the near randomness of most working-class children's reading experiences. They could come in contact with chapbooks or broadsides sold by peddlers, or with small home libraries, generally containing religious works but sometimes containing more (Vincent, *Bread* 110); they might find something to read at their school libraries; they could borrow reading-matter from friends; or they could, if they were lucky, obtain free admission to a circulating library. Thomas Cooper, the Chartist intellectual did this (see below) as did Thomas Carter (Cooper 34; Vincent, *Bread* 117). Some may have had parents who read periodicals. James Watson's mother had "the habit of reading Cobbett's *Register*" (Vincent, *Testaments* 110). Some had less literary sources of reading: besides learning from "the contents of the local papers," Joseph Gutteridge gained knowledge from reading "the sign board literature of public-houses and shops" (Gutteridge 85).[9] Such randomness must certainly figure in the amazing eclecticism of the working-class periodicals these autodidacts contributed to as adults.

But within the great diversity of reading materials, there was clearly a tiny core of commonality. Most working-class readers were more or less acquainted with the Bible, of course. If their households contained any library at all—as many did—the Bible invariably was at the heart of the collection. As David Vincent notes, "The Bible was less the mediator between man and God than a vague symbol of religious commitment, useful as a primer for young children who were learning their letters, an occasional source of entertainment, even, indeed, a particularly suitable item for pawning in times of need" (*Bread* 110). Moreover, most of the schools in which the working class picked up the rudiments of literacy— Sunday schools, schools of the National Society for Promoting the Education of the Poor in the Principles of the Established Church, and those of the nonconformist British and Foreign School Society—used the Bible as the primary, and often the only, text for reading lessons (Burnett 141, 146–47). Some would not look back fondly upon these early and difficult forced-reading experiences. In his autobiography, the poet John Clare, who considered parts of the Bible among his "favourite readings," nevertheless was harshly critical of the Bible as a reading primer:

> I think the manner of learing [*sic*] children in village schools very erronious, that is soon as they learn their letters to task them with lessons from the bible and testament and keeping them dinging at them, without any change, till they leave it A dull boy, never turns with pleasures to his school days when he has often been beat 4 times for bad readings in 5 verses of Scripture. . . . Other books as they grow up be-

come a novelty and their task book at school, the Bible, looses its relish the painful task of learning wearied the memory irksome inconvenience never prompts reccolection. (5)

Clare found solace (and "learning") by reading on his own "the Sixpenny Romances of 'Cinderella,' 'Little Red Riding Hood,' 'Jack and the Bean Stalk,' 'Zig Zag,' 'Prince Cherry,' etc. . . ." (5).

Another autobiographer, the Chartist James Bezer, complains about his Sunday school: "Now, that school did not even learn me to read; six hours a week, certainly not *one* hour of useful knowledge; plenty of cant, and what my teachers used to call *explaining* difficult texts in the Bible, but little, very little else" (quoted in Vincent, *Testaments* 157). The growing Bible literacy of this time was both the product and the promoter of the rise of Methodism and the Evangelical movement. It also could partially explain the persistent linking by working-class thinkers of working-class politics and free thought, since, for some, unpleasant experiences learning the Bible must have shifted to a distrust and dislike of the work itself—or a distrust and dislike of the way their teachers interpreted it. Whatever the case, biblical references are common in working-class periodicals, although attitudes toward the Bible are mixed.

There were other works that working-class children commonly read. The one that is mentioned again and again in working-class autobiography is John Bunyan's *Pilgrim's Progress*, which was found in many working-class homes or school libraries (Vincent, *Bread* 110–11). For many it was one of the first works they *chose* to read—and, for many, it was the first to make a powerful impression. Both Samuel Bamford and Frederick Rogers state that that was the case (Bamford 1, 51; Rogers 6). And Bezer presents Bunyan as the antidote to his dreary Sunday-school education: "My own dear Bunyan! if it hadn't been for you, I should have gone mad, I think, before I was ten years old!" (quoted in Vincent, *Testaments* 166). For Cooper, at nine or ten "the immortal 'Pilgrim's Progress' was my book of books. What hours of wonder and rapture I passed with Bunyan as a boy!" (Cooper 22). References to the *Pilgrim's Progress* in working-class autobiography are overwhelmingly positive; Francis Place is exceptional—unique even—in seeing the work as an "absurd book" (Place 46). Indeed, E. P. Thompson writes that *Pilgrim's Progress*, which posits the value of inner belief against the wiles and falsity of the "other world" is, with *Rights of Man*, one of the two foundation texts of the English working-class movement (*Making* 34–35).

One might expect, therefore, to find *Pilgrim's Progress* promoted enthusiastically as essential reading in the working-class press. But that is not the case at all; even passing references to the work in those periodicals are extremely rare. I can point to only two. The *Sunday Herald*, a London periodical that ran for sixteen weeks in 1832 (Wiener, *Finding List* 56) began its first issue with an attempt to update Bunyan with "A New Pilgrim's Progress; or The Adventures of a Reformer, In Travelling from a State of Slavery and Corruption, to Liberty and Prosperity." In 1845 *Northern Star* published a lengthy excerpt by the editor of *Wade's London Review* that is harshly critical of *Pilgrim's Progress*. The editor of *Wade's* believes that "allegories, emblems, and fables in early education . . . are puzzling and misleading," and describes the malevolent effect Bunyan's work had upon his own childhood: "The result of such reading . . . was to people my young brain with a horrid phantasmagoria of bodiless and misshapen images, from whose midnight tortures and distractions I was happy to escape, after much suffering, with my faculties underanged." The *Northern Star* reviewer, in introducing this excerpt, also admits to being a survivor of childhood night terrors brought on by Bunyan and thanks *Wade's* editor for his "castigation of the mad tinker's printed trash" (15 Mar. 1845: 3).

I have found no other references to *Pilgrim's Progress*—not even a brief excerpt in the wide-ranging and copious collections of literary extracts to be found in several periodicals—collections that, as we shall see, strove to be comprehensive catalogues of valued works.

Why this divergence between autobiographical and journalistic writing, sometimes—as is the case with Cooper—on the part of the same writer? There are a few possibilities.

For one thing, while many autobiographers remembered reading Bunyan as children, none mentioned rereading him at a later age. For many, then, the work may have lost its immediacy, its details having become ghostly images. Or possibly working-class writers perceived the work as one for children and therefore, for whatever reasons, not important for their (largely) adult audiences. In other words, the difference might suggest a conscious or subconscious awareness on the part of these writers of a canon of children's literature—even a canon of working-class children's literature—that is distinct from an adult canon. This may explain another surprising difference between working-class autobiography and journalism: Defoe's *Robinson Crusoe* figures prominently in the childhoods of many working-class autobiographers but hardly at all in working-class periodicals (Vincent, *Bread* 118–19, 127 n, 179 n; Clare 13, 28). If working-class journalists categorized and marginalized *Pilgrim's Progress* or *Robinson Crusoe* as juvenile literature, however, one is hard-pressed to explain the paucity of references in later (and especially Chartist) working-class periodicals, when what children read became more a concern for journalists.

Very likely for many journalists there was more to their silence about these works than the books' inapplicability to adults. Some surely must have seen *Pilgrim's Progress* as dangerous. As I shall argue in chapter 4, many working-class journalists of the teens, twenties, and thirties feared the imaginative in literature and especially in fiction. By these standards a work that was personally liberating for many could be seen as socially dangerous and hardly "useful." This explanation, however, does not explain why Chartist journalists—who generally did not fear the imagination and the imaginative—avoided mentioning the work.

A third possible reason might be found in what, for lack of a better term, I call the "second literacy" one sees described repeatedly in working-class autobiography: a highly-motivated and wide-ranging program of reading, often undertaken years after the reader had first learned to read. The most famous of these, perhaps, is Cooper's, a course of study and memorization so heavy that it resulted in a nervous breakdown (22–68). His directed self-study was only atypical of the working-class intellectual in its obsessiveness. This "second literacy" was always much more deliberate and methodical than the first, since the reader no longer read what happened to be around but sought out, and often sacrificed to obtain, those works that he or she, for whatever reason, believed worth reading. Often one work led to an epiphany that set the reader on a course of autodidacticism. For Clare that work was James Thomson's *Seasons*, a fragment of which he came upon at the age of thirteen and thereafter obsessively sought to obtain. For Alexander Somerville, later (briefly) editor of the *Cosmopolite* and *Political Soldier*, the work was Robert Burns's *Poems*: "I read them under sensations of pleasure entirely new"

(88). For James Watson, the prolific radical publisher of the 1830s, that moment may have come when he happened upon a meeting of radicals who were reading Thomas Jonathan Wooler's *Black Dwarf*, Carlile's *Republican*, and Cobbett's *Political Register* (Vincent, *Testaments* 110). Rationalist texts and poetic works both provided the impetus to self-education, and for many the reading of one sort of work led to the reading of the other. This "second literacy" depended upon choice and not upon accident, and choice depended upon a sense of value. In turn, in presenting in their periodicals a sense of what was and was not valuable, many would naturally refer to this time when they were able to decide what they read. In other words, they relied less upon what books their parents happened to own or what their schools provided for their edification, and more upon those they consciously fixed upon as worthy. But this reason, too, does not fully explain away the discrepancy between private and public values. Whether it was read by choice or not, working-class readers clearly saw *Pilgrim's Progress* as valuable in their own lives. Why would they deny that value in the lives of their audiences? To some extent, then, the relative disregard of *Pilgrim's Progress* and *Robinson Crusoe* in the working-class press remains a mystery; a thoroughly convincing solution must await a systematic comparison between working-class private writing (diaries, letters, memoirs) and public writing (speeches, periodicals, and books).

However working-class journalists obtained the rudiments of literacy, the "second literacy" of each depended upon their own wills and—helped perhaps by knowledgeable colleagues or working-class periodicals—upon their own choices. Their energetic self-pursuit of knowledge, usually against great odds, shaped the form and content of their periodicals in several ways.

For one thing, self-teaching, no matter how thorough—cutting a path as one goes, rather than following any established curriculum—cannot but leave gaps in learning in contrast to a more structured education. Doherty, for one, recognized the gaps in his own education but, in introducing his *United Trades' Co-operative Journal* in 1830, he transformed this deficiency into a point of pride:

> The slender stock of knowledge which we possess has been casually and, as it were, accidentally snatched from the common stock, during

the usual and necessary periods of cessation from labour. . . . We make no pretensions to classic lore. We cannot boast of an acquaintance with what is commonly called the learned languages; nor can we, at present, of course, aspire to a display of the beauties and elegances of composition. The only requisite qualifications which we believe we possess . . . [are] a moderate share of common sense and an accurate knowledge, from experience, of the wants, the wishes, the interests, and the *capacities* of the working classes. (Quoted in Kirby and Musson 2)

In other words, learning from books constitutes only a part of what one needs to become a good working-class journalist and critic; living and learning working-class values is important to promoting those values and to critical evaluation for a working-class audience. Lack of that class-based experience, on the other hand, reduces the value for a working-class audience of middle-class critics, no matter how complete their education.

Another way of dealing with gaps is to deny that they are gaps—to argue that what one has not read is not worth reading. Carlile's pronouncements on Sir Walter Scott's novels illustrate this sort of reaction. Such condemnation is hardly a device invented by working-class journalists; many of the middle-class Evangelical attacks on the novel, for example, were clearly mounted by those who shunned novel reading completely.[10] The tactic is not necessarily an illegitimate or shoddy one. The notion of gaps presupposes an established canon, one that every reader needed to read to have a full education. But working-class critics worked hard to destroy the idea of a universal or class-transcendent canon and to promote an alternate canon that overlapped the established one but served a completely different audience with its own unique values. In that sense, not having read Ovid was no gap at all to Doherty, and he need not have read Ovid to come to that conclusion. For a critic writing for and to a particular class, with a particular culture, at a particular time, Ovid was an anachronism. Moreover, the class interests of these autodidacts led them to read works that were foreign to formal education. William Benbow's *Grand National Holiday*, for example, first published in 1831, certainly helped shape the political philosophy of many autodidacts but probably did not contribute to many university educations. But we could only consider that those university educations therefore had a "gap" if we assume that any work has the exact same value for all people—that there was one canon for all in Britain during the first part of the nineteenth century. Few politically aware autodidacts made that assumption.

Incidentally, pursuing one's own curriculum can have one distinct advantage: such a course of study tends to juxtapose works in a way that a more formal education does not, leading to new angles from which to view particular works. A reading of Shelley's *Queen Mab*, for example, in the context of works by Paine or Comte de Volney—or William Godwin—rather than among Shelley's collected works or those of his poetic contemporaries, would tend to emphasize Shelley's role as a philosopher more strongly than his role as a poet. Works are read in context; one text read in a number of contexts produces, in a sense, a number of different works. A reader today, introduced to Shelley in a course on Romantic poetry simply would not read Shelley in the same way as one who read Shelley after hearing about him in Carlile's *Republican*.

A second by-product of working-class autodidacticism was the energy, and sometimes even obsessiveness, with which these writers promoted their favorite authors and works. These readers did more than learn: they discovered—and, as autobiographies of the time suggest, working-class autodidacts did not forget the emotional and intellectual power that their literary discoveries had upon them. Some, such as Cooper and those several editors who compiled copious literary selections, paid homage to a number of their discoveries in their writings. Others focused upon one writer as their great literary hero: we shall see, for example, Carlile's relentless promotion of—and even possessiveness of—the works of Paine, or Harney's lifelong obsession with the works and life of Byron.

A developing working-class press offered these writers a chance to publicize their own autodidacticism and to promote their worn path to learning as an aid to the working-class readers who followed them. In a sense they worked to promote a working-class curriculum, seeing in their own experience a model for all working-class reading. The obvious egotism of many of the working-class leaders and journalists of this time often proved a hindrance to their political movements: a study of early nineteenth-century working-class journalism is of necessity a study of constant bickering, temporary alliances, and long-standing rivalries, based as much on personality as upon political philosophy. In the matter of literary criticism and canon formation, however, this egotism could be greatly beneficial: faced with the task of building a working-class canon almost from scratch, these writers could only look within for a sense of what was valuable. Their power as critics depended upon their extreme confidence that what was valuable for them was valuable for their class. In other words, their effectiveness lay in transferring the energy and content of their self-study to the working class as a whole.

The Working-Class Periodical

Not every periodical read by members of the working class could, by even the broadest definition, be termed a "working-class" periodical. If that were the case, nearly every periodical published during this time would be "working-class." Coffeehouses and reading rooms regularly carried journals and newspapers supporting a wide variety of political and class interests, and their patrons had access to periodicals such as the London *Times* as well as the *Republican* or *Northern Star*. Describing Doherty's Manchester coffee- and newsroom, Arthur Aspinall writes: "Ninety-six newspapers were taken in every week; they included the principal Manchester and London papers, some from Dublin, Belfast, Liverpool, Glasgow, and Leeds, most of the unstamped (and therefore illegal) ones, and even the *Edinburgh Review* and *Westminster Review* (though not, it may be observed, the Tory *Quarterly Review*)." This variety was not unusual (26, 28). Working-class readers of the 1840s and 1850s also had access to stamped newspapers in mechanics' institutes, although Richard Altick notes that these reading rooms "never attracted many workmen" (201).

Moreover, although buying individual copies of middle-class papers and journals was impossible for most laborers, they could club together to buy them or could rent them out from cooperating news vendors (Altick 323); servants were often obviously in a position to inherit the discarded periodicals of their employers and pass them on; and anyone of any class might find pages of a recent *Advertiser* or *Chronicle* wrapping a purchase from the greengrocer or fishmonger (Webb 23).

As a youth in the 1820s, Cooper, though poor, was a voracious reader of expensive periodicals; through the help of a sympathetic caretaker of a book society for the local Gainsborough gentry, he read "each number of the *Quarterly* and *Edinburgh* Reviews, and of the *European, New Monthly,* and *Blackwood's* Magazines, as duly as they came out." But his "great favourite" was the *London Magazine*, "a periodical which first set before English readers the Essays of Elia, the Picture Galleries of Hazlitt, De Quincey's 'Confessions of an Opium-eater,' verses by Keats and sonnets by poor Clare, and tales by Allen Cunningham, and in the later numbers of which Carlyle's 'Life of Schiller' first appeared" (Cooper 65–66).

Working-class journalists were aware of such middle-class competition. Indeed, they often extracted from middle-class periodicals for their own publications. The many attacks in working-class journals on articles in the *Times* or other newspapers with views seen as hostile to working-class interests suggest that working-class journalists assumed that many readers in their audience knew of such articles and were therefore in need of some sort of political antidote.

To begin to focus the subject of this study, then, I define a working-class periodical not simply as one read by members of the working class but one that self-consciously directs itself toward the working class and its interests.

But how does one judge which periodical is directed toward which class? What may be the most obvious indicator—price—is perhaps the least helpful. It is a mistake to think that the more expensive (and therefore generally stamped and legal) periodicals were directed toward the middle class and that the less-expensive (and therefore generally unstamped and illegal) periodicals were directed toward the workers—or, to put it another way, that the middle class published "respectable" periodicals and the working class did not. If we assume that all expensive periodicals were intended for middle-class audiences, several stamped periodicals clearly directed toward the working class would fall outside the scope of this study. Cobbett's *Political Register*, Carlile's *Republican*, and Wooler's *Black Dwarf* were all stamped and all cost sixpence in the years after the passing of the Six Acts in 1819. In the 1830s Doherty's *Voice of the People*, "the exclusive property of the Working Classes" (1 Jan. 1831: 1) was stamped and cost seven pence an issue. After the stamp duties were lowered from four pence to one penny in 1836, many working-class periodicals, including *Northern Star*, were stamped and cost threepence, four pence, or more an issue.

Prices above a penny or two obviously limited the circulation of working-class periodicals. Cobbett, for example, estimated that raising the cost of his *Political Register* from twopence to sixpence cut his circulation by more than 80 percent (Spater 390–91). But the publishers of such costly periodicals obviously hoped—successfully, in some cases—that an audience large enough to keep them solvent would be interested in their work and would seek out and read their periodicals in the same way they read other expensive publications: in their coffeehouses or reading rooms or by clubbing, borrowing, or buying used copies.

It should not be assumed, either, that all "cheap" periodicals were directed exclusively toward the working class. There were many middle-class periodicals among the unstamped. They were just as illegal as their working-class counterparts but generally were not prosecuted. The *Ladies' Penny Gazette* was directed toward "females in the middling classes of life[:] tradesmen [*sic*] and farmers' wives and daughters" (27 Oct. 1832: 1). Among the middle-class unstamped publications are the innumerable periodicals of the *Figaro* type: *Figaro in London* (and *Figaros* of several other places), *Punchinello!*, the *Whig-Dresser*, and many more. These sometimes excruciatingly arch precursors to *Punch*, which looked satirically at party politics (and which collectively went far toward proving that puns are not simply the lowest form of humor but also a refined form of torture), were, as Joel Wiener points out, "exclusively 'middle class' in orientation" (*War* 178).[11]

Other cheap periodicals were, or tried to be, classless. Editors of many of these periodicals took great pains in their first issues to disassociate themselves from any class interests. Their protestations were in part motivated by a desire to avoid the kind of persecution by the Stamp Office that fell upon their more class-conscious brethren (Wiener, *War* 173). Many of the hundreds of periodicals published during the "War of the Unstamped" proposed this sort of truce with the government in introductory essays. Two of the cheapest of the cheap offer good examples of this sort of distancing. The useful-knowledge London *Halfpenny Magazine* wrote of its audience: "We anticipate extensive patronage from classes very different in rank; just as the fruiterer in Covent-garden-market sells apples and pears to the Duke of Bedford as well as to the little boy at the crossing" (5 May 1832: 2). A northern counterpart, the Edinburgh *Half-Penny Magazine*, aimed itself toward a similarly broad audience, while at the same time drawing a correlation between wealth and intelligence: "We pledge ourselves to produce a *melange*, which, while it may cheer and enlighten the hearth of the ignorant and poor, will not be unworthy of the acceptance of the intelligent and rich" (2 [n.d.] 9).[12] Besides avoiding the wrath of the law, conductors of these periodicals obviously avoided class issues in order to appeal both to the class with more people to buy their magazine and to the class with more pennies and halfpennies to spend on it. This sort of periodical was legion during the explosion of periodical publishing in the early thirties. Other examples are the twopenny *Lincoln Cabinet* (1832), as well as the *Magazine of Interest* (31 Aug. 1833), the *Penny Lancet* (1832), and the *Lawyer* (1833), all of which cost one penny. An earlier example of a periodical that similarly distanced itself from any class is the threepenny Birmingham *Bazaar, or Literary and Scientific Repository*, "adapted to every class of readers" (26 June 1823: 1). A later example is the *Illustrated People's Paper* (1854). Many periodicals of this kind, however, in trying to be everything to everyone, offered nothing of substance to anyone, and most quickly slipped into oblivion.[13]

The *Penny Magazine* of the Society for the Diffusion of Useful Knowledge (SDUK) was a model for both these *Halfpenny* magazines and for scores of other inexpensive publications. That periodical, too, noted in its first issue that "we hope our Penny Magazine will be to *all* classes—a universal convenience and enjoyment." But in the same introduction *Penny Magazine's* editor, Charles Knight, specifically directs the periodical to a more limited group: those "whose time and whose means are equally limited" (31 Mar. 1832: 1). Certainly *Penny Magazine* was read by members of the middle class (Altick 337–39). But its raison d'être was from the start an attempt by middle-class reformers to improve the minds of individual members of the working class, and from its first issue *Penny Magazine's* ideas about individual improvement took on the biases of its publisher's class. Its introductory essay exhibits both the condescension and limitations of the magazine, promising that it "may be taken up and laid down without requiring any considerable effort; and . . . may tend to fix the mind upon much calmer, and, it may be, purer subjects of thought than the violence of party discussion, or the stimulating details of crime and suffering" (31 Mar. 1832: 1). Attempting to divorce the political from the "useful" is, of course, a political act. The "violence" of party discussion and the "stimulation" of crime and suffering informed the working class of their own social and political situation; such "violence" and "stimulation" were therefore among the first things that the working class looked for in their reading and among the first things most working-class journalists gave them. Brougham, Knight, and the SDUK were well aware of all this; by "fixing"—a significant choice of words—the attention of members of the working class, during the little free time they had, upon such "calm" and "pure" subjects as the history of Charing Cross, the antiquity of beer, and the zoo at Regents Park (all covered in the first issue), the SDUK hoped to check any interest their readers might have in political literature and, by extension, in political thought and political activity. The class interests in *Penny Magazine* might be less obnoxiously overt than those of the awkward antiradical periodicals of a generation before, such as *White Dwarf* and the *Anti-Cobbett* (of which more later), but its political intent was equally subversive. That intent was not lost on working-class journalists and readers. A correspondent to the *Poor Man's Guardian* from Poplar, who calls himself "a Labourer," reacted angrily to *Penny Magazine*'s first issue:

> Are we to be amused by the piping of a penny trumpet, sounded weekly to divert our minds?—Pshaw! *Useful* knowledge, indeed, would that be to those who live idly on our skill and industry, which would cajole us into an apathetic resignation to their iron sway, or induce us to waste the energy and skill of man for them all day. . . . I caution the readers of the 'Guardian' against the base and insidious intentions of this Society for the Diffusion of Useful Knowledge. (Apr. 1832: 359)

Among the better-known middle-class propagators of "useful knowledge" besides *Penny Magazine* were *Saturday Magazine*, put out by the Society for Promoting Christian Knowledge, and the remarkably long-lived *Chambers' Edinburgh Journal* (1832–1956). There were many others. Some overtly preached middle-class values. One example of such sermonizing, fascinating in its very transparency, can be found in the story of Goody Two-Shoes in the *Boys' and Girls' Penny Magazine*. Its author offers this argument against working-class political agitation: "The father of Goody Two-Shoes was born in England; and everybody knows, that in this happy country the poor are to the full as much protected by our excellent laws, as are the highest and richest nobles in our land, and the humble cottager enjoys equal share of the blessings of English liberty, with the sons of the king themselves" (5 Jan. 1833: 138). Other periodicals strove for a safe "innocuousness"—a conscious avoidance of discussing or promoting working-class values. *Chambers'* was such a periodical. But, as Altick argues, by striving not to offend the ruling class, the Chambers brothers avoided publishing the very things that would attract a working-class audience: "In his zeal to avoid giving offense on any side, [William] Chambers kept from the *Journal* the qualities necessary to win working-class readers accustomed to the hard-hitting commentary of the political press and the melodrama of both the Sunday newspapers' surveys of crime and the penny numbers of Gothic fiction" (334–35). Altick notes that, after its initial popularity with the working class, *Chambers'* was bought more often by members of the middle class (338).[14] *Penny Magazine*, *Chambers'*, and other periodicals directed primarily toward the working class but not produced by them, fall outside the scope of this study. I do not deny that members of the working class read such periodicals and were influenced by them. I am, however, not interested here in the literary values that one class promoted for another, but rather in those that working-class journalists either saw existing within their own class or that they promoted for that class.

The best evidence for the class orientation of periodicals lies within the periodicals themselves. Most periodicals exclusively and self-consciously directed toward the working class made no effort hide that fact, and many proudly proclaimed their allegiance in their lead article. Thus, in the *Poor Man's Guardian* Hetherington targets his audience on the first page: "We will try, step by step, the power of RIGHT against MIGHT; and we will begin by protecting and upholding this grand bulwark and defence of all our rights—this key to all our liberties—THE FREEDOM OF THE PRESS—*the press, too, of the IGNORANT and the POOR!* we have taken upon ourselves its protection, and we will never abandon our post; we will *die* rather" (9 Jul. 1831: 1). In much the same way in the first paragraph of the first issue of the Chartist *London Democrat* (1839) the conductors of that periodical spell out their class interests: "It is of the utmost importance that working men should be accurately informed of the true state of affairs, and likewise that they should thoroughly understand the principles upon which the present movement is founded; therefore the publication of the Democrat is ventured upon, solely to supply what is considered by many to be a great deficiency" (13 Apr. 1839: 1).[15]

Many "working-class" periodicals, of course, did not spell out their values and class orientation this clearly from the start. Moreover, the first issues of many working-class periodicals no longer exist (as is true of the *Northern Star*).[16] In both these cases the contents of the periodicals—political leaders, letters from readers, reprinted speeches, literary reviews, "varieties," and even advertising—generally offer a clear sense of that periodical's target audience.

A number of periodicals published during the first half of the nineteenth century clearly promoted the interests of the working class while self-consciously working in the interests of the middle class as well. These periodicals differed greatly from those that divorced themselves from class interests; in these, class interests were paramount. Most of the radical periodicals published before 1830 in particular targeted radicals from both the working and middle class, and indeed held that the interests of both groups were the same. Cobbett may have opened the door to a new, working-class reading audience in 1816; he did not thereby slam the door on the many middle-class radicals who had supported the *Political Register* for years. Carlile, Wooler, and William Hone also had feet in both camps. The issues discussed by these editors—postwar debt, the right to form political unions, the vicissitudes of Queen Caroline, and the need for electoral reform, to name a few—were issues important to all classes, and especially to radicals of all classes.

Similarly, the Owenite periodicals of the 1820s, such as the Brighton *Co-operator* and the *Cooperative Magazine*, later known as the *London Co-operative Magazine*, addressed themselves to and had readers among all classes. But their advocacy of a classless society devoid of personal property appealed particularly to laborers, and in the 1820s and early 1830s, as G. D. H. Cole points out, "the driving force of the movement came from the working class" (*Robert Owen* 255). Laborers more often than not produced and wrote for these periodicals; laborers more often than not read them as well.

After the Reform Bill of 1832 severed working- and middle-class radicals into two distinct groups, with largely distinct cultures and sets of interests, fewer journalists found it possible to address working- and middle-class interests simultaneously. At times, for causes such as the struggle against the new poor laws or for factory reform, the interests of the two groups coincided, and some publications catered to both. The

Ten Hour's Advocate, and Journal of Literature and Art, for example, declared in its first issue that it addressed the interests of all (26 Sept. 1846:
1). But for the most part, working-class periodicals of the early 1830s
were directed toward that class alone.

Whether they confined themselves exclusively to working-class interests or self-consciously promoted the interests of other classes as well, any
periodical that exhibited a clear and uncondescending sympathy for
working-class interests I consider a "working-class periodical" and one
relevant to this study.

A working-class periodical, then, is "working-class" because of the
makeup of its audience and because of the relationship between the producers of the periodical and their audience. But this definition raises two
tricky questions: what exactly was the "working-class audience" for these
periodicals, and what exactly is a "working-class journalist"?

Of course there was no such thing as one working-class audience;
there was not one particular group that every publisher and editor of a
working-class periodical tried to reach. Rather, most aimed at smaller interest groups within that class. Some publishers and editors appealed to
laborers in a certain trade. Some focused on certain issues—trade unionism, say, or factory reform, or specific local issues—issues that limited
their audience. Some, such as editors and publishers of Owenite or free-
thought periodicals, sought out a working-class elite that was relatively
conversant in the specialized ideas they discussed. One periodical targeted common soldiers: Carlile's short-lived *Political Soldier* (1833–34).

Moreover, many working-class periodicals, consciously or uncon-
sciously, at best appealed directly to only half of the working class, direct-
ing their periodicals specifically to "working men." That is how the *London
Democrat* prefaced its opening number. Cobbett draws the same line, at
least partially, by addressing his first discourse to the working class to
"Journeymen and Labourers." Many periodicals aimed toward a male audience in their titles: among these are two of the best-known working-
class periodicals of the 1830s, the *Poor Man's Guardian* and the *Poor Man's
Advocate* (1832–34).

This blindness to the latent energy and power of ideas held by the
women of the working class helps explain the almost complete exclusion
of female working-class journalists in the first half of the nineteenth cen-

tury. Not counting working-class poets published in these periodicals, and acknowledging that some anonymous submissions most certainly were written by women, I have been able to discover only five women who were intimately connected with working-class journalism. Three of them were connected in some way with Carlile: his wife, Jane, and his sister Mary-Anne, both of whom at one time shared his imprisonment, helped with his business, and published his works while he was in prison; and the fascinating Elizabeth Sharples, who, impressed by Carlile's free-thought ideas, began to give free-thought lectures of her own. She became Carlile's mistress and assisted him with his later projects. She was also the only known female editor of a working-class periodical, the free-thought *Isis* (Wiener, *Radicalism* 81–85, 191, 196–97).[17] The other two were Chartists: one Sophia, a Birmingham Chartist who corresponded with several periodicals, including the *National Association Gazette* (1842) and the *English Chartist Circular*, and Helen MacFarlane, the translator of the *Communist Manifesto* for Harney's *Red Republican*, who was probably the "Howard Morton" who wrote regularly for that periodical and its successor, *Friend of the People*, and whose leaving prompted Engels to criticize Harney for breaking with "the most outstanding and capable contributor to *The Friend of the People*."[18]

But these five women were exceptions in a fraternity of male publishers, editors, and writers, who, in leaders, addresses, essays, and exhortations, often depicted their audience as a brotherhood or as "brethren." Later, many Chartist periodicals explicitly or implicitly recognized that women did indeed have a place in a working-class audience. The *Northern Star*, certainly, tried to be a full-feature family newspaper. In another case, a writer for the Glasgow *Chartist Circular* advised Chartist mothers what to read to their children.[19] But even in the few cases in which women had a legitimate place in a periodical's audience, it was often a place apart from that of their fathers, sons, and brothers. Harney might appeal to both sexes in the literary page of *Northern Star*, but O'Connor, in that newspaper's political leaders, constantly addressed himself to men: "Fustian jackets, unshorn chins, and blistered hands." Such gender-based exclusion of both staff and audience, we shall see, strongly influenced views of literature in these periodicals.

In almost no case, then, did working-class journals—even those with massive circulations—target the entire working-class as their audience. "Working-class audience" is a term of convenience denoting any audience composed of members of the working-class: everything from the smallest local interest group to the broadest mass audience. By describing each periodical individually as it comes up in this study, I hope to give some idea of the particular composition of its audience.

One important point remains in defining a working-class periodical. Some of the periodicals published during this period were produced by one person alone; most were produced by a very small group of people. In either case, most periodicals of the day strongly reflected individual preferences and values. Because of this, the class standings and values of the journalists behind these periodicals are crucial in determining whether a periodical is "working-class" or not. In many cases, writers (and, more rarely, publishers and editors) of these periodicals were anonymous; all our evidence about their values lies wholly within the texts themselves. In cases in which the journalist is known, I apply the same tests to them and their writings as I do to the periodicals: if their lives and works show a clear sense of sympathy with the aspirations of the working class—and especially if members of the working class realized that sympathy—I consider them and their writings relevant to this study, in spite of their class origins or even class standing. Therefore, the periodical writings of Cobbett and Robert Owen have a place here, even though calling Cobbett "working-class" would be problematic, and calling Owen "working-class" would be downright ridiculous. Or, to take a later example, Jones, one of the last great Chartists, was the son of Major Charles Jones, who was equerry to the duke of Cumberland. He was educated at the aristocratic St. Michael's College at Lunenburg in Hannover and attended the Middle Temple and became a barrister before dedicating himself to Chartism in 1846 (Baylen and Gossman 2: 264). After that date, few seriously questioned his efforts on behalf of his adoptive class; as Engels wrote to Karl Marx, "he was the only *educated* Englishman among the politicians who was, at bottom, entirely on our side" (Marx and Engels 116)—a statement that reveals as much about Engels's view of education as it does about Jones's class values. Working-class readers of *Northern Star*, the *Labourer, People's Paper,* and other periodicals that Jones wrote for saw him as a fellow traveler; these periodicals, and his writings in them, figure importantly here.

For the purposes of this study, then, I define a working-class periodical as a periodical that is self-consciously directed toward the working class and that clearly reflects working-class interests; I define a working-class journalist as one who self-consciously promotes those class interests. Hundreds of periodicals and writers fit within the limits of these definitions.

2

A Sense of Canon

A Literary History

The Influence of Paine

THE FIRST periodical directed intentionally toward the working class, an inexpensive edition of Cobbett's *Political Register*, came out on 2 November 1816. Any history of the working-class press of this period, however, literary or otherwise, must begin not in the nineteenth century but in the eighteenth, and not with William Cobbett but with Thomas Paine.

The massive sales of both parts of Paine's *Rights of Man* demonstrated the readiness of the "swinish multitude" (as Edmund Burke had dismissed them in his 1790 *Reflections on the Revolution in France*) to receive and discuss political ideas. Paine is, in *Rights of Man*, intensely aware of that audience, and indeed derives much of his rhetorical power from them. In particular, his constant use of a communal, popular "we" argues strongly, as Olivia Smith puts it, "that there exists a public understanding that is intellectually adroit and competent to deal with political questions" (52). Paine presented himself in *Rights of Man* not just as an educator of the people, but also as the articulator of their basic political aspirations; the publication of his ideas proclaimed the value of their own. That assumption of popular political ability was nothing short of revolutionary in Britain in 1791, and it was that revolutionary assumption that underlay every working-class periodical published in the first half of the nineteenth century.

Throughout the period from 1816 to 1858, but especially at its beginning, working-class journalists acknowledged Paine as their model in matters of politics and rhetoric—and sometimes in matters of religion. They had other influences in these areas, of course. Volney's *Ruins . . . of Empires* (1791), Elihu Palmer's *Principles of Nature* (1801), and the works of d'Holbach, Voltaire, Rousseau, Godwin, and Bentham often appear in articles of working-class periodicals or in the lists of working-class publishers. But Paine was obviously the father figure to many journalists. As a contributor to Thomas Davison's *Medusa, or Penny Politician* wrote, concluding a memoir of Paine: "Thus have we humbly attempted to pay a tribute of gratitude to this great man whose pen has done more to benefit the human race than all the writers that have preceded or followed him" (27 Mar. 1819: 41). In July of the same year, William T. Sherwin, an early radical journalist, published a highly laudatory biography of Paine. Carlile, Sherwin's sometime collaborator, followed with his own *Life of Thomas Paine* in 1820 (Wiener, *Radicalism* 28).[1]

In all his many periodicals it was Carlile more than any other working-class writer who coveted the role of Paine's political and theological son and heir. He lavishly praised Paine in every one of his periodicals. Indeed, Paine seems the only mortal that the extremely egotistical Carlile believed his superior—or at least his equal—as a politician or theologian. Carlile wrote in the *Republican*, "I hold him to be the most useful man that ever trod the soil of the United States, or of any other states" (1 Aug. 1823: 124). Carlile's *Republican* energetically promoted and then diligently reported the many birthday dinners held annually on 29 January in honor of Paine, often with Carlile himself as the guest of honor. Indeed, Carlile held that Paine's birthday was a "Festival of Reason" of far greater significance to humanity than another birthday, Christmas (*Republican* 1 Feb. 1822: 129). Such dinners were held throughout the country until well into Chartist years.[2]

Another journalist who assumed the mantle of Paine was Cobbett, a man who had hated Paine during Paine's lifetime but who had reversed himself completely by 1816.[3] Cobbett's economic ideas in particular owe much to Paine's *Decline and Fall of the English System of Finance* (Williams

20; *Political Register* 18 Sept. 1819: 131–32). But while Carlile accepted all of Paine as his gospel, Cobbett considered the free-thought ideas of Paine's *Age of Reason* to be "nonsense" (15 Jan. 1820: 635). This difference between the two men was partly responsible for two attacks on Cobbett by Carlile in his *Republican*; attacks mounted with the virulent flavor of a bitter sibling rivalry (10 Feb. 1826: 161–65; 11 Feb. 1854: 168–79).[4]

One of Cobbett's more quixotic enterprises was to bring Paine's bones from their original resting place on Paine's farm in New Rochelle, New York, to England in 1819, when Cobbett returned from a two-year exile. That action was ridiculed in drawing and verse—by Byron and others.[5] The recurrent image of most of these drawings and verses—Cobbett with Paine's bones strapped to his back—is surely an emblematic cut at Cobbett's deep debt to Paine.

Paine offered Carlile, Cobbett, and their successors much more than a class-based view of the political system. He offered them the possibility of using their minds and pens to add their own ideas to the struggle against the prevailing political state. Paine's writing—in *Rights of Man* and other works—is situational; he wrote political analysis motivated by the interplay of class values and current events. What he did in 1791 others could do in 1819, 1832, or 1848. *Rights of Man* was not a periodical, but it showed working-class writers what a working-class political periodical could do and should be.

More than this, Paine's style—loaded with verbs and nouns, shorn of ornamental adjectives, elegant and thorough, but at the same time simple, concise, and above all accessible—was the perfect rhetorical model for working-class journalists.[6] Few slavishly tried to copy Paine's style, and the best among the working-class journalists were fine and original stylists in their own right. Cobbett, for example, has a lively and personal style that is purely his own, as anyone who has read even a few pages of his *Rural Rides* knows.[7] But for an example of prose that sought out a specific audience, one with widely differing literacy skills, and that spoke uncondescendingly to that audience with clear, simple, and yet comprehensive prose, and for an example of prose that articulated the attitudes of the working class in the language of that class, many looked to Paine.

In one other way *Rights of Man* is a seminal work for working-class journalists. It can in no way be construed as a work of literary criticism, but nonetheless it suggested a bold new way for members of the working class to view literary texts. Paine argued in *Rights of Man* that the best government was one that changed to represent the shifting will of the people, and that the worst government was one stagnated by traditional values upheld because of tradition alone—a tyranny by the dead over the living. He exhorted the people to judge and rejudge government by their own constantly evolving values and to reject and replace a government that did not respond to their present needs. Many working-class journalists heeded his call and became popular political critics; many applied the same judging and rejudging, the same willingness to reject and replace, to literary texts as well. Most working-class critics refused to accept without careful consideration the literary values either of the dead or of writers of other classes. Instead, they judged works of literature using their new, class-based values. Such a strongly antitraditional approach to texts made some working-class journalists iconoclasts, desiring nothing more than to condemn outright the (to them) irrelevant works by writers of other ages and classes. Others, however, approached literary works with a breadth of mind rare in any age. They were extremely receptive to new literature and willing both to reject any so-called classics that offered nothing to their own class and also to reapproach, reinterpret, and recanonize old literature for their new audience.

1816–29

It is no accident that a working-class press came to life in the second half of the 1810s. The long war with France had ended in 1815, leaving a staggering national debt. The Industrial Revolution had reshaped British society, destroying the industry and livelihood of many skilled artisans and creating a steadily growing force of unskilled and semiskilled labor, which generally worked under oppressive conditions. The year 1816 was one of hunger for many. In no other period of British history, perhaps, was the division between the interests of the ruling classes and the economic underclass so great. This division led to an increased sense among the working class that they were indeed one class with common aspirations, and this sense in turn led to a greater need for outlets in print to voice those aspirations. For in a world of "us" and "them," it was clear that the press belonged to "them" completely.[8]

A number of periodicals sprang up between 1816 and 1820 in an attempt to remedy all these problems. Most were literary as well as political from the start.

At the end of 1816, aware that food riots were erupting throughout Britain and believing that the "hirelings" of the established press did nothing to promote the true interests of the people, William Cobbett decided to address the "Journeymen and Labourers" himself, by lowering the price of his *Political Register* from 1s. ½d. to 2d.—a difference of 10 ½d. Cobbett put out his first reduced-price issue on 2 November; he described the results in his *Register* some months later:

> The effects of No. 18, were prodigious. It occupied the conversations of three fourths of all the active men in the kingdom. The whole town was in a *buz* [*sic*]. The labouring classes of the people seemed as if they had never heard a word on politics before. The effect on their minds was like what might be expected to be produced on the eyes of one bred up in the dark, and brought out, all of a sudden, into broad daylight. Every body was permitted by me, expressly to *re-publish* this Number, and, in town and country, there were, in two months, more than *two hundred thousand* of this one Number printed and sold; and this, too, in spite of all the means which the Government, the Church, the Military and Naval Half Pay, and all the innumerable swarms of Tax-gatherers and Tax Eaters, were able to do to check the circulation, not forgetting their fast allies, the great Manufacturers, Loan-Jobbers, and some of the Yeomanry. (2 Aug. 1817: 551)

In issue after issue of the inexpensive *Register*, Cobbett presented himself as an extremely self-confident articulator and shaper of the political, moral, and economic values of the working class. He also presented himself as an articulator and shaper of their literary values.

Cobbett, proud of his origins as a plowboy, was largely self-taught and was extremely well read. George Spater, in his biography of Cobbett, notes the breadth of Cobbett's reading:

> We know that he had read *A Tale of a Tub* as a small boy, and by the time he became a journalist he had read a great deal more of Swift. He

seemed as familiar with Shakespeare as with the Bible, and quoted him more often than any other author. By the peak of his career he had read the poetry of Dryden, Pope, and Goldsmith, who were his favorites, and he also read Milton, Marvell, Butler, Cowley, Churchill, Thomson, and Cowper. He knew all 400-odd lines of Goldsmith's poem "The Traveller." He had read some Byron, and mentions Wordsworth and Southey, but not Keats or Coleridge. The novels Cobbett read included those by Fielding, Sterne, Le Sage, and Cervantes. In addition to the plays of Shakespeare, he was familiar with those of Wycherley, Congreve, Beaumont and Fletcher, Otway, and Foote, as well as those of his contemporary Sheridan. He read some of Molière, Voltaire, La Fontaine, and Rousseau. He occasionally mentioned Virgil and Horace. He had carefully studied Blackstone's *Commentaries*, Watts's *Logic*, and Blair's *Lectures on Rhetoric*. He had read some of Fortescue, Bacon, Evelyn, Gibbon, Addison, Paley, Samuel Johnson, and William Temple. (1: 18)

Much of Spater's evidence for Cobbett's reading comes from the pages of the *Register*. Cobbett usually revealed his literary learning in that periodical in two ways. First, his style—vigorous, flashing with irony, presenting the enemies of the people as stupid or evil caricatures—owes much to Dryden, Pope, and Swift, to "the great political satirical tradition of the eighteenth century" (Birell 215).[9] Second, he showed his literary influences in the *Register* through direct quotations. Usually when Cobbett used established writers he distilled their ideas into short snatches, presenting a brief quotation here, a headnote there, almost every one yoked to the service of a nonliterary point, most often attacking the present political or economic state of affairs. After quoting three couplets from Goldsmith's "Deserted Village," for example, Cobbett argues that Goldsmith depicts accurately the state of the working class in 1821, not 1770: "Dr. GOLDSMITH, if he used a little of poetical licence, only *anticipated* the literal and melancholy truth" (5 May 1821: 319–20).

Cobbett rarely published any literature at length, or any discussions of literature. The few times he did overtly take on the role of literary critic in the *Register*, he did so to serve distinctly nonliterary purposes. His harshest criticisms of Scott, for example, appear in a missive instructing "Tree Planters and Gardeners"; his lively assault upon Shakespeare and Milton appears in an essay attacking potatoes.[10] His reluctance to enter often into literary discussion in a periodical that ranged freely over a host of subjects, says much about Cobbett's conception both of himself as a journalist and of his audience. Cobbett saw himself as the working-class autodidact whose self-education had brought him in contact with the great works of writers of other classes. In the *Register* he took on the role of an intermediary between those writers and the working class. Long before the SDUK existed, he saw himself as the great diffuser, the one to bring the class in which he was born out of the dark and into social and literary daylight.

Obviously, many works and writers canonical to other social classes were of very limited use, in Cobbett's eyes, to the working class. Though he might use Shakespeare at times to back up his own points, he dismissed him out of hand on several other occasions as a writer unworthy in his own right of the attention of Cobbett's audience. He similarly dismissed Milton and Scott. He ridiculed Johnson more than once, presenting him at one point as a rhetorical and political failure when compared to Paine (18 Sep. 1819: 132). Cobbett's *Political Register* was the filter through which a tiny amount of Cobbett's huge store of literary knowledge passed on to the working class. His reticence in promoting the "classics" implies that while the literature he read might have entertained him, he felt that only a small amount had any place in a working-class canon.

While Cobbett "occasionally mentioned Virgil and Horace," as Spater notes, Cobbett's *Political Register*, like most other working-class periodicals, is virtually free of classical quotations, translations, and allusions. Such quotations and allusions were common in the middle-class periodicals of this time. Certainly, Cobbett and most other working-class journalists never received a substantial classical education; but that does not fully explain this particular difference between working- and middle-class periodicals. Cobbett was among the first in a long line of extremely well-read journalists for the working class who consciously rejected the supposed value of a classical education. As Cobbett wrote in 1807, "learning, truly so called, consists in the possession of knowledge and in the capacity of communicating that knowledge to others; and, as far as my observation will enable me to speak, what are called the *learned* languages, operate as a bar to the acquirement of real learning" (*Political Register* 10 Jan. 1807: 36, quoted in Williams 45). This statement does not reflect any bitterness on Cobbett's part about an education denied him. His linguistic abilities were unquestionably strong; he was the author not only of the very popular *A Grammar of the English Language*, but also of a grammar for students of French (1824). He simply believed that Latin and Greek were useless for himself and for his audience. So did others: a writer in John Wade's *Gorgon* (1818–19) argues that those languages are "despised and useless" (30 May 1818: 12).[11] Both this writer and Cobbett, and those who succeeded them, failed for the most part to publish or discuss Latin or Greek works, not because they lacked education or culture, but because they believed in and promoted very different educational and cultural values.[12] In this way, too, Cobbett worked to create a new, distinctly working-class sensibility about literature.

Richard Carlile spent his young manhood as a tinplate worker. He was twenty-seven years old before changing careers to radical journalism. In 1817, influenced by Cobbett, Wooler, and other radical thinkers, he began collaborating with Sherwin, another pioneering working-class journalist, on *Sherwin's Political Register*. Sherwin abandoned his *Register* after the 1819 Peterloo massacre, apparently because of the frightening level of political tension and the repressive governmental reaction to that event. Carlile took over, renamed the periodical the *Republican*, and "by the end of the year he was recognized as the standard-bearer of free expression" (Wiener, *Radicalism* 18–21, 33, 42–43). Carlile was a leading working-class journalist until well into the 1830s, and more than any other he suffered for his ideals. He spent much of his adult life in prison, was constantly harassed by the authorities, and his stocks (and therefore his livelihood) were seized several times. Despite the relentlessness of these attacks, he wrote and published a huge body of periodical literature. Besides the *Republican*, which ran until 1826, he published the *Lion*, the *Prompter*, the *Gauntlet*, and several other shorter lived periodicals. Some of these works were more free thinking than political, others more political than free thinking. Most combined politics and free thought in large doses and ranged into many other subjects as well. One of these subjects was literature.

Carlile was far less grounded in the established canon than was Cobbett, as the relative lack of literary quotations and allusions in his writings suggests. His suspicions of the Bible carried over to texts in general.

What texts he did publish and promote were those the truths of which he believed to be absolutely self-evident. This, of course, explains why he published many editions of Paine's writings. He judged texts exclusively for their didactic effectiveness and was always wary of the imaginative in fiction or poetry. He may have published both Byron and Shelley, but he published them, as we shall see, for their truths and in spite of—indeed, in denial of—their imaginative qualities.[13] For the most part Carlile shunned the imaginative literature of other classes and was even wary of their didactic literature. He is the great literary iconoclast among early working-class journalists.

Thomas Jonathan Wooler was apprenticed to a printer as a youth and became the first of several journalists to apply a background in printing to producing a working-class journal. He was the editor and printer of two periodicals before 1816, the *Reasoner and Statistical Journal* (1808) and the *Stage* (1815–16), but these, though radical, were not directed toward the working class. From 29 January 1817 on, however, he "appealed to a larger public" with his immensely popular *Black Dwarf* (Stephen and Lee 21: 899). That four penny periodical was particularly targeted toward the working class, and no less a witness than Viscount Castlereagh noted that the *Dwarf* indeed found that target: the *Dwarf*, according to Castlereagh, could be found in the northern colliery districts "in the hatcrown of almost every pitman you meet" (Hendrix 108).[14]

Forced by the Six Acts to raise his price to six pence, Wooler maintained the *Dwarf* with a limited circulation until 1824, when he ceased publication, bitterly recriminating his audience: "In ceasing his political labors, the Black Dwarf has to regret one mistake, and that a serious one. He commenced writing under the idea that there was a PUBLIC in Britain, and that public devotedly attached to the cause of parliamentary reform. This, it is but candid to admit, was an error. Either there is no public, or that public is indifferent upon the subject" ("Final Address," 1824 n.p.). After publishing a short-lived periodical, the *Mechanics' Chronicle* in 1825 (Prothero 187), Wooler retired from journalism until well after the "War of the Unstamped"—indeed, until well into the Chartist period. At the end of 1848, Benjamin Steill, a veteran of the periodical struggles of the 1830s, asked Cooper, a Chartist, to collaborate with the "aged" Wooler in a weekly penny periodical, the *Plain Speaker*. In describing their collaboration in his autobiography, Cooper shows no love for Wooler: "'He was, at one time, the finest epistolary writer in England,' said Mr. Steill in his commendation. But the stilted style of the *Black Dwarf*, however it had been relished by the men of a former generation, was not in favour with the men of my generation. . . . Nor was Wooler's conversation more animated than his style: it was 'flat, stale, and unprofitable'" (Cooper 317). Certainly, Wooler's *Black Dwarf*, the product largely of one man, epistolary in style, directed toward issues that had lost much of their significance by 1849, was in some ways very different from the working-class periodicals that Cooper was familiar with. But in other ways, it was far closer than Cooper acknowledged; in a literary sense especially, *Black Dwarf* is the most forward-looking of the earliest working-class periodicals. Despite the disgust with his audience Wooler displayed when quitting them, he shows in that periodical a fuller conception of the essential humanity and humanism of a working-class audience than do either Cobbett or Carlile.

Wooler believed that his periodical should offer as much entertainment as education. *Black Dwarf* promoted itself in its first year as "a survey of the DRAMA, and the literary world in general" ("Prospectus," 1817 n.p.). Interspersed with stinging condemnations of the Six Acts and reports of the events at Peterloo are reviews of Edmund Kean's *Othello* (26 Feb. 1817: 78), of an 1817 revival of Philip Massinger's *A New Way to Pay Old Debts* (12 Mar. 1817: 110), and a very early stage version of Mary Shelley's *Frankenstein* (6 Aug. 1823: 207–8), among other plays. Those reviews and others are concerned primarily with the ability of plays to entertain, not to teach. The idea that a working-class audience should watch, say, Shakespeare purely for pleasure is one that Carlile and Cobbett never seemed to recognize. With such reviews, Wooler departed boldly from his contemporaries.

Wooler strove to entertain with his own writings as well. Like Cobbett, Wooler shows the influence of the great British satirists—especially Pope—in his lively personal style.[15] Moreover, his work strongly shows the influence of the satirists of his own day, such as George Cruikshank and his friend Hone, both of whom he flattered by publishing a "Reformer's House That Jack Built" obviously derived from their "Political House That Jack Built" (1819). He shows their influence as well in his satirical advertisements and in features such as his "State

Theatricals," which reviewed the doings of Parliament as a drama, or his "A New Political Herbal," which compared certain public figures to plants, connecting the then poet-laureate, Robert Southey, for example, with the "Spurge, or Common Laurel."[16]

No one has yet compiled a list of the literature that Wooler read, but that list is obviously an extensive one. Wooler, like Cobbett, was fond of quoting established literature to make his own points—as, for example, when he compares the concoction of the Six Acts to the strange brewing of the Weird Sisters in *Macbeth*. But unlike Cobbett, Wooler published extracts of English, American, and European literature independently of his own points, as writing worth reading by his audience solely for its own sake. Many of these extracts appeared in an extraordinary series Wooler began publishing in 1820 called "The Blackneb."[17] The introduction to that series argues that the working class of the present should find value in many of the works of the past:

> In beating up the quarters of our old friends, we shall occasionally ascend the high latitudes of time, and traverse the various districts of life. Now and then we may relieve the severe gravity of the argumentative, by excursions into the fields of Anecdote and Poetry . . . and we hope to produce some proof, that a sense of Liberty is not a thing begotten on the poverty of yesterday, by yesterday's oppression; that Liberty is not the trimming shifting ignis-fatuus, which the servile would have us believe, but a real entity, unchangeable, eternal, and one of the chief blessings of social existence. (26 Jan. 1820: 89)

During the two years that the series lasted Wooler published fully 698 quotations by "old friends," quotations from (among many others) Locke, Benjamin Franklin, Bacon, Hazlitt, Thomas More, Swift, Cowley, Francis Quarles, Milton, Marvell, Aristotle, Holinshed, Sterne, Hume, Thomas Browne, James I, the *Paston Letters*, Machiavelli, Chesterfield, Erasmus, Erasmus Darwin, Blackstone, Bentham, and Johnson, and ending with, as number 698, an early publication of the "Star-Spangled Banner" (*Black Dwarf*, 9 Oct. 1822: 524).[18] Despite the abundance of sources here, the selections were obviously chosen carefully, as expressions of liberty. Wooler may have published far more literature than Cobbett did in his *Political Register*, but *Black Dwarf*, too, acted as a very selective filter between established writers and the working class.

Wooler shows in *Black Dwarf* a broad-minded approach to literature that anticipated the views of many later working-class journalists. Wooler was the first to reexamine established writers systematically, to separate what was applicable to his audience from what was useless, and to give old writers a new greatness by letting them speak directly to a new class. While Carlile distrusts these literary voices and promotes himself as a replacement for them, and while Cobbett respects those voices insofar as they back up his own dominant voice, only Wooler lets them speak for themselves. His *Black Dwarf* celebrates the multiplicity of these voices, not their unanimity.

While Cobbett's, Carlile's, and Wooler's periodicals were the most popular of this period, there were others. Some of these did not last long enough to establish more than the barest literary identity. Cumulatively, however, they show a belief in the power of Paineite rhetoric, a healthy sense of themselves as a new literary power, and a general willingness to apply established works to their own ideas. They also show a strong belief in the literary ability of members of their class, publishing many of their poems. In this they are similar to their better-known contemporaries: Carlile, Wooler, and, to a lesser extent, Cobbett also published working-class poetry. Most of the poems stridently or satirically comment on the events and issues the poets saw as important to their class. Many of the poems in periodicals such as Davison's *Medusa* and the *Cap of Liberty*, as well as *Black Dwarf*, demonstrate convincingly that Shelley was far from the only writer to commemorate the Peterloo massacre in verse (see chap. 5).[19]

These periodicals occasionally looked to established writers to make or emphasize their own points. *Hone's Reformists' Register*, Davison's *Medusa*, and a Glasgow periodical, the *Spirit of the Union*, all published, without commentary, passages from Hazlitt; they reflect the obvious fondness that early working-class journalists held for that essayist.[20] Hone also presented his audience with long passages of verse from Cowper and Defoe, "one of the closest observers of mankind" (5 July: 733–36; 4 Oct. 1817: 337–41). A writer in the twopenny *People*, a periodical that only lasted from April to July of 1817, noted a strong parallel between the ways Macbeth and Richard III used hired assassins and the ways Liverpool, Castlereagh, and Sidmouth employed "spies, informers, and hatchers of plots and treasons and conspiracies" to do their dirty work (28 June 1817: 319–20).

Reviews are rare in these short-lived works. One in particular stands out. *Hone's Reformists' Register* is perhaps the only working-class periodical of the first half of the nineteenth century that today is known primarily for its literary commentary. Hone was the first to notice what he saw as the brilliance of Southey's recently published (though long-before-written) *Wat Tyler,* and the first to compare unfavorably the reactionary poet-laureate of 1817 with the revolutionary young poet who wrote the poem in 1794.[21]

Perhaps no stronger compliment—albeit a backhanded one—was paid to the political power of all of these periodicals than that of their imitators: periodicals published by members of the government or parties loyal to the government in an attempt to "combat the seditious and infidel publications of the day," as one of them, the *Green Man, or Periodical Expositor,* states. Other such periodicals include the *Anti-Cobbett,* written by George Canning, William Gifford, and Southey; Gibbons Merle's *White Dwarf,* subsidized by the Home Secretary, Sidmouth; and *Shadgett's Weekly Review of Cobbett, Wooler, Sherwin, and Other Democratical and Infidel Writers.*[22] These imitations also paid tribute to the rhetorical and literary power of working-class periodicals. Their writers often tried to use Paineite rhetoric to serve their own reactionary ends. Some bravely tried to imitate Wooler's or Cobbett's satirical style. They also carried reams of imitation working-class poetry. But while these periodicals contain the same forms as their originals, they are infused with a patently false energy. Trying to speak to the people, not with them or for them, they are mannequins of early working-class periodicals.

In the 1820s a new kind of periodical began to appeal to members of the working class. Although Owen's Co-operative ideas found few working-class adherents in the days of Peterloo, when he was denounced by Cobbett, Wooler, and others, by late in the decade a number of laborers had embraced Owenism—or, to be more precise, had adopted some of his ideas and adapted them to suit their class. According to E. P. Thompson, the Owenite movement owed as much to ideas of the working-class as it did to Owen himself:

Owenism from the late Twenties onwards, was a very different thing from the writings and proclamations of Robert Owen. It was the very imprecision of his theories, which offered, none the less, an image of an alternative system of society, and which made them adaptable to different groups of working people. From the writings of the Owenites, artisans, weavers and skilled workers selected those parts which most closely related to their own predicament and modified them through discussion and practice. If Cobbett's writings can be seen as a relationship with his readers, Owen's writings can be seen as ideological raw material diffused among working people, and worked up by them into different products. (*Making* 868)[23]

In the late 1820s and into the 1830s a number of Co-operative periodicals began to appear, conducted largely by members of the working class and appealing especially to an audience of that class. Two of the best known of these early Co-operative magazines are the Brighton *Co-operator* and the *Co-operative Magazine*. In general these periodicals had a serious, millennial tone, a far cry from the ironic style of some of the earlier working-class journals. This tone was reflected in the literature they chose to discuss or publish. These periodicals, like Carlile's, were relatively free of imaginative literature. Their own literature consisted largely of fables, simple moral tales, and didactic poetry. When established writers do appear, their ideas are firmly linked to the Co-operative movement. In the *Co-operative Magazine*, for example, Burns, Shelley, and Southey all earn honorable mentions, because a few carefully chosen lines from the poetry of each show a leaning toward Co-operative principles.

The Co-operative magazines had small circulations and appealed to a very limited segment of the working class. They survived largely upon the energy of the movement and the events within it, such as the development of Co-operative societies and labor exchanges, and not because they supplied the working class with news about revolutionary events, as had the press of 1817–20. That more popular press lingered on, but without the energy of its first years. The Six Acts of 1819, which so rigidly defined a newspaper as to make every production of the working-class press liable to the four-penny stamp, dampened that press. A gradual lessening of the political tension within that class during the years before 1830 had much to do with shrinking circulations as well. The events of the early

1830s threw the working class as a whole into a new ferment, and a renewed working-class press exploded into action.

1830–36

William Carpenter, one of the first working-class journalists to enter the fray in the "War of the Unstamped" of 1830–36, gave his first periodical the ponderous title of *Political Letters and Pamphlets, Published for the Avowed Purpose of Trying with the Government, the Question of Law—Whether All Publications Containing News or Intelligence, However Limited in Quantity or Irregularly Issued, Are Liable to the Imposition of the Stamp Duty of Fourpence.* Hetherington, one of the most famous working-class journalists active during this period, stated on the masthead of every issue of his *Poor Man's Guardian* that that periodical had been "ESTABLISHED, CONTRARY TO 'LAW,' TO TRY THE POWER OF 'MIGHT' AGAINST 'RIGHT.'" Both journalists thus loudly asserted one of the primary purposes of their periodicals, and indeed a major purpose of most of the working-class periodicals of the time: to combat the provisions of the Six Acts of 1819, provisions that made any periodical that appeared more often than once every twenty-six days, sold for less than six pence, and contained "any Public News, Intelligence, or Occurrences, or any Remarks or Observations thereon, or upon any Matter in Church or State" a crime, one punishable by imprisonment and high fines (Wiener, *War* 4–5).[24]

Combating laws that had been on the books for more than ten years does not completely explain why an enormous wave of working-class periodical publication began in 1830 and continued for six years. The idea that all the working-class journalists of this period were obsessed with the one issue of "taxes on knowledge" is, quite simply, wrong. Such thinking only dulls any sense of the energy of what was one of the most spirited and colorful periods of British working-class journalism—indeed, of British working-class history. Fighting the Six Acts and the class oppression that they codified was, during this time, one struggle among many. As E. P. Thompson argues convincingly in *The Making of the English Working Class*, the early 1830s were the very years in which this class came of age. A revived working-class press reflected that new-found awareness; it reported and discussed the events and issues that were of interest to the working class, those moreover that reinforced the working class's awareness of itself as a class, with common needs and aspirations.

Many working-class concerns in the early 1830s were not new, of course. The Co-operative movement continued into the decade, and new Co-operative periodicals appeared, most important among them the *Lancashire Co-operator,* which became the *Lancashire and Yorkshire Co-operator* (1831–32), and the *Crisis* (1832–34), which was edited by Owen himself, as well as by his son, Robert Dale Owen, and James E. "Shepherd" Smith. That periodical, at one time subtitled *National Co-operative Trades' Union and Equitable Labour Exchange Gazette,* dealt also with another concern vital to the working-class: trade unionism. This concern was far from new. Wooler had written on union issues; in 1825 John Gast had produced the *Trades Newspaper and Mechanics' Weekly Journal,* a periodical representing several trades and "governed by a committee of the trades" (E. P. Thompson 853 n).[25] In the 1830s, however, more working-class periodicals than ever before focused on trade-union issues, among them the *Herald to the Trades Advocate, and Co-operative Journal,* the *Scottish Trades' Union Gazette,* and the *Tradesman,* all published in Glasgow; James Morrison's *Pioneer;* and a series of periodicals edited by Doherty, the most popular of which were the stamped *Voice of the People* and the unstamped *Poor Man's Advocate.*[26]

Some periodicals, such as the twopenny *Radical,* later the *Radical Reformer,* Carpenter's short-lived *Political Unionist,* and Carlile's *Union,* championed the cause of political unions. Others, such as the *British Labourer's Protector, and Factory Child's Friend,* a periodical out of Leeds, focused on factory reform. Periodicals such as Cleave's and Cruikshank's *A Slap at the Church* (1832) attacked organized religion. Other periodicals, including two papers published by Charles Penny, the *London Policeman* and the *People's Police Gazette,* censured legal and police abuse of the working class. One periodical, the *Advocate,* saw as its purpose opposing the use of machinery in any form.

There were other concerns as well: the Poor Law Amendment Act of 1834, the hated "bread tax" (or the Corn Laws), and the celebrated cause of the Tolpuddle Martyrs (1834). Most working-class periodicals aimed at comprehensiveness, addressing in turn each issue they felt was important to their audience and using those issues to promote the idea of a separate class with a distinct and valuable consciousness. Some of the more successful periodicals of this kind were James H. B. Lorymer's *Republican*, the *Poor Man's Guardian*, the *Cosmopolite*, the *Destructive and Poor Man's Conservative*, Joshua Hobson's *Voice of the West Riding*, and Richard Lee's *Man*, as well as later, full-size newspapers such as *Cleave's Weekly Police Gazette* and *Hetherington's Twopenny Dispatch*.

One issue of importance to most working-class periodicals of this period was the Reform Bill of 1832. Although there was much debate among working-class journalists as to the value of the bill before it passed, most of them agreed in hindsight that the bill signaled a betrayal of the working class by the middle class, and that it left their class alone without direct representation in government. From 1832 on, these journalists knew that working- and middle-class interests were forever severed and that the working class had to take control of its own destiny. More than ever, their political values were class-based. So, more than ever, were their literary values.

It is often difficult—indeed, even impossible—to connect specific ideas or statements about literature in these periodicals with specific writers in the way I have done with Cobbett, Wooler, and Carlile. This is not because the 1830s lacked colorful and industrious champions of the working class: Cleave, Watson, Hetherington, and Carpenter in London, Doherty in Manchester, Hobson in Leeds, and many others were just as active and productive as their predecessors and, if anything, even more strident and class conscious. The 1830s was a decade unsurpassed in the history of the British working class and its journalism in the variety of its movements, writers, and ideas.

Therein lies a problem. This period was one of committees and combinations, of short- and long-term alliances and collaborations, of the National Union of the Working Classes, the National Association for the Protection of Labour, the Grand National Consolidated Trades' Union, the London Working Men's Association, and many other political, trade, and Co-operative unions. In much the same way, working-class periodicals of the time were generally the products of a combination of journalists. Periodicals published, edited, printed, and largely written by one man—those, in other words, like Cobbett's *Political Register* or Wooler's *Black Dwarf*—did exist during this period, and they can tell us, for example, that Carpenter, in his *Political Letters and Pamphlets*, was somewhat familiar with the works of Shakespeare. But such one-person efforts were rare. Most periodicals had a publisher, a separate editor, and a number of contributors. The *Poor Man's Guardian*, for example, was published by Hetherington and edited, for the most part, by James "Bronterre" O'Brien. Both men influenced the ideas in that periodical. So did others: Thomas Mayhew, Cleave, Watson, and possibly Julian Hibbert (Wiener, *Finding List* 46).[27]

Moreover, in many cases a periodical's publisher, editor, or contributors, or even its name, could change in mid-run. Describing one of the more popular periodicals of the day, for example, Patricia Hollis notes that "the *Cosmopolite* was launched in March 1832 by eight vendors, including [Edward] Hancock, [George] Pilgrim, [James] Knight, and [Joseph] Walker." But by the end of 1833 Carlile and his son Richard were "the anonymous publishers, writers, and proprietors" of that periodical (134, 151).[28] Eventually, *Cosmopolite* merged with Lee's *Man* (Wiener, *Finding List* 12). Such confusing transitions are not unusual. Trying to trace the family history of these periodicals can be at times incredibly difficult. And this already complicated situation becomes even more complex when we consider the latter part of this period, when the smaller, pamphlet-size papers such as *Cosmopolite* and *Poor Man's Guardian* gave way to full-size, full-feature newspapers such as *Cleave's Weekly Police Gazette* and *Hetherington's Twopenny Dispatch*. Since most writings in working-class periodicals were not given bylines, trying to assign individual pieces to identifiable writers is in many cases an exercise in futility.

So while we are often stopped from saying with certainty what John Cleave thought about John Milton, for example, or what Lorymer thought about Scott, we can draw some general inferences about how these journalists approached literature.

Most working-class journalists of this time obviously believed that literature had some value to them and to their class. Almost every one of their periodicals carried literature in one form or another. Whether or not these journalists made references to the literary lights of the past or the established writers of their own day, almost all published a huge amount of working-class poetry. Like the poetry in earlier working-class periodicals, this poetry—satirical, occasional, or didactic—was almost always directed toward overtly political ends. Just as working-class poets of 1819 strove to immortalize the eleven martyrs of Peterloo, for example, so the poets of 1834 strove to immortalize the six martyrs of Tolpuddle.[29]

Besides publishing working-class poems, the editors of this period were far more likely than their predecessors to publish long excerpts from other works and even, on occasion, to republish entire works. The works that these publishers and editors chose to print or reprint—those, in other words, that they considered to have literary value and therefore to deserve a place in a working-class canon—include, as would be expected, a number written by the working class or directed particularly toward that class. One of the most commonly reprinted (and reviewed) works during this period, for example, was Rowland Detrosier's *An Address Delivered to the Members of the New Mechanics' Institution . . . on the Necessity of Extension of Moral and Political Instruction among the Working Classes.* Parts of this work—independently, or in reviews—appear in, among other places, *Berthold's Political Handkerchief* (1831; "Literature," 19 Sept. 1831 n.p.), *Cleave's Weekly Police Gazette* (2 Apr. 1836 n.p.), and from an unknown issue of *True Sun*, from which the passage in *Cleave's* is excerpted.[30] To take another example—one that must have scared the life out of the overseers of the unstamped in the Home Office—a supplementary number of the *Poor Man's Guardian* consists entirely of eight closely printed pages of excerpts from Francis Macerone's *Defensive Instructions for the People*, a manual on street fighting that describes, among other things, the proper way to construct pikes and barricades and the most effectively damaging use of burning acids (11 April 1831).

But for every such example of exclusively class-based literature, an instance can be found taken from works already canonical to the middle class. The journalists of this period, too, culled from that canon to create their own. Continuing in the tradition of Wooler's "Blackneb" series, at least two editors during this time created whole periodicals—*Materials for Thinking*, and *Every Man's Library of Republican and Philosophical Knowledge*—solely to bring the best and most relevant ideas of established authors to the working class. *Materials for Thinking*, compiled by John Taylor, went through at least three printings, the last in 1852. In that periodical Taylor brought Addison, Sterne, Pope, Johnson, and many others to a working-class audience. No copy of *Every Man's Library* is now known to exist, but according to the *Poor Man's Guardian* and Lorymer's *Republican*, that periodical carried the writings of Paine, Locke, and Voltaire (Wiener, *Finding List* 16–17).

Generally, working-class journalists during this period chose to publish an established work if it had obvious political and social value for a working-class audience. As long as a work had such relevance, the actual class standing of its writer hardly mattered. In the second issue of the *Political Soldier*, for example, two poems appear, one beside the other: a working-class poem, "The Soldier Flogged," and Thomas Hood's "A Waterloo Ballad" (14 Dec. 1833: 11). No distinction is made between the two poems or between their writers; the implication is that no distinction should be made, as long as each work speaks to the working class.

These journalists did more with literature than just excerpt it. They were far more likely to review individual works than their predecessors. Generally, critics in these periodicals felt that, to serve their audience, they had to operate within a completely new set of standards. In other words, most working-class reviewers rejected outright the many critical models offered by middle-class commentary of the past and present. A writer in the *Poor Man's Guardian*, noticing a new periodical called *The Truth!*, recognized the absence of a good middle-class model for the working-class literary critic: "All that we have heard of [*The Truth!*] is, that it is to contain political as well as literary criticisms; what room there may be for the former, we know not, but we do know that the latter is absolutely wanting" (18 Aug. 1832: 501)[31]

Working-class journalists generally believed that middle-class commentary and critics were hopelessly corrupt. A writer in a working-class critical journal, the *Literary Beacon* (1831), saw as the purpose of that periodical less reviewing individual works (although it did contain many reviews) than "breaking down the system of corruption which has been for so long a period permitted to exist under the name of criticism" ("Introduction," [Sep. 1831?] n.p.). Another periodical, the popular *Destructive*, clearly attacks middle-class reviewers in a blanket diatribe upon "men of letters," showing their literary corruption to be at least partially class based:

> People are but too apt to attach vague notions of excellence to what are called "men of letters." It is a grievous error. They are among the most worthless of society. Their trade is "phrase-making"—their habits loose and idle—their knowledge confined to books, and their characters in general a compound of envy, sycophancy, and fretful vanity. . . . Ever ready to lick the dust from under the feet of rank, when it notices them, their spite is equally vigilant to revenge every little neglect, real

or fancied, to which their exorbitant vanity subjects them at its hands. Thus, while they are the most querulous of mortals respecting their own wrongs, they treat the "lower orders" with ten-fold more superciliousness than they can themselves endure from their patrons. (16 Mar. 1833: 53)

Generally, working-class reviewers believed that their articles, which promoted the truth, stood in opposition to the lies of such middle-class reviewers. That belief entailed a rejection of middle-class attitudes toward literature in general. That rejection in turn necessitated a complete renunciation of those values that made a work canonical for the middle class. By promoting their truthful views over the lies of the middle class, the working-class journalists of this period deliberately sought a new canon, one composed of works that had direct value for their own class.

While working-class critics' standards may have been class based, they reviewed—and sometimes approved—the works of writers from all classes. Of course, they were especially eager to recognize the efforts of fellow working men and women. Perhaps the most frequently reviewed writer during this period was Ebenezer Elliott, especially his *Corn Law Rhymes* (1830). Reviews of Elliott's work appeared, among other places, in the *Literary Beacon* (16 July 1831: 33–36) and the *Weekly True Sun* (17 Jan. 1836: 997). These reviews make it clear that despite the problems the literary historian might have in seeing Elliott as "working class"—after all, he was the owner of a Sheffield foundry—working-class reviewers of the time clearly felt he was a proletarian. Charles Cole, the "London Mechanic," is also a frequent subject for review.[32] The poems of these two were also published frequently in working-class periodicals during this time. But few periodicals restricted the works they published or reviewed to working-class productions. Generally, when reviewers saw writers of any class attacking, neglecting, insulting, or otherwise offending the working class they were merciless in their assaults. But when writers of any class promoted truths valuable to the working class, described conditions in a way that accorded with that class's view of things, or otherwise reached out to that class, reviewers would heap praise upon their work. Many examples can be found of reviews hostile or complimentary to established writers; many can be found that both compliment and attack. Thus, a reviewer of *Eugene Aram* in the *Literary Test*. . . . (1832), for example, angrily enumerates the many ways that Edward Bulwer insults the working class (7–14 Jan. 1832: 17–22, 37–39);[33] a reviewer of Benjamin Disraeli's *Alroy* and his *Rise of Iskander* in the *British Liberator* prefers the second over the first because of its simple, more generally comprehensible style, which makes it more accessible to the working class (17 Mar. 1833: 80); and two periodicals, the *Schoolmaster, and Edinburgh Weekly Magazine* (1832–33) and *Cobbett's Magazine* in 1832, greeted enthusiastically the long-delayed publication of Shelley's class-sympathetic *Mask of Anarchy* (*Schoolmaster* 8 Dec. 1832: 291–93; *Cobbett's* Jan. 1833: 17).[34]

These reviewers were willing to look to other eras and classes for works relevant to their own class, works that they felt were worth placing side by side with the best of those written by members of the working class. Their literary integrity matched their political integrity. Staunchly sticking to their working-class literary ideals, they refused to meet established writers halfway; for a writer to enter the working-class canon, he or she had to come all the way to them. If a work did not serve the interests of the working class in some obvious way, these journalists ridiculed, condemned, or ignored it as useless.

The working-class journalists of this period, then, promoted a canon for their class that at first glance appears to be half old and half new, made up both of works valuable to their class exclusively and those taken from the middle-class canon. In reality, however, the working-class canon the journalists of this period promoted had very little in common with that of the middle class. The journalists looked at every work they quoted or reviewed from a completely new, class-based point of view and wanted their audience to look at literature in the same way. To examine a work with an entirely different set of values and beliefs about what "literature" actually is, is, in a very real sense, to look at a different work. Everyone read Burns, for example, but, as we shall see, the poems by him the working-class respected and the ways they read them differed from those the middle class read and the way they read them. This was the period when the working class first fully recognized itself as a class, and just as working-class politicians saw for the first time that their class had its own interests, apart from and in opposition to those of any other, so working-class writers first fully recognized that their class had its own literature and literary principles, apart from and at times in opposition to those of other classes.

1837–58

In the spring of 1836 Parliament passed the Newspaper Bill that lowered the tax on newspapers from four pence to one penny and increased the penalties imposed on publishing or selling the unstamped. The act was met with bitterness and anger on the part of working-class journalists and the politically aware working class in general, who saw it as serving to make "the rich man's paper cheaper, and the poor man's paper dearer" (D. Thompson 40)[35]—but by 1837 the bill all but killed the issue of "taxes on knowledge." It did not kill the working-class press, however: the "War of the Unstamped" ended just as Chartism was beginning.[36]

The People's Charter, with its six points—universal male suffrage, the ballot, equal electoral districts, payment for members of Parliament, abolition of property qualifications for candidates, and annual elections—was drafted and published by the London Working Men's Association in the spring of 1838. Its ideas were not new; they had been discussed for years. What was new was the yoking of these points together into a specific program for mass agitation: the Charter popularized working-class philosophy. Chartist literary ideas as well were not born in a vacuum; they were continuous with and developed from earlier working-class literary ideas.

Such a continuity of ideas is only to be expected. The leading working-class journalists of the early 1830s—Hetherington, Cleave, Watson, Carpenter, Lorymer, Lee, Hobson, and others—welcomed Chartism and were active in the early Chartist press. Several leading Chartist journalists began their careers working with the unstamped. Bronterre O'Brien, we have noted, was the editor of the *Poor Man's Guardian* and the *Destructive*; he was also an early contributor to the *Northern Star*, the editor of several Chartist periodicals, and one of the leading political thinkers of Chartism. Harney, one of the most active of all Chartist journalists, began his career as a shop boy for Hetherington (Schoyen 6).

Holding that Chartism centered exclusively upon the six points obscures any sense of the variety of concerns during this time. Working-class thought was no more fixed upon these six points than were the ideas of earlier working-class thinkers limited to the Six Acts or "taxes on knowledge." There were a variety of submovements within Chartism; there were moral-force Chartists, physical-force Chartists, "land-plan"

Chartists, teetotal Chartists, Christian Chartists, knowledge Chartists, O'Connorites, O'Brienites, Lovettites, and complete suffragists. Most of these submovements were represented in one or more periodicals. Moreover, there were many issues important to the working class not at all connected to the Charter. Those issues—trade unionism, free thought, Co-operation, and others—were discussed in Chartist periodicals and in a number of non-Chartist periodicals directed toward the working class, chief among them Richard Oastler's factory-reform periodicals, *Fleet Papers* and *Champion of What Is True and Right and for the Good of All*, and George Jacob Holyoake's free-thinking periodicals, *Oracle of Reason*, the *Movement*, and the *Reasoner, and Herald of Progress*. Most of the periodicals of this time, Chartist or otherwise, like their predecessors, were the work of more than one person.

The most popular working-class periodical of the Chartist era was, without question, *Northern Star*, a full-size, full-feature weekly. Some historians of Chartism, such as Mark Hovell, have argued that the *Star* "was an expanded O'Connor"—that the *Star*, in other words, existed solely as the outlet for O'Connor's demagoguery and as the means by which he could control the raw and stupid power of the mob (96).[37] That view is, quite simply, ridiculous, and can only distort our view of O'Connor, Chartism, and the mass of the *Star*'s working-class readers. The *Star* represented the voices of many apart from O'Connor. According to Gertrude Himmelfarb, O'Connor was "thoroughly latitudinarian in his editorial policies" (258). Dorothy Thompson writes:

> Anyone who has read the *Star* knows that it is very far from being the kind of one-man paper that was traditional among radical journals. The paper had an editor who was a determined and opinionated radical, the Rev. William Hill, a Swedenborgian pastor from Hull who had formerly been a linen handloom weaver in Barnsley. Editorial control rested with Hill, and later with the other editors, Joshua Hobson from 1843 to 1845, and G. J. Harney from 1845 to 1850. O'Connor's role was as a major contributor—most weeks he wrote a front-page *Letter*, he occasionally wrote other columns, and he always ensured that his speeches were reported in full. But for the rest—the greater part of the paper—he allowed his editors and other staff considerable freedom. The *Northern Star* was run in accordance with O'Connor's idea of what a radical newspaper should be—and this was much more like a radical

Times than like a reincarnation of Cobbett's *Political Register*. The paper succeeded because it was considered by its readers to be the paper of the Chartist movement, not simply the voice of Feargus O'Connor. (46–47)

Almost every issue of the *Northern Star*, every week for fourteen years, carried a literary page. The many different writers for that page (including Harney and Ernest Jones, but *not*, apparently, O'Connor) obviously believed their audience had both strong political abilities and strong literary comprehension. They were not talking to a mob.

Northern Star is crucial to this study for a number of reasons, chief among them its obvious value to thousands of working-class readers of the time and its sheer volume of literary information. No other periodical in the 1840s offers such a sense of what members of the working class took literature to be.

Northern Star folded in 1852, leaving no national newspaper for Chartism. Jones quickly tried to fill that void, putting out the first issue of *People's Paper* on 8 May 1852. *People's Paper* never had the success the *Northern Star* did. It struggled to survive from issue to issue, pleading again and again to its readers for donations to keep it going. Keep going it did, however, from 1852 to 1858, and it served in those years as the national outlet for the political and literary ideas of many among the working class. It, too, had a literary page, much like the *Star*'s; it, too, offers the scholar a wealth of literary information. While I do not mean to downplay the importance of the many local working-class papers of this period, or of the shorter-lived and smaller-circulation national periodicals, I think it is hard to overstress the importance of these two papers. From the *Northern Star* and *People's Paper*, more than any other periodicals, we can get some sense of the working-class canon between 1837 and 1858.

The literature and literary values found in the working-class periodicals of this time reflect both the literary ideas of earlier working-class intellectuals and the vitality and evolution of working-class critical thought in the 1840s and 1850s. These periodicals, like their predecessors, were crammed with working-class poetry; most of it, as before, was directed specifically toward working-class political ends. Working-class journalists show that they inherited the literary sensibilities of their predecessors in their reviews and extracts as well: many also judged or published works by established writers based on overtly political, working-class standards. But a new way of viewing literature began to develop during this period. A number of reviews and extracts in Chartist periodicals were not obviously political—or rather, not overtly, immediately, and primarily political.

The extracts in these periodicals continued in the tradition of Wooler's "Blackneb" series. Some periodicals contained selections in departments such as the "Flower Gatherer" ("we cull the choicest") of the *Northern Star* or the "Gleaner" of the *People's Paper*. Other periodicals were wholly composed of extracts: William James Linton's *National: A Library for the People* is perhaps the best example of these. Like the editor in *Northern Star* who in 1840 extensively quoted Shakespeare as a political poet to support the tenets of Chartism,[38] many of these editors used established writers to support specific working-class points. But interspersed among the usual political thinkers are such apparently nonpolitical writers as Captain Frederick Marryat, James Fenimore Cooper, and Charlotte Brontë (all of whom were extracted in *Northern Star*). Linton, in his *National*, excerpts 125 writers; his three favorites—Milton, Shelley, and Godwin—are overtly political, but he also published Keats, Spenser, Confucius, Robert Herrick, Izaak Walton, Socrates, and Chaucer.

Reviewers, too, tended to take a broader view of literature than their predecessors did, and were concerned as much with the pleasure of the text as with its value—or, to put it more accurately, they saw more value than their predecessors did in the simple pleasure a text offered. Individual reviews praised both the politically correct and the aesthetically pleasing. For example, in the April 1850 issue of the *People's Review of Literature and Progress*, a non-Chartist periodical put out by self-professed "Members of the Working-Classes" ("Preface," [1850] vi), a reviewer of Henry David Thoreau's works cites two passages worthy of special attention. The first is Thoreau's politically appropriate statement about refusing to pay taxes to support an unjust cause from his lecture on "Resistance to Civil Government." The second is a distinctly nonpolitical description of a Concord sunset from *A Week on the Concord and Merrimack Rivers* (1849). The reviewer offers no suggestion that the first excerpt's political power is any more valuable than the second's aesthetic impact.

Such a broadening to include literature that is not strictly political does not at all imply a turning away from the political—or a softening of working-class sensibilities. Far from it. Rather, it shows a growing maturity of literary thought on the part of working-class thinkers and a more sophisticated sense of the political in literature. These later working-class thinkers did not see literature as simply a collection of political facts that, properly disseminated, would result in political action on the part of their audience. They did not see their audience as "little vessels . . . ready to have imperial gallons of facts poured into them until they were full to the brim," as Thomas Gradgrind sees his audience of schoolchildren in *Hard Times* (2). In a number of ways, but particularly in literary ones, these journalists served their class not simply by exhorting members of that class to collective action, but also by working toward their holistic individual improvement. Whether moral-force or physical-force Chartist, or not Chartist at all, these journalists generally believed that human and imaginative improvement was linked to political improvement.

Perhaps the best evidence that these journalists placed great value on the imaginative in literature is that many of them, unlike their predecessors, were poets and novelists in their own right. Linton, Gerald Massey, Jones, and Cooper were major Chartist poets, as well as important journalists. Jones, Cooper, and even, apparently, O'Connor, were writers of fiction.[39] A number of periodicals—*Cooper's Journal* for example, or Jones's *Notes to the People*—existed largely to carry the imaginative writings of their producers. These writers were not any less political than others in either their journalism or their creative writing, of course; rather, they showed with their own fiction and poetry that the imagination could effectively serve the political and the social.

The prefaces to many working-class periodicals of this time exhibit not just a greater belief in the imagination, but an increased certainty of the power of beauty and the inseparable interconnection of the beautiful, the imaginative, and the truthful in literature and in the minds of readers. Linton states in the preface to his *National* that his role is not simply to enlighten his audience, but to "respond to their feelings" (5 Jan. 1839: 2). A writer in the *People's Paper*, probably its editor, Jones, writes in the first number, "Features of romance will not be wanting to temper and harmonise the more stern and serious portions of the People's Paper, and to commend it as a household companion of the leisure hour" (8 May 1852). This statement says as much about the writer's idea of the psychological makeup of the paper's individual readers as it does about the editorial components of the paper itself.

The literary values of working-class journalists widened in one other way during the Chartist period. The 1840s and 1850s were decades of growing internationalism on the part of working-class thinkers, engendered in part by the growing number of political exiles from Europe after 1848, among them Mazzini, Marx, and Engels. Many Chartists, including Cooper and Linton, were supporters of Mazzini; many, including Jones and Harney, were friends of Marx and Engels. In fact, and without really stretching our definition, Mazzini, Marx, and Engels could all be considered "British working-class journalists" during this time: Mazzini contributed to Linton's *English Republic* and Harney's *Red Republican*; Engels was, for a time, the foreign correspondent for *Northern Star*; and Marx was actually a temporary co-editor of *People's Paper*. Further, Marx's and Engels's *Communist Manifesto* was first published in English in *Red Republican* on 9 November 1850 (F. B. Smith 52, 106; Saville 40, 50; Schoyen 129, 142–43; Cole, *Chartist Portraits* 294).

The growing political internationalism parallels a growing literary internationalism on the part of working-class journalists. That internationalism was a part of some earlier Chartist periodicals. The last two numbers of the *English Chartist Circular*, for example, carry articles on "The Living Political Poets of Germany," writing about Johann Ludwig Uhland and Anton Alexander von Auerspurg (n.d. [Jan. 1843?] 397, 403–4). But the internationalist flavor is strongest in the later periodicals, which carried or discussed work by George Sand, Eugène Sue, and Victor Hugo—all three of whom were well known to British working-class journalists as political radicals—as well as John Greenleaf Whittier, Pushkin, and many others. These late Chartist thinkers believed that international political class interests transcended national ones and obviously felt the same way about literary interests and values.

The sense of canon that working-class journalists promoted in this period, therefore, was in several ways broader than any promoted before. Almost any writer, from Elizabeth Barrett Browning, to Massey, to Ferdinand Freiligrath, was eligible for entry into that canon. The criteria for canonization were various and sometimes complex and reflected the sense these journalists had of their audience, and of what they saw as valuable and "literary" for that audience. Earlier working-class journalists had held that the ability of a work to promote working-class political progress was the simple standard for allowing a work entry into a working-class canon. The view many Chartist journalists held of their audience was more complex, subtle, and human; every member of that class needed the "Charter and something more," as Harney put it in each issue of *Red Republican*. That "something more" included a sensitivity to beauty as well as a sense of humanity, self-esteem, and self-reliance. And that "something more" could be found in a number of "great" and not explicitly political works. In that sense, *Jane Eyre* is a political work.

Perhaps the most rewarding discovery to be made from an investigation into the working-class periodicals of the first half of the nineteenth century is what they tell about the amazing and ever-increasing depth of the working-class canon, a depth that forces us to rethink working-class literary, psychological, and political history. I notice that as I have discussed this study with a number of people, the exact same questions come up again and again, all concerned with middle-class works about the working class: "What did they think about *Alton Locke*?" "What did they think about *Mary Barton*?" "What did they think about *Hard Times*?" These questions are important ones. Working-class critics rarely accepted depictions of their own class by middle-class authors without some criticism; their criticism of such outside views gives us a new perspective from which to view these middle-class writers and also says much about working-class journalists and the class as a whole.

But I think it significant that the works of literature I have been asked about are almost completely limited to contemporary middle-class depictions of the working class. The uniformity of this line of questioning implies a distorted and limited view today of working-class critics and readers of the first half of the nineteenth century, and especially of the Chartist period. The fact is that in all the working-class periodicals I have looked at, I have found not one reference to either *Hard Times* or *Mary Barton*. I have, however, found references to *Nicholas Nickleby*, *Paradise Lost*, *Faust*, *Don Juan*, and *Hamlet*. Working-class critics of the 1840s and 1850s were not so narcissistic and narrow-minded as to recognize only works of literature strictly depicting their own condition. Many working-class critics had as strong a sense of analogy as their middle-class counterparts; they also saw how Shakespeare, say, or Goethe or Byron, could speak to them and help them understand and better their own lives.

Instead of wondering, then, what they thought of *Mary Barton* or *Hard Times*, I find it more rewarding to ask "What did they think of Thoreau?" or "What did they think of Rabelais?"—or Sand, or Herrick, or Chaucer? Only by investigating the extent of the working-class canon, by investigating their views of writers we might consider (wrongly, in many cases) to be at the periphery of an early-nineteenth-century working-class canon, can we begin to realize the growth, breadth, and literary and political sophistication of the working-class canon of this time. The more I read, the more I am convinced that that canon is at least as broad and sophisticated as any other in Britain at the time.

3

"Imagination Flaps Its Sportive Wings"

Views of Fiction

ALTHOUGH THE attitudes of working-class journalists toward all literary genres changed greatly between 1816 and 1858, toward no genre was there a more discernible and sweeping change than toward fiction. A study of the periodicals written for and by that class during this time indicates that working-class thought about fiction changed from an absolute rejection of the genre to general acceptance. Such a change parallels the slow shift in middle-class attitudes toward fiction, documented in such works as John Tinnon Taylor's *Early Opposition to the English Novel,* with an important difference: working-class journalists solidly based their reasons for rejecting or promoting fiction upon distinctive and identifiable class grounds.

There are three reasons for this change in attitude toward fiction. First, the genre itself changed considerably, in the minds of working-class reviewers. Almost all these critics from the 1830s on noticed the different and, to them, more relevant uses to which, say, Dickens, or Ernest Jones, put the genre than did Scott.

Second, the ideas working-class journalists had about what their readers should read changed. Early journalists perceived fiction as a dangerous diversion from serious literature. They felt that the earnest working-class reader should be concerned only with factual and rational literature instead of imaginative works. In this they echoed the sentiments of middle-class literary reformers such as Charles Knight, editor of the *Penny Magazine*, put out by the SDUK. Unlike Knight, however, whose "useful knowledge" in that magazine steered clear of politics, early working-class journalists felt that the most useful knowledge was political, and that that knowledge was best found in their own periodicals. Later working-class writers and editors saw room for—indeed, a necessity for—imagination, recreation, and diversion and began to understand that political and social truths could be conveyed through imaginative as well as factual literature.

Finally, later working-class journalists themselves changed; they were in general very different from Cobbett, Wooler, and Carlile, who restricted themselves almost exclusively to facts and to the epistolary essay as the medium for conveying those facts. Most later journalists realized that political essays alone would not hold their audience and reacted accordingly. They were, of course, able to turn out a rousing political essay if the situation demanded, but many—for example, Linton, Cooper, and Jones—were fiction writers themselves, as well as essayists, and saw value in both forms.

Early Views: Fears of Fiction

The three major working-class journalists from 1816 through the mid-1820s—Cobbett, Wooler, and Carlile—all attest to Scott's popularity as a fiction writer by confusing, in almost all their pronouncements about fiction, the writer with his genre. To them, all fiction and Scott's fiction were largely the same. References to Scott in journals produced by these men appear with far greater frequency than do those to any other storyteller. Not one of the three mentions Jane Austen or any of her works.[1] Henry Fielding, Sterne, Ann Radcliffe, and other early nineteenth-century novelists might earn passing comments, and on rare occasions these journalists might notice a contemporary novel by a now-forgotten author. Scott, however, is the only writer of fiction who appears repeatedly, and the only one the journalists continually scorn for writing within a corrupt and useless genre. Study of the views of fiction by these early journalists, then, is largely study of their views of Scott.

One might wonder how a working-class audience could read Scott, when his books were, at this time, commanding record prices for fiction, as high as 31s. 6d. (for *Kenilworth*). Cheap reprints of his works were not available until the late 1820s (Altick 263, 274). Clearly, many readers simply did not read Scott at all; rarely did the early critics assume that their audience had any specific knowledge about Scott's plots or characters. On the one occasion I have found in which any of these writers deals with specific details from Scott, Wooler is discussing a stage version of *Kenilworth*, of all books (see below). The theater was obviously instrumental in bringing Scott's work to the poor; as Louis James writes in his *Fiction for the Working Man*, "The impression remains . . . that the main impact of Scott on the lower classes came through the numerous and popular dramatizations of his works" (103). It is clear, however, that even if part of their audience read or saw Scott, not one of the early critics assumed that his readers were familiar with him in any detail.

Although Cobbett maintains that as a young man, "novels, plays, history, poetry, all were read, and nearly with equal avidity" (quoted in Spater 18), he rarely mentions fiction in his *Political Register*. Besides calling Hannah More "that Old Bishop in Petticoats" and mentioning that "Mother" Harriet Martineau "is a vain gossiping creature, talking nonsense" (20 Apr. 1822: 188; 3 Jan. 1835: 12), those few times he mentions fiction he is discussing Scott. He mounts several strong personal attacks on Scott, whom he calls a man "I have always despised" (26 Jan. 1827: 85). His attacks on Scott's fiction, however, and on fiction in general, are far less direct. In only one place, a digression in a letter "To the Planters and Gardeners" in his *Register* of 10 November 1827, does he straightforwardly develop his thoughts on the dangers of fiction by Scott and others like him. Discussing what he sees as good books on gardening, he turns to describing bad books, by which he means "the circulating library trash, abounding with WALTER SCOTT'S amusements." Those "amusements" are dangerous, not to laborers or their families, but to a limited segment of the middle class: "the dirty-necked daughters of the Jews and jobbers, and the lazy wives, who sit and almost rot by the fire-side, stuffed with the drugs of the apothecary instead of being bustling about the house, and taking care to spare the purses, and make pleasant homes for their husbands and their children" (397–98). This disruption within the domestic economy of this small class leads, Cobbett maintains, without saying how, "to the destruction of the good morals of the country."

Cobbett was not the first to argue that fiction is a time waster that keeps people from their proper duties.[2] Certainly he is not the first to argue that fiction is especially dangerous to women. What is strikingly new about his view is its class bias. Earlier assaults on fiction had generally been directed toward all classes, although previously, if one class had been singled out for attack it was the "lower orders." Cobbett turns that attack on its ear, targeting instead the worst elements of the middle class: nonlaboring and nonproductive middlemen. In essence, Cobbett argues that Scott's fiction is useless, and leads the wives and daughters of useless members of society to be themselves useless. Fiction causes this class, already a heavy burden on society, to become an even heavier one.

In his personal attacks on Scott, Cobbett argues the uselessness of the genre of fiction by arguing the uselessness of the most popular novelist. He repeatedly notes that Scott was the first person to be "baronetted" by George IV, and often includes Scott among the placemen and pensioners he hates so intensely. Indeed, Scott is a pensioner for pensioners; he earns his £100 a year as a member of the Royal Society of Literature by writing "heaps of stuff for the amusement of the idle hours of those who live on taxes." Cobbett is obviously galled that Scott, a "sentiment-monger," should be esteemed more highly in some circles than Cobbett is. He notes with some chagrin that the Spanish refer to him as "Sir William Cobbett," "thinking, doubtless, that it was utterly impossible that the author of such a work [Cobbett's *Protestant Reformation*] should escape *Baronetting*, while WALTER SCOTT, who had put forth nothing but what may well be called the dish-washings of literature, had not been able to escape the piercing eye and unsparing hand of the distributors of English honors."[3] Whether this conceit of Cobbett's is a fiction or not is impossible to say. Clearly, though, Cobbett compares genres and writers here, and sees himself and his form of writing as more valuable than Scott and his novels. Just as in his *Grammar of the English Language* and in grammatical articles in the *Register* he attacks earlier prose writers in order to promote a new working-class rhetoric with his own writing, so in his attacks on Scott and his fiction Cobbett indirectly emphasizes the importance of his own work and form by belittling another's.[4]

Although Wooler, like Cobbett, has very little to say about fiction as a genre or about individual works of fiction, curiously enough he almost certainly took the name for his journal from a work of fiction—by Scott.

Scott anonymously published his *Black Dwarf* in November 1816 (Johnson 557); Wooler published the first issue of *Black Dwarf* on 29 January 1817. The character of Elshender of Mucklestane-Moor, Scott's "Black Dwarf," is similar in many important respects to the persona of the Black Dwarf that Wooler takes on in many of his political and critical essays: both are stunted, philosophic, and superficially misanthropic; both are fully sensitive to the failings of human society; and both strive to improve it. While such borrowing shows that Wooler was at least somewhat aware of the popular fiction of the day, it does not necessarily mean that Wooler admired Scott's fiction in general. Wooler in 1817 could not have known that Scott wrote *The Black Dwarf*; at the time almost no one in Britain knew. Nor does Wooler's adoption of a fictional persona imply that he approved of novels. Like Addison's and Steele's Isaac Bickerstaff, Wooler's Black Dwarf may be an imaginary character writing to imaginary correspondents, but his subject matter is completely factual.

Wooler does offer several indirect views on fiction. In a review written in the persona of the dwarf, Wooler criticizes one of the many stage versions of *Frankenstein*, attacking "the taste for the marvelous" in fiction and drama, which he feels prevails "in all ignorant countries." Wooler has nothing but contempt for Mary Shelley's romanticism, and for the fantastic in fiction:

> The story is taken from a novel, by Mrs. Shelley; who, dissatisfied with the ordinary means of introducing men into the world, sets Frankenstein upon the task of *making a man at once*! She does not furnish him with the best materials, for she sends him to the corruption of the grave to look for the principles of life; as if that which had left the body before the process of putrefaction began, was likely to be found there after the decomposition of the mortal corpse. The authoress however had the business in her own hands; and by putting together the largest and finest bones he could find, and covering them we suppose by flaying the most recently deceased body; borrowing the whitest teeth, and the longest and blackest hair, with the superaddition of some secret process wisely transacted behind the scenes (lest other ladies should grow enamoured of the new process of man-making, and every boarding-school miss set about making a lover for herself) a sort of non-descript devil is produced, from which the poor frightened Frankenstein shrinks with as much horror as other people.

Wooler ends his account with amazement that the audience, including the *"learned,"* found this stuff at all entertaining—though "the pit did not relish it so much" (6 Aug. 1823: 207–8). The hierarchy of the theater apparently parallels the social hierarchy; the groundlings are unaffected by such an imaginative flight, which only appeals to those in the higher seats and the higher classes (including, one assumes, the "boarding-school misses"). Obviously, as far as Wooler is concerned, those classes can keep their strange fancies.

Wooler's other remarks about fiction are almost exclusively limited to attacks upon Scott. In a prospectus for a new series of the *Dwarf*, promising a greater variety than before, Wooler moves smoothly from the generic to the specific and back again: "Our next novel feature will be, a *regular* notice of modern literature. We have occasionally referred to this topic, on political subjects; but since Sir Walter Scott has begun to *pervert history* in his *novels*, to serve the despotism which he loves for the favours it has conferred upon him, a closer attention is necessary, to expose such frauds" (31 Dec. 1823: 920–21). Wooler himself gave his readers a clearer idea of one way that Scott perverts history in a review of a stage version of *Kenilworth*. There he maintains that Scott "has only put himself in hooped petticoats, laced stomacher, and large frill, and called it Queen Elizabeth" (7 Jan. 1824: 28). Later working-class journalists expanded upon Wooler's political reading of Scott's fiction and his charge that Scott is hostile to their class interests.

Every reference Wooler makes to fiction is negative. The *Dwarf*'s primary political purpose is to attack political abuses, and one of its literary purposes is to attack generic abuses. Nowhere does Wooler provide a model of good fiction; he can only look upon the genre with derision. Imagination invested in romances, Gothic nonsense, and pseudohistorical charades is misdirected. As a correspondent to *Black Dwarf* writes: "Sir Walter Scott may have imagination; so has a green sickness girl" (6 Aug. 1823: 196–97).[5]

Carlile is the first journalist to deal with the political and social aspects of fiction at any length in a working-class periodical. He is also more doctrinaire and strident in his attacks than any other working-class journalist. He wages his struggle against fiction as violently as he struggles against the established system of political power and the established church. In a footnote to an article entitled "Fiction," he writes "we

should, as lovers of truth, war even with the fiction of the poet, the novelist and the romance writer, and give it no quarter" (*Lion* 24 Oct. 1828:
523). Carlile's belief about fiction, and that of several of his correspondents, is simple: fiction is not truth; therefore it is a collection of lies;
therefore fiction is dangerous. He and his correspondents take this philosophy to extreme lengths, spelling out in wild and colorful detail the
pernicious effects that fiction has on the human constitution and the
body politic. And although they may cite this or that writer for particular
censure, they never focus their attacks upon specific subgenres of fiction—upon "silver-fork" novels, for example, or Newgate novels—because they felt that the genre as a whole was corrupt.[6]

Such an attack nearly corresponds with previous and contemporary
views about fiction held by two other groups: the Utilitarians and the
Evangelicals. Leslie Stephen noted that for the Utilitarians "it was difficult to distinguish between fiction and lying" (367). During the first
dozen years of its existence (1824–36), the Utilitarian *Westminster Review*
mirrored the working-class press by displaying its hostility toward imaginative literature and in particular toward the "historical" romances of
Scott (Nesbit 96, 105–9).[7] Richard Altick cites several Evangelical views of
fiction that—we shall see—are remarkably like Carlile's and his correspondents': they, too, saw novels, "the most dangerous of all literary
forms," as a kind of lotos fruit diverting the reader from profitable contemplation and positive moral values, overstimulating the imagination,
and eventually leading to general debility (108–15).[8] Considering that
both movements were involved in bringing literacy—and transmitting
their own ideologies—to the poor, such a connection is not surprising.
Although the militantly free-thinking Carlile would certainly have been
loath to acknowledge it, early religious training had a strong role in shap-
ing the minds of many working-class readers and writers. Like Carlile,
many from the working class got some, or often all, of their skimpy formal education from Sunday schools or church-run day schools, and it
should come as no surprise that the generic views of their teachers found
fertile soil.[9] Working-class intellectuals did not simply parrot their
middle-class teachers, however. Rather, using much the same argument,
they substituted a class basis of criticism for a religious one; they were not
concerned with fiction's effect on the soul, but upon society.

Carlile's first attack on fiction (as an editor, at least) comes in the *Re-*

publican in the form of a letter from a "Lancashire Weaver" who calls himself Epicurus and whose views on fiction Carlile highly commends: "He calls himself my pupil; but it seems that he is going on a fair way to become his master's master" (6 Feb. 1824: 188). Epicurus's subject is mental improvement, and he stresses the importance of knowing literature and the fine arts but questions the value of novels. Epicurus does admire Fielding, Smollett, and Richardson—why, he does not say—but he attacks the successors of these writers, "the bastard species of novelists, who have imitated the faults of their great originals, and whose volumes are fit for nothing but to be sold to grocers, tallow-chandlers, &c. for waste paper" (185–86). Again, the specific faults of these writers, and therefore of "their great originals," Epicurus does not describe. Instead, he launches an attack on the novel itself: "Novels in general are a corroding poison in society, embittering the reader's pleasures, which otherwise he might enjoy, pure and untainted" (186). To this weaver, novels are a drug, debilitating the ordered mind. He describes the mental effects of novel reading in lurid and often incomprehensible detail, restricting his description at first, but only at first, to effects on the bodies and minds of women, "the only exclusive novel-readers," and presenting the novelist as a sort of seducer and rapist: "The novelist sports with female affections—dabbles and wantons with innocence itself—releases every fibre of the frame—unstrings almost every cord of life—plays with the vibration of the ears, produces, destroys, and produces again, the most nervous and painful sensations, until the animal machine is disordered by an action and reaction, of conflicting feelings and passions" (186). Women may be the most easily seduced by the novelist, but they are not alone:

> The human mind ceases to be a mind when order and regularity are no longer predominant, but forced and beaten down into comparative non-existence. The fancy is courted; hundreds of illusions are admitted as realities; imagination flaps its sportive wings, and skims over the surface of things like a swallow over a lake, occasionally twittering and fluttering round particular objects, and having prevailed upon the memory to follow in the same fairy-like course, they finally write [*sic*] with their myriads of progeny to destroy the judgement, by compelling it to take a tour through regions where she [*sic*] inevitably gets lost and bewildered, and at last falls a victim to the powerful and capricious tyranny of the imagination. (186–87)

Epicurus's highly representational description of the human psychology, with its cords to the body, birds, and mysterious "regions of thought," as well as his abrupt and confusing transitions—from women to all people, from some novels to all, and later, from novels to religious writings—make it hard to try his letter by the test Epicurus sets for literature: "the touchstone of reason" (187). His passionate denunciation of fiction is at least as emotional as those of his Evangelical predecessors. Unlike the Evangelicals, however, the hell he fears is clearly one of this world. This avowedly self-taught weaver cries out a warning to those would-be autodidacts who are following him to avoid the trap of fiction—or of any purely imaginative writing. Instead, others should read, as he has, only "books that are written in favour of the liberties of mankind" (188).

In his next periodical, the *Lion* (1828–29), it is Carlile himself who wars against the genre and against three correspondents who champion fiction in different ways and who, in doing so, show that not all readers of radical periodicals agreed completely with Cobbett, Wooler, or Carlile. The first of these champions of fiction, R. T. Webb, notes "the beauty and utility" of some novels, citing a novel he or she thinks is by Godwin, *Ann of St. Ives*, as an example (*Lion* 21 Mar. 1828: 377).[10] Webb believes that this story belongs to a new subgenre: the "skeptical novel." Two such novels, Webb believes, are *Tremaine; or the Man of Refinement* and *The Mummy*.[11] Both promote free thought; *The Mummy*, for example, "hazards some thoughts about the soul, and resolves the body to its elements, to the full denial of a resurrection." Such works use fiction to make hard truths palatable. As Webb writes: "to draw a simile from the shop: we must sweeten physic for children, and sometimes gild a pill for grown persons" (378). Carlile in reply denies that fiction can somehow improve truth, or improve the ability of people to comprehend truth. Instead, fiction cloaks or covers truths, which are most effective unadorned: "We deprecate the fiction of novels, as part of the common evil of fiction, and the timidity that shelters its desire to promulgate useful truths under the guise of fiction" (379).

Another correspondent to the *Lion*, Anti-Parson, carries to extremes the idea that fiction is an adornment of truth. In the poem "Truth and Fable," Anti-Parson allegorizes the positive relation between the two. Fable,

cover'd with a gorgeous cloak
And deck'd with jewels rare,
(Most part were *false*, but all were fair)

comes upon "poor naked truth," shivering and alone. Fable suggests
that Truth share her cloak, so that

"By the same interests united,
No more will silly man be frighted;
For me—in wisdom's ear
My dear,
You'll whisper a kind word;
And by the senseless fool,
Nurs'd in blind folly's school,
Thro' me—your sober accents shall be heard—
With tastes distinct—but in one cause connected
Your harsher features will not be detected,—
And in whatever circle we appear,
Trust me you need not fear:—
Thanks to your reason, and my folly,
We shall be thought good company." (14 Nov. 1828: 624)

Curiously charitable, Carlile concedes "the general correctness of moral
or character of this Apologue," and then proceeds to condemn it: "Still it
is an evil, that should be corrected; and as in this publication, the aid of
fiction to truth is not found useful, I have to request that no correspondent will hereafter forward any thing of the kind, as I have resolved most
strenuously to assert the propriety of exhibiting truth without the garb
of fiction" (624). Carlile puts himself, his periodical, and his readership above needing the crutch of fiction, here feeling that fiction is not
so much damaging as it is useless, at least for the educated reader. "In
other quarters," he writes, fiction "may be useful; but cannot be useful in
mine" (624).

The third proponent of fiction in Carlile's *Lion* is one Juvenis, whose
essay, filling several pages with small type, takes some empiricist ideas to
strange lengths, attempting to prove that fiction is a part of nature (29

Nov. 1828: 683–88). Briefly put (and would that Juvenis were), he argues that since all ideas can only be received through sense impressions, then all thoughts are born of those impressions, and must "express only what nature dictates." Therefore, "on these remarks, I think I have a right to establish the conclusion, that in giving birth to the wildest vagaries of the imagination, we are still conforming to nature, and therefore to deprecate fiction is, in fact, to revile nature. . . . In short, if fiction be dangerous, you must admit that nature teaches us dangerous and unserviceable lessons, and we must no longer take nature for our guide" (685). Carlile, whose temper flies forth in the form of angry footnotes throughout the essay, notes here with exasperation, "This is a jump. I do not see the chain to this conclusion." Certainly, Carlile is not wrong to question the logic of this confusing essay. Within its pages of questionable logic, however, the essay does take up and further develop Anti-Parson's arguments for the utility of fiction. "Abstruse and laborious disquisitions, though they be recommended by the most profound erudition, will seldom meet so much attention as when they are set off by a flourish of the imagination . . . for I hold the mind to be in one point of view, like a stomach, which sometimes requires to be flattered by dainties, and will refuse a plainly dressed dish" (686). Carlile appreciates this idea even less here than he did when Anti-Parson posited it, and he uses the editorial privilege of getting in the last word to dismiss his correspondent's laborious disquisitions with scorn. "In all romance writing, or novel writing, or poetic fiction, there must be in the mind that indulges it, a sense of trick and dishonesty, which to encourage is to encourage that same sort of vice, which makes general or more enlarged trick and dishonesty successful and socially mischievous. The difference can only be in the degree and not in the action. I hate it, and war against it in every degree; and can find no use for it in the present state of society in this country" (687). Carlile's subject here seems a generic hash, but to him, the romance and the novel are exactly the same. Northrop Frye argues that the contrast between romantic and realistic "is a nineteenth-century one" (45), but the idea that a novel could present any realism relevant to the working class is one foreign to Carlile.

Despite the contentious tone Carlile adopts toward all three of his correspondents, they are not wholehearted proponents of fiction. Each one seems somehow above fiction; even Webb, who praises the new school of skeptical fiction and mentions that he has half written a couple of novels, states that he is slightly embarrassed to be discussing fiction in the sober pages of the *Lion*. The other two make it clear that fiction is useful only to those who need it: for Anti-Parson, the type of person who most needs fiction is "the senseless fool / Nurs'd in blind folly's school"; for Juvenis, using fiction "is like giving medicine to a spoiled child, who will not take it, unless it be covered with sugar" (624, 687). In short, to all three, fiction is a tool with which the intelligent communicate truth to the ignorant. High on Carlile's long list of intolerances, however, was one for ignorance; he has no desire to try to sweeten truths for those who cannot take them straight. Moreover, he sees no escape from ignorance in the lies of fiction. His correspondents may see fiction as a crutch; he sees it only as a snare.[12]

Besides sparring with his correspondents, Carlile discusses fiction directly in two generic essays. The first, "Literature and the Fine Arts," he published in the *Lion* on 14 November 1828 (609–12). The second, "Literature," appeared in *Gauntlet* on 10 February 1833 (2–3). Both clearly show that while Carlile may have taken the germ of his arguments from ideas of middle-class thinkers, he clearly reshaped them to suit a working-class audience. In these articles he maintains that literary reform is inseparably entwined with political reform. If literature were reformed to exclude fiction, society itself would improve.

In the earlier essay Carlile's position is less clear, for it is not certain exactly what he is attacking. He places fiction in the more general and confusing category of "the perversion of letters" that constitutes "light reading," a category that includes "the novels of Sir Walter Scott, and every piece of fiction that has been presented to mankind" (609)—what the total category includes can only be guessed at. Carlile's target is clearer in *Gauntlet*: "Letters are the last remaining spark of the English Republic, and they, too, like state affairs, have fallen under the dominion of madmen. He whose insanity can body forth the greatest number of strange ideas, has been deemed pre-eminent in literature. Sir Walter Scott has been an instance of this kind, and verily it grieves me to see such a man as William Godwin bothering his brain to educe a mass of fiction under the name of a novel" (2). That Carlile includes Godwin in his condemnation suggests that the genre can only muddle the ideas of the most rational of thinkers. Both essays batter Scott relentlessly. "I had rather bear a year's imprisonment where I now am," Carlile writes in *Gauntlet* from Giltspur Street Compter, where he was imprisoned for seditious libel, "than be compelled to read the forty-five volumes of Scott's novels. The idea that the writer is an habitual liar, rises on every page" (3; see Wiener, *Radicalism* 176). In each essay Carlile moves from an attack on Scott to an attack on the genre in order to show that fiction writers enslave their readers, that "they who furnish mankind with light readings are their enemies, and the qualifiers for all the oppressions, degradations, and deprivations that are found among them" (*Lion* 610). Novels are "a despotism in letters, that fetters the mind and degrades the body" (*Gauntlet* 2). While novelists may be the madmen who write this "trash unworthy the notice of being" (*Gauntlet* 3), Carlile is just as angry at the novel reader, who, instead of reading those texts that will elevate and liberate, has a "sickly appetite" that "pores over the source of its own disease, and drains every current of health to gratify its own depraved cravings" (*Gauntlet* 2).

Fiction does more, though, than pose a threat to individuals; it endangers the whole social system. Carlile, like Cobbett and Wooler, maintains that fiction imperils the higher classes. He writes of the class of "drawing-room dolls" in this same issue of *Lion*: "Well as they are, as far as all the luxuries of life are in question, they shrink from the labour, and dread the process of thought. . . . They give fashion to that which is nationally useless, rather than useful, and decry the innovation of original thought, or any thought, that thinks there is room for improvement in the present, and to them delightful, constitution of things" (611). But to Carlile, the working class is besotted by fiction as well. Their penny fiction may differ from the novels only the higher classes can afford, but the effects are the same. In his latter essay Carlile draws a direct parallel between the reading choice of some laborers and their intellectual, physical, and social degradation: "I have noticed in Lancashire, where the bodies of the children are debilitated by the factory exertions of labour, with their inflamed eyes and shrivelled frames, and to whom a few hours in Sunday-school has brought the faculty of reading, that they crave nothing but the wildest kinds of fiction in pictures and little books, feeling and acting as if they themselves were creatures of another world, and a blotch on this" (*Gauntlet* 3). To Carlile, fiction blinds such laborers to oppression and thus allows that oppression to happen. In short, fiction paralyzes all society, and each class perpetuates an unfair political system by encouraging fiction writers.

The solution, of course, is to substitute good reading for bad. In the *Gauntlet* essay Carlile offers himself as a savior to smash the political stasis caused by novels: "I throw down the gauntlet against this state of things, and will strive mightily to make literature of more importance than to fashion fiction" (3). Obviously, Carlile feels that Britain would be a far better place if the aristocratic dolls and suffering factory children alike threw away their *Ivanhoe*s and penny dreadfuls and began to read *Lion* or *Gauntlet*. Like Cobbett, Carlile sees his writing as a model, not simply for the rising working class of his day but for the society of the future. He offers a vision of the literature of this new society in the *Lion*, a society in which fiction has no place: "After purging the country of its political errors and its superstition, an order of literature and arts will arise, exceeding any that has hitherto existed or even been contemplated" (612). This statement is syntactically confusing; it is unclear exactly what or who purges the country in this way. It is clear, however, from Carlile's statements about literature and from his life's work, that he is proud to place himself prominently among the purging forces.

Later Views: The Uses of Fiction

When Carlile published his last full attack on fiction, in the *Gauntlet* in the early thirties, he was not alone in his views about the genre. Others echoed his criticisms and developed new ones. Two writers in particular, one in the journal partially edited by Owen himself, the *Crisis*, and another in the hotly radical *Destructive* see nothing but physical and social dangers in fiction reading. The *Crisis* article, "On the Late Sir Walter Scott," begins as a study of Scott but soon becomes an attack on novels, charging that they are psychologically ruinous to their readers: "Persons whose minds are filled with works of fiction, frequently make serious mistakes in their calculations of real life, and are often swamped, stranded, or wrecked. Their wrecks should inspire succeeding voyagers with caution. We know some persons who became comparatively useless, and now hang and are likely to hang burdens on their friends, from incessantly reading works of fiction." This writer, one A. B. C., believes that a nation of such derelicts "can be formidable to nothing but their own welfare, and serviceable to none but their own enemies"—a statement with class implications as well as national ones, for the poor especially suffer from this genre, "which diverts the mind from the distress which requires relief" (20 Oct. 1832: 131–32).

The *Destructive* carried a long excerpt from Thomas Macconnell's *Lectures*. Macconnell lashes out at the "Sweet Nonsense" of fiction, again attacking the genre by attacking Scott and presenting novel readers as useless social drop-outs: "The intellect of all novel readers will be found stunted, dwarfish, debilitated, and indolent. Such persons cannot take the pains to think, and are consequently disqualified from forming any sound or stable opinion upon any important public matters, which require public opinion for their adjustment" (*Destructive* 13 Aug. 1833: 243).[13]

One criticism that these two essays and others make is that novels are by nature effeminate, and that they feminize society. Criticism of women as the principal readers of a useless genre is as old as is the novel itself (Taylor 52–86). Among working-class critics, Cobbett, Carlile, and Carlile's correspondent Epicurus all take this sexist approach. The essays in *Crisis* and *Destructive* take this point a step further by arguing that novelists prize "feminine" qualities of beauty and imagination and care little for the "masculine" qualities—reason, factual knowledge, and understanding—that are to be found in more sober literature. Celebrating and indulging the feminine, fiction writers divert readers from, and even destroy, the masculine; they "emasculate the intellect, and disqualify it for deep thought and laborious investigation" (*Crisis* 13 Oct. 1832: 132). A writer in the *Artizan's Miscellany, or Journal of Politics and Literature* (1831), a mildly reformist Edinburgh paper conducted by "several members of the Working Classes," bemoans "this effeminate and novel-hunting age," about which he wonders "whether the *he* animal does not pay more devotion to the novel than [does] the other sex, thus entailing, as it does, a disgrace upon us, and ridiculing our pretensions to nobler and more masculine ideas, or to a better knowledge of human nature" (25 June 1831: 39).[14] Macconnell likewise declares that he has no doubt that such is indeed the case, and such a feminization of letters endangers the national literature, the individual novel reader, and the public in general:

> The once masculine character of our national literature has been very
> seriously injured by this effeminate species of writing, which can only

proceed from the pens of she-men; and, which if the public mind was in a high energetic and healthy tone, would have none but she-men and children for its readers. But it is lamentable to be obliged to acknowledge that it can boast its thousands and tens of thousands, and *hundreds of thousands* of male readers; and hence, we have so many pigmies [*sic*] in understanding, and giants in imagination; so many capitalists in ignorance, and paupers in knowledge. (243)

Besides scorning women and femininity, these critics show their dread of inactivity and leisure, which they see as particularly feminine behavior. The many movements the working class supported in the thirties found their power in relentless activity and agitation. In the eyes of these spokesmen, to give in to diversion or inactivity—to read fiction—was tantamount to class betrayal.

Just as the number of working-class periodicals increased considerably in the early 1830s during the "War of the Unstamped," so did instances expressing the views they held about fiction. Seen in the context of the many other working-class writings about fiction of this time, the antinovel pronouncements of A. B. C., Macconnell, and the writer for *Artizan's Miscellany* seem a rear-guard action. During the 1830s most working-class journalists and editors began to accept fiction and to use it themselves to serve working-class ends.

This change necessarily involved a major shift in critical technique. Working-class journalists before and into the thirties refused to separate fiction writers from the genre of fiction, and their reviews are almost always simultaneous attacks on one writer, usually Scott, and on fiction. From the thirties on, however, most journalists clearly separate individual writers of fiction from the genre and recognize that fiction is not generically bad, but rather that individual works of fiction can be good, bad, or indifferent. To put it another way, they began to realize that fiction need not always be a romantic flight far removed from class reality. Moreover, these journalists realized that their readers were now readers of fiction as well. The thirties saw the development of cheap reprints of novels and part publication, and an explosion of inexpensive magazines publishing fiction (Altick 273–80). Journalists could not simply reject a genre that was becoming more and more a part of the everyday life of the working man and woman.

Two reviews of Scott's work illustrate these changes. The first, from the radical and literary Edinburgh *Schoolmaster*, was written on the occasion of Scott's death and is one of the few essays in any working-class periodical that effusively praises Scott.[15] The article is an incredibly far-fetched attempt to rehabilitate a writer—to shape that writer's beliefs to fit a radical creed. According to this article, Scott's biggest mistake was in believing himself to be a Tory: "If Sir WALTER SCOTT has gone to his grave in the belief that he is a Tory writer, no man was ever the dupe of so gross self-delusion" (29 Sept. 1832: 132). The essay argues that Scott consistently holds the peers, lawyers, "country gentry," and especially the monarchy in contempt: "Has the railing of the most violent Radical, or the strongest arguments of Paine, struck a more fatal blow at monarchy than the popular narratives of Scott?" (132). To the writer of this essay, Scott's heroes are all of the working class:

> It is among them, the poor or the unregarded, that we are taught to look for shrewdness, intelligence, generosity, fidelity, disinterested attachment, religion that is not hypocrisy or mummery, and patriotism which is not ambition in flimsy disguise. We have from among the very offscourings of the degraded *castes*, spae-wives and gaberlunzies, who, by the grandeur of their elementary character, their generosity, eloquence, and enthusiasm, make gentles and nobles look small in comparison. There is no need to run over the catalogue of poor schoolmasters, post-boys, fish-wives, idiots, and such rag-tag, whose prepossessing qualities, steady virtues, and redeeming points, it is the study and delight of this truthful writer to bring out. (132–33)

This view of Scott as a champion of the working class could not be more opposed to the view in an article in one of the earlier and better-known Chartist journals, the *Chartist Circular*. Scott is the first of many subjects of that periodical's long-running series called "Literary Sketches," and is the only one that the writer of those sketches attacks relentlessly. The thesis of the essay is that Scott enslaves the working class.

> I do not know any great modern author, whose writings have a stronger tendency—by the fascinating charm they throw around the knights and dames of olden times, and the obloquy they contemptuously heap on the people, degraded by serfism and vassalage—to increase and prolong the feelings of veneration, which his genius artfully excites in young minds, for *aristocratic* deeds, and makes them bow their knees with slavish awe, and admire the bold feats of noble desperadoes,

(who, if in common life, would have been designated ferocious ruffi-
ans) than the renowned Sir Walter Scott. (13 Feb. 1841: 305–6)

This writer believes that Scott heaps praise upon titled characters simply
because they are nobly born, and has nothing but contempt for the working class:

> The minor machinery, composed of the people, he metamorphoses
> into "Cuddy Headriggs," and "Doogald Creatures," with a sheeplike
> train of "Goose Gibbies" and fanatical "Kettledrummels," including
> serfs and slaves, and contemptuously describes them as a cringing,
> fawning, creeping, half-crazed vermin, executing the despotic will of
> their masters, without compunction, or like "Burley," gloating over the
> deeds of blood, which he recklessly performed in the guise of puritani-
> cal fanaticism. (305–6)

The enormous differences between the two essays are of course striking,
but the similarities, when compared to the earlier attacks on Scott by
Wooler, Carlile, and other genre bashers, are equally striking. Neither of
these writers makes a criticism of Scott that is also a criticism of fiction in
general. Indeed, there are no statements at all in either article about fiction as a genre; Scott's strengths and weaknesses are his alone, and not
those of his medium. In both articles it is Scott, not fiction, on trial,
tested both for literary quality and, more important, for political propriety. In the *Schoolmaster*, Scott passes all tests (in spite of what he might
have thought he was doing). In the *Chartist Circular*, he fails all tests miserably, but his failure is not the failure of fiction. The many stories published in that periodical make clear that fiction had its place there. In
neither article does the fact that Scott chose to write fiction disqualify
him as a writer from the start. Both articles show a belief that fiction
could tell the truth if its writers properly directed their talents to serve
humanity, and especially to serve suffering humanity.[16]

The leap that these two working-class critics, and most of the others
of the 1830s and beyond, make from the earlier critics is enormous and
indicates a number of changes. For one thing, the working-class journalists from the 1830s on had far less reason to fear that fiction of any kind
threatened to divert laborers from reading their own periodicals. From
1830 to 1836, during the "War of the Unstamped," the working-class
press proved itself able to survive and even thrive under the most oppres-

sive conditions. O'Brien and Hetherington, the editor and publisher respectively of the *Poor Man's Guardian*, were so confident that fiction offered no threat to their sales that they even sold magazines such as the *Parterre* (1834–37), which contained, according to an irate correspondent who bought a copy from Hetherington, "empty tales, devoid of sound and sense, [that] fetter the understanding and delude the people with a show of words." Unashamed, O'Brien agreed with the correspondent that such tales are useless, but felt that such periodicals as the *Guardian* have nothing to fear from them and that "the gloomy mists of mystery and fiction will shortly dissolve before the rising sun of political and moral science" (*Poor Man's Guardian* 20 Sept. 1834: 262).[17]

This flourishing of a working-class press meant that the working class as a whole had a larger amount of reading matter to choose from, and that working-class editors could (and, to survive, should) diversify. Moreover, the many periodicals published by members of the middle class for a working-class audience—for example, *Chambers' Edinburgh Journal*—provided models of variety for these journalists. Much more common at this time than the one writer, one- or two-essay political periodicals of Cobbett or Wooler were journals featuring a number of writers and several departments: political leaders, useful knowledge, excerpts, poetry, and sometimes prose fiction.

By the early thirties, fiction as a genre was changing, too, and many working-class journalists recognized this. No longer did most working-class critics hold, as did Carlile, that realism had no place in fiction. Dickens, Bulwer, William Ainsworth, and many others could offer a kind of fiction very different from the romances of Scott: or, as a critic in *Northern Star* stated retrospectively in 1845, "Charles Dickens and others like him have effected a revolution in novel writing. It is the *many*, not the few, who now form the materials from which are quarried the heroes and heroines of fiction" (11 Jan. 1845: 3). That Wooler, Carlile, and many other working-class writers simultaneously directed their criticisms both at Scott specifically and at fiction in general demonstrates the dominance of Scott and the romantic over fiction in the eyes of these men. Works of the early thirties, such as Bulwer's *Eugene Aram* and Martineau's *A Manchester Strike* (both published in 1832), forced these journalists to reappraise such beliefs (see below). New writers were writing a new sort of story. A writer in *Johnstone's Edinburgh Magazine* (1833–34) writes of this new fiction in his aptly titled "New Novels for 1834":

> The true, the natural, the probable, if not yet eagerly sought after, are already more valued when they come in the way. The Dynasty of the Bandit and the Bravo, with all their terrific tributaries and illegitimate descendants, is wearing to a close. The Corsair can scarcely be longer pronounced sea-worthy. . . . One begins to look for something in a story, which shall, whether faintly or more vividly, resemble the real history and ordinary goings-on of the men and women of this strange work-a-day world in which we find ourselves placed, to suffer and endeavour, along with them. (Jan. 1834: 319)

In the thirties for the first time, for most working-class reviewers good fiction was equated with truthfulness. The new task for the critic was to guide rather than condemn out of hand, to point out which works were truthful and which were not, and to dissect individual works, separating fact from fancy.

One of the earliest working-class periodicals that criticized works of fiction individually and not simply as indicators of a completely corrupt genre is the aptly titled *Literary Test*. Although the *Test* lasted only five weeks, from the beginning to the end of January 1832, it helped pioneer a critical stance that would become commonplace later, especially in Chartist periodicals. In both his prospectuses (to be found in the *Poor Man's Guardian* [1 Oct. 1831: 104; 31 Dec. 1831: 231–32]) and in his first "Review of Books" (1 Jan. 1832: 2–4), the editor of the *Test* states his intention to revolutionize literary criticism. The traditional aim of all writers should be "to instruct and improve, by light and interesting means, the condition of their fellow creatures" (2). Surveying society, however, with all its political and social abuses, the editor concludes that most writers have only been hirelings and entertainers of the rich, and have done little to correct "this fearful perversion of nature and right," and that most critics, under the control of publishers, authors, and advertisers, have been even more slavish than the writers they have criticized.

The editor's response to this state of letters is to turn the Golden Rule into a critical tenet, noting "that I 'do unto others as I would that others should do unto me'" (1). That idea controls every critical article in the *Test*. The writers in the periodical (there seem to be several, each one designated by a separate letter of the alphabet) all infuse that saying with a strong working-class sensibility. Indeed, the periodical seems so concerned with working-class political causes that Joel H. Wiener describes the *Test* as "a literary miscellany that features radical political comment in the guise of literary and theatrical views" (*Finding List* 27).[18] This is misleading. The writers in the *Test* attempted to disguise neither their literary nor their political views. The linkage the *Test* makes between the political and literary is not very different from the political/literary editorial stances of the quarterlies—the Whig *Edinburgh*, Tory *Quarterly*, and middle-class radical *Westminster* reviews. Close readings of individual literary works on the basis of political propriety as well as literary merit were far from new at this time. What was new was that members of the working class were reading in this way.

One work that the *Literary Test* dissects is Bulwer's *Eugene Aram* (7–14 Jan. 1832: 17–22, 37–39). The critic, identified as B., attacks the then anonymous author of that work for misrepresenting or insulting the working class both in his style and in his plot. Stylistically, Bulwer may be a good writer, even "very superior to most of his fraternity," but B. feels that Bulwer is guilty of one "fault of the worst description":

> the one of *pedantry*—and pedantry, too, of the most insulting kind: not a character does he introduce, but he makes him quote a something or other, at the same time . . . adding insult to offence, by prefacing it with "Every one knows what Cicero has said," or, "all persons are acquainted with" this, or with that, thereby conveying by it an imputation of ignorance to all persons, who may not have wasted so much valuable time, as the author, in making themselves acquainted with a whole library of almost obsolete and useless literature, which, however interesting to the book-worm, was never intended for the nineteenth century. (19)

Bulwer's "pedantry" narrows his audience, excluding with its "every one" and "all persons" almost all of the working class; any laborer can only approach such a work as an illegitimate intruder.

In his criticism of *Aram*'s plot, B. attacks Bulwer's distortions of class. Analyzing a scene in which Aram meets a prince and in which Bulwer presents Aram's "native dignity" on an equal level with the prince's "royal dignity," B. observes that only the former sort of dignity has any value: "A man, possessed of one tenth part of a mind with which *Eugene Aram* was gifted, could look upon no person with reverence or humility; and indeed, there are few 'princes of the blood' on whom such a man could look otherwise than with a most sovereign contempt" (39).

By far Bulwer's greatest fault, to B., is that he completely misrepresents the poor in his story. B. lashes out at Bulwer's apparently intentional use of fiction to distort truth, citing Bulwer's comment in his preface that "With the facts on which the tale of EUGENE ARAM is founded, I have exercised the common and fair licence of writers of fiction: it is chiefly the more homely parts of the real story that have been altered" (18). Bulwer's idea of the license of fiction is very similar to Nathaniel Hawthorne's idea of the license of romance in his preface to *The House of the Seven Gables* (9); it is exactly this connection between romance and fiction that B. finds so reprehensible. Bulwer's "altered" parts serve only to give the working class "credit . . . for a great many of the bad and vindictive feelings, which belong to a state of barbarism;—and seldom making them appear, except in rather an objectionable light . . . and if, alas! he could say no good for the poor, the weak, and the oppressed, there was not the least occasion for him thus gratuitously to accommodate his rich reader with additional reasons and excuses for treating them with unkindness and persecution" (18). B. feels that Bulwer may have distorted his narrative because "the author may have felt himself incompetent to the task of depicting a class to which he himself did not belong," though he feels that Bulwer is a good enough writer to present an undistorted view if he wished. More likely, B. maintains, Bulwer restricts his audience to the few and writes to please those readers, "keeping out of their way whatever objects they might deem objectionable." Truthful depictions of the working class are "too humble, too common, too natural,—not sufficiently *exotic* to flatter the pampered, refined—the hothouse senses of 'society'" (18).

B. even criticizes Bulwer's dedication (to Scott) because dedications imply writing for an individual rather than for the public (18). In every respect, B. writes the review from the outside looking in; Bulwer's novel is a middle- and upper-class fantasy that he and the class he represents cannot directly engage in. However much B. dismisses Bulwer and his type of novel, though, he does not attack the genre itself. The fact that B. gives a particular novel this kind of close reading demonstrates that novels are not all class-exclusive romances and cannot be dismissed out of hand, as they were by people such as Carlile. Fiction may be badly in need of reforming before it can serve the working class, but B. shows that working-class critics were beginning to understand that the genre was important enough to deserve reformation.

Before B. dissects *Eugene Aram*, he examines the political opinions of its author. Using only textual evidence (for, at the time B. wrote, there were only rumors about Bulwer's authorship, which B. discounts), B. concludes that "the author . . . is a Whig, approaching more toward the Radical" (17). Such an analysis is an integral part of the review as a whole and not a digression; to this writer, a test of the work on literary and political grounds is a test of its author. The review indicates the large distance in political thought between the working-class radical B. and the middle-class Whig/Radical Bulwer. B. deplores Bulwer's halfhearted radicalism in his depiction of the poor and his ideas about class; though B. assumes that Bulwer must feel he has been "very original and startling" in his equating the prince's dignity with Aram's, B. believes that that kind of lukewarm political sensibility leads only to a false sense of reverence and a further tyranny of rank.[19]

Such a textual reading of an author's political views, and a corresponding class advocacy on the part of the critic, is common in the *Test*. The writer of a slashing review of *The Opera* (1832), one of Catherine Gore's "silver fork" novels, mounts an attack on the type of elitist fiction the book represents, the class that reads it, and the authors who write works like it. "It is one of those sickening fictions which the authors of the day are compelled to invent for the amusement of the idle and luxurious, who have rendered real life too unnatural and miserable to afford an interesting description, and who would find a picture of things as they ought to be, too dangerous and revolutionary to suit their views or interests" (21 Jan. 1832: 58). "Real life" here takes on a sense of working-class reality, and real truths are "dangerous and revolutionary" working-class truths. Gore, unaware of such life and truth, is useless to this critic.

Even a rare positive review of a novel in the *Test* shows that the critic recognizes the distance between the author and the working class. *Newton Forster; or the Merchant Service* (1832) is written by "a humane man, who has risen above a great many of the prejudices and follies of that class of society, to which he evidently belongs:—he is an officer in the Navy, and has seen the cruelties which are inflicted there with a kind and pitying eye" (14 Jan. 1832: 39). Frederick Marryat, the author of the novel, may be aware of the cruelties inflicted, but to this critic, he is above them. In all the works reviewed in the *Test*, as in the review of *Eugene Aram*, working-class critics seem eavesdroppers; at best they can hope for sympathy from novelists, but they can find no direct advocates.

It is important to remember the cultural context of the *Literary Test*. The year in which it was published was the year that the first Reform Bill passed, and its critics show cultural aspirations similar to the political aspirations of working-class leaders. The opportunity for political and social equality seemed for the first time a possibility; such equality necessarily called for a new cultural orientation. In criticizing Bulwer's pedantry, his misinformation, and his (and Gore's) narrow appeal to a pampered audience, the critic is protesting working-class exclusion from what other classes see as the ranks of the literate. These criticisms make it clear that working-class agitation at this time was far more complex than a simple clamor for the vote and was in fact also a struggle for literary and cultural authority. In all its reviews the *Test* anticipates the critic who, speaking several years later for another working-class movement, cried out "Where is the Bulwer of Chartism?" (*Labourer* Aug. 1847: 94).[20]

The *Test*'s way of reviewing is similar to that found in many working-class periodicals of the thirties, forties, and fifties. An excellent example of this continuing tradition can be found in the *Northern Star*. For ten weeks in late 1844 and early 1845, Harney, the editor of the literary page, carefully analyzed with painstaking thoroughness the first third of Disraeli's *Coningsby*.[21] Just as B.'s reviews of Bulwer are essentially a working-class radical's literary battle with a middle-class Whig/Radical, so these articles amount to a literary duel between a leading Chartist and the then leading exponent of the Tory/Radical Young England movement. Harney praises the few points, such as the call for universal suffrage and a dislike of Castlereagh, on which most Chartists and Disraeli would agree. Most of his comments, however, are combative; he disputes, for example, Disraeli's favorable views of George Canning, his ludicrous presentation of Manchester as a "Lancashire Eden" (22 Feb. 1845: 3), and especially the obvious relish with which Disraeli and Young England view feudalism: "It is not to the vaunted 'wisdom of our ancestors' we must look for political or social remedies for present wrongs and sufferings. The 'good old days' are a pleasing illusion; nothing more. It is equality, not feudalism, that is the hope of the many; and though that hope will not be all at once accomplished, onward we must march. The 'golden age' is before, not behind us; and only through the triumph of democracy may we hope to hasten its reign" (14 Dec. 1844: 3). We have here, as in the review of *Eugene Aram*, an analysis that is largely political, that sorts the good from the bad, and that shows a novel—even a mostly bad one—to be worth careful attention. There is a major difference between the 1832 review and this one, however. Harney writes with far more confidence and with the perception that he and his audience are and should be part of the readership of *Coningsby*. B. speaks for a class outside the genre, wanting in. Harney speaks with the authority of a member of a well-organized movement; he tests his movement against Disraeli's, and finds his own much more sensible and viable. B. seeks a position of power; Harney writes from one.

Working-class critics of fiction in the thirties, forties, and fifties never unanimously supported any established writer as the "Bulwer of Chartism" or of any other working-class movement. They alternately praised or found fault with Bulwer, Marryat, Ainsworth, and other storytellers, largely basing their opinions on how close those writers came to meeting working-class standards. Although in *A Manchester Strike* Martineau, as Catherine Gallagher writes, "left . . . an ambiguous legacy, for she had at once ennobled workers and bound them in chains of necessity" (61), a critic for the Manchester *Poor Man's Advocate* found enough realism and sympathy for the working-class in that novel to write "certainly have we rarely met with a book which has afforded us more delight, or so completely riveted our attention. Every incident of the tale is drawn from real life" (29 Sept. 1832: 5). Several months later, however, a critic in *Cobbett's Magazine* (1833–34), edited by William Cobbett's son, John, argued—quite rightly—that Martineau's views about the unpopular poor laws in her *Poor Laws and Paupers Illustrated* are sheer propaganda; she is guilty of perverting the genre, of "the employment of fiction in the cause of Doctrinaire government" (Jan. 1833: 10).[22]

Even Dickens was not seen by all as the worker's advocate. He, too, was subject to a literary test with each serialized installment he published.[23] He may be called by Harney in the *Northern Star* the "poet of the poor" (21 Dec. 1844: 3), but another critic in that periodical calls

Dickens's romantic *Haunted Man* "the latest (would that we were sure we might say the *last*) volume of trash coined from the muddled brains of Dickens" (10 Feb. 1849: 3). Yet one more critic, William Maccall, calls Dickens "a writer whose genius is not of the first order" who "is brave enough in attacking vices which no one cares to defend" (*The People* 11 Sept. 1852: 293–94). The best praise a critic in the *People's Paper* can muster for a collection of stories by Dickens is that he "has appeared this time with less pretension than usual" (20 Jan. 1855: 5). This comment is even more insulting than it first appears because the critic fails to notice that, in *The Seven Poor Travellers*, Dickens wrote only the first and last tales, and the stories the critic praises the most were not even written by him. Again in that periodical, perhaps the same critic complains that "the ever self-repeating Boz . . . exaggerates [and] gives caricatures of humanity for the sake of appearing original" (25 Nov. 1854: 8)—a harsh accusation from a critical perspective that valued "real life."

Most Chartist literary critics clearly demanded that established writers approach Chartist views to earn any praise. The closer Dickens seemed to come, the greater the praise lavished upon him. During the last two weeks in 1844, in a Christmas version of the *Northern Star*'s literary page, the "Christmas Garland," Harney copiously summarized and reviewed the previous year's *A Christmas Carol* and the present year's *The Chimes*. Harney agreed with Dickens that *The Chimes* was "a great blow for the poor,"[24] and sensed in that work a class sympathy unlike any Dickens had exhibited before:

> In the *Chimes*, expressing views of man and society far more comprehensive than he has before put forth, Mr. DICKENS enters the public arena, as the *champion of the people*! *Wellerisms*, however happy, would be out of place in a work of this description. The masses are the victims of undeserved suffering; their case is a solemn one; and solemnly, with an eloquence that was never excelled; in "thoughts that breathe and words that burn," Mr. DICKENS pleads that cause against the cruel, canting, unnatural, blaspheming doctrines and actions of the ruling classes of society. (*Nothern Star* 4 Jan. 1845: 3)

Harney did not ignore the several faults of *The Chimes*: "in plot and construction, we think it decidedly inferior to any other production of Mr. DICKENS's pen." Plot and construction were less important than political character to Harney; in that respect *The Chimes* "*is decidedly the best work Mr. Dickens has produced*" (3). That an influential working-class critic in the most influential working-class periodical of the nineteenth century can argue that Dickens's best work is *The Chimes* is a strong sign that political character, not author, style, or story, was a work of fiction's primary test. No established author passed that test all the time.[25]

Copiously summarizing and then analyzing Dickens's Christmas stories was a tradition for the *Northern Star*; the *Star* treated *The Cricket on the Hearth* in 1845 and *The Battle of Life* in 1846. Considering the prohibitive price of Dickens's Christmas books for many of the working class, the lengthy summarizations in the *Northern Star*, Chartism's most popular paper, and the several dramatizations of those books must have been the media through which a huge segment of the working class first connected Dickens with the spirit of Christmas. But the *Star* was not always effusive about Dickens's Christmas books. The vehemence with which a critic attacks *The Battle of Life* (while dutifully summarizing it at length), calling it a "thorough failure," as well as the abrupt dismissal of *The Haunted Man* (above), make it clear that the gushing praise for *The Chimes* is not simply because of an excess of Christmas cheer on the *Star*'s or Harney's part.

Harney's generic views show a far greater sense of class power than those of Carlile or other early working-class critics. The early journalists not only feared fiction but feared that the class they wrote for would be unable to withstand the evils of that genre. Harney, on the other hand, believed in the ability of his class to cope with bad fiction. He wrote with a confidence that his class had achieved cultural and political awareness equal to, if not greater than, that of any other class. He perceived that any fiction worthy of the name not only could but *must* serve his class.

Fiction Published in Working-Class Periodicals

The fiction that working-class journalists chose to publish indicates as clearly as their critical articles that through time they gradually acknowledged fiction as a genre of potentially great value, and shows as well that they assumed a growing literacy and sophistication on the part of their audience. Early periodicals published next to no fiction, and those of the late twenties and early thirties published little; the Chartist periodicals of the late thirties, the forties, and the fifties published a vast amount of fiction by a great number of writers, native and foreign, working-class and otherwise.

Wooler never published fiction. Carlile, curiously enough, considering he denounces fiction more loudly than any of his contemporaries, does carry one story in his *Republican*: Voltaire's "Story of Bababec and the Fakirs" (9 June 1826: 711–13). The simple free-thought moral of the tale—that matters of this world deserve more attention than those of the next—must somehow have raised the story above the lies of fiction in Carlile's eyes. Whatever the case, Carlile, the arch fiction hater, has the distinction of being one of the very first British working-class editors to publish fiction.

Most of the tales that found their way into the working-class periodicals of the late twenties and early thirties were, like Voltaire's story, simple tales with simple and explicit morals or, very often, fables. Cobbett used the form in the last years of the *Register*. In 1831 he published one fable by Aesop, "The Fox and the Eagle," with the moral, provided by Mrs. Trimmer, that "the rich, though ever so highly exalted, should beware *how they provoke the poor by injuries.*" In introducing this fable, Cobbett explains that he had just read Aesop "in preparing a Spelling-Book, as an introduction to my Grammar." He published that work, *Cobbett's Spelling Book*, and Carlile responded by publishing a broadside attacking Cobbett's use of fables (*Political Register* 28 May 1831: 527–28; Wiener, *War* 160). Cobbett, however, was unrepentant. Several years later he referred to another fable to make a point about Parliament (26 Apr. 1834: 203). In one instance he adopted Aesop's form and published his own fable, "The Wolves, the Zealous Hound, and the Perfidious Hunters," in which he obviously presents himself as the zealous hound, beset on all sides (30 July 1831: 310–11).

Co-operative writers, especially, used fables to teach. A writer in the *Co-operative Magazine*, reviewing a Co-operative allegory called *The Revolt of the Bees*, while deploring much of fiction allows that it can elevate and notes that "writers in the line of fable have been probably as useful in teaching the best rules of life, and impressing moral conduct, as even our best preachers and sermon-writers" (Apr. 1827: 126). *The Revolt of the Bees*, incidentally, should not be confused with Bernard Mandeville's *Fable of the Bees*, its "in many respects . . . very different predecessor" (126).[26] The

Co-operative *Crisis*, which carried A. B. C.'s tirade against all fiction, contains several fables, all of which consist of a short narrative and, just in case the reader has not the literary acumen to derive the proper meaning from the text, a stated moral. That moral could be almost as detailed as the fable it explicates. For one fable, "The Ocean and the Mountain Stream," by Allen Davenport, the moral is fully half as long as the fable itself (18 May 1833: 151). For another, a fable about the conflict between workers and drones in a beehive (a favorite subject for Co-operationists), the writer offers a moral that conflates allegory with political reality, making the lesson more confusing than the allegory it is supposed to explain:

> Working men—follow the example of the Working Bees, and if the Rich will not give up the honey they unjustly possess—do ye commence making fresh honey, and consuming it,—to obtain this object, form yourselves into Associations and no more sell your labour, but Exchange it for Equal Labour with your brother workmen: and by these honest means you will be enabled to enjoy the entire value of what you produce, and the Drones of Society can no longer consume what they do not produce—leaving you, the producers, with your unfortunate wives and children in want of the common comforts of life. (9 Feb. 1833: 40)

The condescending tone and sometimes silly attempt at one-to-one allegorical correspondence in this passage and in the entire fable suggest that the writer doubts strongly the ability of his reader to understand any but the simplest text.[27]

Fiction other than fables in early journals is rare, and likely represents an attempt to imitate publications of other classes or—though space in working-class periodicals was generally precious—to fill space, rather than to publish fiction that would rival in worth political essays. John Cobbett, in publishing in parts a portion of *The Marauder of Mitford: An Historical Tale of the Year 1317* throughout *Cobbett's Magazine*, seems to be joining the ranks of Scott's imitators. Doherty published part of a story called "The Gridiron" for two weeks in *Poor Man's Advocate* and then wisely dropped it; it is a tale that goes nowhere and says nothing, very slowly (7 July 1832: 198–200; 14 July: 207–8). Many of the major working-class periodicals of the early thirties—*Poor Man's Guardian, De-*

structive, Carpenter's Monthly Political Magazine (1831–32), and *British Labourer's Protector, and Factory Child's Friend*, among others—carried no fiction at all.

It was in Chartist periodicals that fiction first found a secure place. Many of the Chartist periodicals are as stuffed with fiction as they are with reviews of fiction. The published fiction takes several forms: excerpts from longer works by established British writers, extracts and whole works from foreign writers, and, most common and most important, the first working-class fiction.

In publishing extracts of fiction, Chartist editors generally had the same ends in mind as they did in their reviews: to point out the best of the writers of the middle and upper classes, or to promote Chartist points by non-Chartist writers. Linton extracts Fielding, Sterne, and Defoe (twice) in his *National: A Library for the People.* The *Chartist Circular* excerpts *Tristram Shandy* and *Gulliver's Travels. Northern Star* extracts from Dickens, Ainsworth, Bulwer, Thackeray, and many others, sometimes prefacing extracts with titles such as "Common Crimes in Polite Society" (for an extract from Thackeray's *The Newcomes*, 4 Apr. 1840: 3), or sometimes providing introductions that emphasize the Chartist meaning of an extract, as, for example, the introduction to a long excerpt on the Eatanswill elections from *Pickwick Papers* arguing that such corruption is no more and that Chartism has changed British election practices for the better (31 July 1847: 3). Mostly, however, extracts in the *Star* are left unintroduced and untitled; readers were assumed able to draw their own morals from fiction.

Chartist editors reviewed and excerpted American and European fiction writers and also, unhindered by copyright laws, published whole stories by them. *People's Paper* was especially enamored with American fiction: a long-running section called "American authors" carried, abridged, Edgar Allen Poe's "A Tale of the Maelstrom" (8 May 1852: 7) and other tales by Poe, and published quite a lot by Hawthorne, including parts of *The House of the Seven Gables*, "one of the most splendid expositions of the human heart written" (17 July 1852: 3). The section also devoted eight weeks in 1853 to offering six stories from Harriet Beecher Stowe's *The Mayflower.* Another periodical, *The People: Their Rights and Liberties. . .* (1848–52), extracted selections from Hawthorne's *Blithedale Romance* (21 Aug. 1852: 265–66) and carried the whole of Hawthorne's

"The Procession of Life" (16 Jan. 1852: 22–23; 23 Jan. 1852: 32; 6 Feb. 1852: 43–44).

As for European fiction, Chartist editors showed a marked preference for French authors. In 1845 *Northern Star*, "in accordance with the universal rage at the present time" (25 Jan. 1845: 3) reviewed and extracted at least four different works by Eugène Sue, whose *Mysteries of Paris* alone, according to the reviewer, guaranteed the "sterling" quality of all his writing (4 Jan. 1845: 3). For this reviewer (or these reviewers), Sue unerringly promoted a radical viewpoint that spoke as clearly to the British working class as to the French. One review, for example, highly approves of Sue's sympathetic depiction of the poor, citing, for example, a chapter in *Thérèse Dunoyer* that describes, "in touching, nay, even sublime simplicity, the sufferings of the industrious poor—and that accompanying 'soul of goodness,' which, animating thousands of the heroic children of labour, prompts them to feel for the sufferings of others, inducing them to succor the wretched, at the expense, to themselves, of a deprivation of the commonest necessaries" (29 Mar. 1845: 3). Sue's *Matilda, or the Memoirs of a Young Woman*, on the other hand, "is an index of fashionable life and the impurities which spring from it—of society as it is, not as it should be" (25 Jan. 1845: 3); and Sue's *Wandering Jew* attacks "priestcraft" (2 Feb. 1845: 3).

Ten years later, Sue's *Janet and Louisa* was proudly translated "for the [*Northern*] *Tribune* exclusively." The Chartist press published other French writers as well. *Northern Star* carried an extract from Victor Hugo in 1838 (26 May: 7). *Chartist Circular* serialized Alexandre Dumas's "A Legend of Peter the Cruel" (beginning with 9 Apr. 1842: 551–52); a short part of his *Count of Monte Cristo* found its way into the *People's Paper* (18 Dec. 1852: 6).

Working-class journalists' new awareness of foreign writers, particularly those who clearly sympathized with their class, and their intent to broaden the literary base of their readers cannot be attributed to lower costs and lack of copyright protection alone, but surely indicates a sense of class solidarity that transcended nations as well as a growing awareness of foreign political movements.

This growing connection between foreign politics and foreign fiction can be seen in the treatment later Chartist editors accorded George Sand. *Northern Star* was the first to notice Sand, in 1847, writing of her

Consuelo: "For its intrinsic merits, and as the production of a woman's pen, this is a singular and interesting work; displaying greater power of reasoning, more knowledge of life and human character, and far greater boldness of utterance, than often characterize the writers of romance. The plot is not so well constructed as it is brilliant and original . . . breathing throughout the spirit of truth" (2 Oct. 1847: 3). The events of 1848, which raised Sand to political importance as a propagandist for France's new provisional government, also brought her to the notice of several Chartist editors. In 1848 Linton, representing one group of Chartists, traveled to Paris in support of the provisional government; he used the opportunity to interview both Sand ("a handsome matronly woman") and Hughes de Lamennais (F. B. Smith 73). George W. M. Reynolds, a latecomer to Chartist leadership (in 1848), himself a novelist with strong class sympathies, regularly devoted the opening pages of each issue of his *Reynolds's Political Instructor* (1849–50) to profiling important English or European proletarian figures and devoted the front page of his 5 January 1850 issue to Sand—the only fiction writer of any nation to earn that distinction.[28] The first paragraph of that article promotes Sand as both novelist and political thinker, maintaining that she is more closely linked to a British working-class audience than many British writers are.

> George Sand, or to use a more correct appellation, Madame Dudevant, has acquired for herself a reputation, that has spread into every corner of the civilized world. Her writings in no way resemble the trashy productions of our own fashionable authoresses, but are in every respect above the general standard of the popular modern romances. Instruction is carefully blended with entertainment, and a profound current of politico-philosophical sentiment and reasoning pervades every book to which the name of George Sand is affixed. Mawkish love-tales, with strained and uninteresting scenes of fashionable life, so much admired by aristocratic readers, are not to be found in the pages written by Madame Dudevant. Her language is powerful, eloquent, and enthusiastic; her ideas grand, philanthropic, and far in advance of the present age. Those that are willing to appreciate depth of thought, humanity of sentiment, and a thorough knowledge of the defects existing in the social and political relations of Europe, will read the works of George Sand with unfeigned delight and derive vast instruction from their perusal. (65)

In 1850 Harney began to publish Sand's *Consuelo* in weekly installments in his *Friend of the People*, prefacing the serialization with an introduction to Sand by Guiseppe Mazzini. In the same periodical, earlier in the year, Harney was the first to publish Marx's and Engel's *Communist Manifesto* in English.[29] Such a combination is no accident, of course; Sand, Mazzini, Engels, and Marx, in Harney's mind, all offered British workers a vision of social, political, and personal improvement that most British writers simply could not.

In Chartist periodicals the British writers who could offer the best fiction to a British working-class audience were usually Chartists themselves.[30] Most Chartist journals either offered their editors a means to publish their own fiction or provided laborers with their only opportunity to have their stories published. Linton, in his *National*, shows that the simple moral tale is not dead in Chartist periodicals; his series "Records of the World's Justice" offers scenes of poverty "combined with allegorical characters and plots. The characters act out their parts (Honest Age, Corrupt Parson, Faithful Child, etc.) to formula, leading to a Chartist moral" (Vicinus 116). The *Chartist Circular* printed at least eighteen stories, some long serializations, by working-class writers. The names alone of many of these tales—"The Basket-Maker: A Tale for Aristocrats and Non-Producers," "Don't Enlist," *The Revolutionist* (by Ernest Jones), *Albert, or the Spirit of Freedom*, for example—demonstrate that these stories offer a clear alternative to any other fiction written at this time.

The *Northern Star*, usually a trendsetter in literary matters, lagged surprisingly behind other Chartist periodicals in printing working-class fiction. In 1847, late in its run, it offered a number of "Tales written expressly for the *Northern Star*," some by Chartius, and some unsigned, perhaps by others. Still later it published a serialized novel, *Sunshine and Shadow* (1849–50), by Thomas Martin Wheeler, who in a dedication to Feargus O'Connor complains that "the fiction department of literature has been neglected by the scribes of our body." To Wheeler, such a lack is politically dangerous, for "the opponents of our principles have been allowed to wield the power of imagination over the youth of our party, without any effort on our part to occupy this wide and fruitful plain" (31 Mar. 1849: 3).

Most other Chartist periodicals, however, were open earlier to working-class fiction. The *Ten Hour's Advocate*, the *People*, the *Labourer*, *Notes to
the People*, and *People's Paper* all offered working-class short stories and serialized tales. Jones, co-editor (with O'Connor) of the *Labourer* and editor of both *Notes to the People* and *People's Paper*, apparently had ambitions
to be a writer and poet long before he became a Chartist, and did more
than any other Chartist, as both an editor and a writer, to bring Chartist
fiction to a proletarian audience. In every one of the several periodicals
he edited or helped edit, and in others as well, he disseminated his politics through both essays and fiction. In the preface to his *DeBrassier* (also
called *The History of a Democratic Movement*), published in parts in *Notes to
the People*, Jones argues that fiction can be much more powerful than
other forms of writing: "I do not see why Truth should always be dressed
in a stern and repulsive garb. The more attractive you can make her, the
more easily she will progress. Let the same moral be conveyed in a tale,
and preached in a sermon, the former will make ten proselytes, when the
latter will secure but one (10 May 1851: 19).[31] Chartist doctrine, the most
solid and important for a working-class audience, needed its Bulwer, or
rather, needed a writer who could present their truths in a way a Bulwer
could not. Jones is probably the critic who asks "Where is the Bulwer of
Chartism?" and he, more than Cooper, with his once-famous Chartist
poem, *The Purgatory of Suicides*; more than Linton, with his stories or
"Hymns for the Unenfranchised," indeed more than any other Chartist,
fills that role and is, in the words of a writer in the *Northern Star*, "as original in his sphere as Boz" (6 Jan. 1844: 2). In all his periodicals, but especially in the last, the long-running *People's Paper*, he elevated fiction of all
kinds, especially that of the working class, to a higher importance than it
had ever had in a working-class periodical. In the pages of the *People's Paper* there were, as we have seen, reviews and summaries of Dickens and
others and serializations of Stowe; there was an enormous amount of
working-class fiction as well. Much of that fiction was written by writers
other than Jones; Wheeler is one of the few contributors who is actually
named, but the paper is filled with fiction by pseudonymous and anonymous writers. In terms of sheer bulk, however, most of the fiction in the
People's Paper was written by Jones himself, in long serializations; he published *Lovers and Husbands; or the Wrongs of Man* from late 1853 into 1854

and *The Maid of Warsaw* and *The Serf Sisters* in 1854 and 1855. The last two novels show a different kind of international awareness; they were timely attacks on Russian tyranny written during the Crimean War.

The change in attitude toward prose fiction in working-class journalism from Cobbett, Carlile, and Wooler to the writers for Chartist periodicals like the *Northern Star* was a sweeping one. A critic in the *People's Review of Literature and Progress*, noting the change, maintained that: "novel writing has long been elevated to the level of an Art, and it will ere long be raised to the level of a Power. It is one of the weapons of the fourth estate, that heterogeneous compound of intellectual forces which recruits its rank and file from all classes and from all castes" ("Recent Novels," Mar. 1850: 84).[32] Such a statement would have been ridiculous thirty years before. Within just a generation, working-class journalists had helped expand the audience for all fiction to include the working class. Their views about fiction show clearly that their readers were not simply class conscious but were also culturally class proud.

4

"Impassioned Truth"

Views of Poetry

ALMOST EVERY working-class journal issued between 1816 and 1858 published poetry; even the generally prosaic periodicals of Wooler, Cobbett, and Carlile—journalists who had all shunned the imaginative horrors of fiction—included at least a little verse. Still, the sense on the part of working-class journalists as to which poems were valuable to their class developed significantly in the first part of the nineteenth century. Indeed, their ideas about what poetry should be and about what was valuable in it evolved as considerably as had their concepts about fiction. All working-class journalists in the first half of the nineteenth century operated within a canon of verse particular to that class, a canon that overlapped the middle-class canon of the time but that had its own distinct emphases. The canon broadened considerably during the years from the teens to the fifties.

Early working-class journalists approached poetry guardedly. While generally deploring the imaginative in poetry, they allowed that a limited number of poetic types could serve a useful purpose. The poems they published, almost always political and occasional—characterized by ridicule of the oppressor and uncompromising support for the people— included satires, poems honoring a politically correct historical figure, and those praising abstract qualities such as freedom or reason.

The journalists of the thirties, forties, and fifties, on the other hand, generally had much more liberal ideas about what poetry could be and should do. They still admired the overtly political but found political justification for their views in the poetry of all ages and many countries—in poetry very often neglected or rejected by their predecessors. In other words, they ranged far beyond verse strictly linked to one occasion. They also approved of poetry that was at best only indirectly political, at times not apparently political at all, and often not directly relevant to British working-class issues. Chartist journalists were almost as likely to discuss or publish an excerpt from Tennyson's "May Queen" as from Shelley's *Queen Mab*. Later working-class journalists increasingly realized that each member of their audience was an aesthetic as well as a political being and they believed that while political poetry was always important, the cultural improvement of the working class necessarily entailed its political improvement. Such an evolution of thought necessarily meant an expansion of the body of poetry that could be considered part of a class-based canon; later working-class critics worked wholeheartedly toward that expansion.

Views of Poetry in the Early Working-Class Periodicals

In the 1810s and 1820s, working-class journalists took what seems at first glance to be a confusing stance toward poetry. In their periodicals early journalists often published poems with one hand and condemned poetry with the other. Carlile was especially prone to this sort of apparent hypocrisy. It is worth remembering that Carlile was the one who declared war on the fiction of the poet as well as that of the novelist and romance writer (*Lion* 24 Oct. 1828: 523). After publishing a poem by Captain Bosquet "of the Navy," he states: "It is our intention to exclude all Poetry from the future pages of 'The Republican,' unless it be something very superior in its powers of instruction. We are among those who do not think [poetry] any ornament to common sense, and bad Poetry is calculated to spoil it!" (17 May 1822: 627). In subsequent issues, he must have decided that a number of poems passed that test, for he published as many after writing this statement as he had done before.

Despite this antigeneric pronouncement, it was Carlile, more than any other working-class figure of his day and perhaps of any time, who brought Shelley and Byron to a mass audience. In 1822 he published an unexpurgated version of *Queen Mab*, providing, where Shelley did not, translations of those parts of the notes originally in other languages; and in the same year he published *Cain: A Mystery* and *The Vision of Judgment* (Wiener, *Radicalism* 68).[1]

Carlile offered two reasons for publishing Shelley and Byron. For one thing, Carlile held that by publishing them, he had fired another salvo in the struggle for the freedom of the press. He published *Queen Mab* in 1821 soon after an edition printed by William Clark was suppressed and *The Vision of Judgment* soon after John Hunt's 1824 trial for publishing his edition of that work. In announcing his edition of *Queen Mab* in the *Republican*, Carlile explained that "the Vice Society, by an indictment, had succeeded in suppressing its public sale. They are now solicited to try what they can do again in that respect. If they please, they shall make it as common as they have made the 'Age of Reason'" (8 Feb. 1822: 145).[2] With Byron's works, Carlile at times seems to hold that fighting for a free press is the only reason for publishing them at all: "*Cain is a Mystery*, and there is but little to be learned from it. I republished that and the VISION OF JUDGMENT, not from my admiration of the works; but, because I saw them menaced by my enemies" (11 Feb. 1825: 164). Carlile was not always as uncharitable toward Byron's works, although he did see Byron as being greatly inferior to Shelley. Elsewhere, Carlile allowed that *Cain* "is a ponderous blow at superstition." Shelley, or at least Shelley's *Queen Mab*, he always respected.[3]

Carlile also maintained he published Byron and Shelley because of their political and free-thinking ideas; on the level of argument, both were worthy of publication. Whether that argument happened to be in verse or prose made not a whit of difference to him. As he wrote, "I am not a poet, or a lover of poetry, beyond those qualities which it might have in common with prose—the power of instructing mankind in useful knowledge." As far as Carlile was concerned, the prose notes to *Queen Mab* were as good and as valuable as the poetry, "of equal bulk, equal beauties, and equal merit." In all Carlile's pronouncements about Shelley or Byron, I have found only one instance in which Carlile makes an aesthetic judgment about the work of either: in passing, he calls *Queen Mab* a "beautiful poem."[4]

But what was such beauty? Carlile took a prosaic approach to poetry and sought in it what he looked for in prose: political and religious truth and relevance to a working-class audience. *Queen Mab* had those things and was therefore beautiful. Other works—even some by Shelley—did not have them and were therefore not beautiful. Carlile was far less sympathetic, for example, toward Shelley's *Revolt of Islam*. In *Lion* he wrote:

> It appeared to me to be poetry without any other purpose than poetry, subject without sense, or to make the most of it, *a discouragement to political virtue*, by setting it forth as certain of defeat and destruction. There is an imaginary revolt against tyranny; but so far out of all time and locality, so unlike any thing historical or futurely probable, so badly exhibited, so completely subdued by tyranny, and a great deal of superstitious exhibition of future state reward only, to political virtue and constant love, that I could not but feel contempt for the author of Queen Mab. (3 Apr. 1829: 417)

Not only are the political principles wrong in the poem but the setting and culture that Shelley presents are, in Carlile's mind, so distant from those of the early nineteenth-century British working class as to make it senseless to such an audience.

The failure to achieve an exact correspondence of setting and culture to those of the present—in other words, a lack of occasion—disqualified other works of poetry as well from having any value for Carlile. While disparaging the theaters of the day in his *Republican*, Carlile turns his attention to a performance of *Macbeth*:

> Here the assassination of a good man by a villain is the leading trait of the play and a woman exhibits herself on the stage with her hands bathed in blood, holding two blood-stained daggers that have just done their work, after having stimulated her husband to commit the murder by a union of the art of the syren with the fury of the vixen. It is possible, that the reality of such a scene might have passed; but it is not likely to occur again, and therefore, not a fit subject to be remembered by an exhibition on the stage. (13 Feb. 1826: 56)

Carlile believed that there were two sorts of poetry: poetry as imaginative fiction—to him a form as loathsome as fiction; and poetry as argument—argument strictly relevant to the political and social affairs of the day. The latter was the only form suitable to Carlile, although he apparently saw no reason why anyone would trouble to yoke good argument to irrelevant versification.

Carlile was almost certainly influenced in such views by his hero, Thomas Paine, who stated in Part 1 of *The Age of Reason*, "I had some turn, and I believe some talent, for poetry; but this I rather repressed than encouraged, as leading too much into the field of imagination" (434). Carlile had, as well, other influences for his views. Like his ideas about fiction, his notions of poetry are strikingly similar to those of the middle-class denouncers of imaginative literature, the Utilitarians and Evangelicals. Bentham and other Utilitarians intensely distrusted poetry; Bentham would have excluded poetry and all imaginative literature from his ideal republic (Altick 133–34) and held that there was "no more reason for teaching [poetry] than chips and cards" (Manning 106). It was this very exclusion from his own education, of course, that led to John Stuart Mill's famous crisis, his turning to Wordsworth for therapy, and surely his later criticism of Bentham's "deficiency of Imagination" (Mill 61).[5] Strict Evangelicals, too, harbored a deep dislike of the genre. Richard Altick notes one extreme Evangelical sect that, as late as the 1860s, saw Shakespeare as "a lost soul now suffering for his sins in hell" (11–12, 126).[6] Although probably familiar with these views, Carlile was not a slave to them; he infused his dislike of poetry with his distinctly working-class bias.

Cobbett and Carlile rarely agreed on anything, but their views on poetry were largely in accord. Cobbett, too, looked for the qualities of good prose in poetry and denounced the imaginative. His views can best be seen in his discussion of Byron's *Vision of Judgment* and his many denunciations of Milton and Shakespeare.

Cobbett devoted almost all of the 24 January 1824 issue of *Political Register* to *The Vision of Judgment*—or, to be more exact, to the trial of John Hunt for publishing the poem (193–237). The article included a long excerpt of the transcript of the trial taken from the *Morning Chronicle*, and therefore provided Cobbett with a legal way to present extracts of the poem itself. Certainly, Cobbett was delighted with the barbs in the poem directed toward George III, George IV, and Robert Southey. But in his lengthy commentary on the case and the poem, Cobbett says nothing at all about the work as poetry or about Byron as a poet. Instead, his explains how James Scarlett, Hunt's lawyer, bungled the case and failed to get his client acquitted. Scarlett's defense, Cobbett thought, consisted of hairsplitting about technicalities: of "pretty distinctions between public libel and private libel" (211). Scarlett should have defended Hunt by arguing that Byron was absolutely right in his accusations, and that George III was a miserable failure as a king. That is exactly what Cobbett proceeded to argue in the article. Cobbett's intent, which he feels should have been Scarlett's, was to flesh out Byron's versified arguments with his own prose ones. Argument is everything, and genre is irrelevant; without the extracts from Byron that Cobbett provides, it would be hard to tell in this article that *The Vision of Judgment* is not itself prose.

Nowhere are Cobbett's views about poetry clearer than in his persistent attacks on Milton and Shakespeare. His first salvo was in an article of 18 November 1815 with the unlikely title "To the Editor of the Agricultural Magazine: On the Subject of Potatoes." The essay connects two of Cobbett's better-known aversions: his hatred of potatoes, which he saw as an unhealthy and agriculturally unsound substitute for grain, and his apparent hatred of the works of Shakespeare and Milton.[7] In it he proclaims that promoting "this worse than useless root," the potato, is now the fashion, just as it was in his time merely fashion to like Shakespeare and Milton. To prove that both poets and tubers were fashionable rather than good, Cobbett savages them as worthless. He attacks Milton's invention in *Paradise Lost*, arguing that the work is stuffed with unnatural and ludicrous happenings foreign to heaven and (more important) to earth. According to Cobbett, Milton writes of

> God, *almighty* and all *foreseeing*, first permitting his chief angel to be disposed to rebel against him; his permitting him to enlist whole squadrons of angels under his banners, his permitting this host to come and dispute with him the throne of heaven; his permitting the contest to be long, and, at one time, doubtful; his permitting the devils to bring cannon into this battle in the clouds; his permitting one devil or angel, I forget which, to be split down the middle, from crown to crotch, as we split a pig; his permitting the two halves, intestines and all, to go slap, up together again, and become a perfect body; his, then, causing all the devil host to be tumbled head-long down into a place called Hell, of the local situation of which no man can have an idea; his causing

gates (iron gates too) to be erected to keep the devil in; his permitting him to go get out, nevertheless, and to come and destroy the peace and happiness of his new creation; his causing his son to take *a pair of compasses* out of a *drawer*, to trace the form of the earth. All this, and, indeed, the whole of Milton's poem, is such barbarous trash, so outrageously offensive to reason and to common sense, that one is naturally led to wonder how it can have been tolerated by a people, amongst whom astronomy, navigation, and chemistry are understood. But, it is the *fashion* to turn up the eyes, when Paradise Lost is mentioned; and, if you fail herein you want *taste*; you want *judgment* even, if you do not admire this absurd and ridiculous stuff, when, if one of your relations were to write a letter in the same strain, you would send him to a madhouse and take his estate. It is the sacrificing of *reason* to *fashion*. (193–94)

As far as Shakespeare is concerned, "the case is still more provoking." Cobbett disdains "his ghosts, witches, sorcerers, fairies, and monsters . . . [and] his bombast and puns and smut, which appear to have been not much relished by his comparatively rude contemporaries" (194). His onslaught continues with unabated energy for two more pages before Cobbett finally turns to his main subject: those hated potatoes.

In subsequent articles, Cobbett reiterated his attack on these two "writers of bombast and far-fetched conceits and puns" (26 June 1824: 797).[8] Almost every time that Cobbett brought up Milton or Shakespeare, he used the attack on them to support another point— here a warning against potatoes and elsewhere a fierce denunciation of Malthus's then-fashionable "population lie" (26 June 1824: 797). Exaggeration to prove a point is a characteristic weapon of Cobbett's, and he surely exaggerated in his attack on Milton and Shakespeare. The essay itself shows that he had read Shakespeare and *Paradise Lost*. Although he rarely quoted Milton in the *Register*, he quoted Shakespeare often. Indeed, George Spater notes in his biography of Cobbett that Cobbett quoted Shakespeare's works more than any others except the Bible (538).

Cobbett attacked Milton and Shakespeare for their content and style, and it is in these areas that Shakespeare and Milton differ from Cobbett. They used puns and conceits to create "lies"; Cobbett used facts to create "truths." They, like Scott, often ignored useful truths in favor of useless fantasies. Cobbett's displeasure is not with the genre but with its misuse. Poetry could tell truths, and other poets could put the genre to good use. Both T. A. Birrell and Spater provide a long list of the poets whom Cobbett was decidedly influenced by in his own writing. Birrell connects him "to the great political satirical tradition of the eighteenth century: Dryden, Pope, Swift, Gay, Johnson, and Churchill—but especially Pope" (214–15). Spater concurs partially with this assessment, holding that Dryden, Pope, and Goldsmith "were his favorites" (18).[9] Cobbett himself wrote several poems for the *Register*. Moreover, he mined the poems of Virgil, Dryden, Swift, Pope, Goldsmith, and Byron for quotations and had nothing but praise for Burns, "one single page of whose writings is worth more than a whole cart load that has been written by WALTER SCOTT" (17 Nov. 1832: 415).

Despite the fame William Hone earned for his satirical verse and parodies he presented little poetry or discussion of it in the short-lived *Hone's Reformist's Register* except for an extract from William Cowper's *Task*, a few satirical poems, including some by Defoe, and an excerpt from William Hazlitt's just-published commentary on *Coriolanus*.[10] The most notable discussion of poetry in the *Register* is Hone's assault on Southey. The occasion for Hone's remarks was the publication during the same month (Feb. 1817) of Southey's *Wat Tyler*, a work he wrote in 1794 while still a strong republican but that was published only now by his enemies, "as proof of his political apostasy" (Madden 231). From the moment of its publication the republican sentiments in *Wat Tyler* made it an important work within the working-class canon. Hone was the first working-class journalist to notice the poem and the first to compare with scorn the (to the working class) now-servile poet laureate with the true poet of years before:

> The present poem appears to have been written many years ago, when Mr. Southey had not merely reforming opinions, but very wild notions indeed. In consideration of a Court pension, he now regularly inflames his muse, in praise of official persons and business, at certain periods throughout the year, as precisely stated and rehearsed in verse, as the days whereon his pension is made payable and receivable. His present muse, however, is no more like to that which he formerly courted, than the black doll at an old rag shop is like Petrarch's Laura. Poor Southey! a pensioned Laureate! compelled to sing like a blind linnet by a sly

pinch, with every now and then a volume of his old verses flying into his face, and putting him out! I have no doubt, he would at this moment exchange his situation, fleshpots and all, for that of the Negro, who earns his 'daily,' by sweeping the crossing at Mr. Waithman's corner! (22 Feb. 1817: 157–58)[11]

Hone here, largely by contrast, implies what a good poet is and therefore, by extension, offers something of an idea about what good poetry is. The craft is irrelevant to him; the quality of a poem lies not in its rhyme and rhythm but rather in its political truth and power.

Hone's attack on Southey was the first of many directed at the poet laureate by working-class journalists, attacks that continued to appear in Chartist periodicals long after Southey's death in 1843. For working-class journalists, Southey was the whipping boy of poetry, just as Scott was the whipping boy of fiction.

One month after Hone's essay appeared, his friend Wooler published an even more scathing attack on Southey in *Black Dwarf*. To Wooler, Southey's apostasy was more detestable than it was to Hone. As far as he was concerned, Southey was hardly a silly bird warbling pointless songs, but was rather a traitor to the people, a former ally who had turned against them. Citing an apology Southey had written excusing himself from the sentiments of *Wat Tyler*, Wooler writes: "He has confessed himself guilty of throwing opinions like fire-brands amongst the people, which he now says would lead them to destruction, and to cure which he has dared to mark his own disciples as fit objects of ministerial vengeance, and deserving of a halter as traitors to the state. In what does such a man differ from the received opinion of the character of the Devil? The agency of hell can do no more, than first seduce to sin, and then betray to punishment" (26 Mar. 1817: 144).[12] Southey's present villainy, then, stems largely from his disavowal of his previous poetic heroism. Wooler asserts in the review of *Wat Tyler* that Southey has been able to suggest ideas in his poetry that Paine, Cobbett, or Henry Hunt would not have dared express in their prose writings or speeches. To Wooler, *Wat Tyler* is a great poem not simply because of its political sentiments but because of its power to excite. Wooler holds that there is something generically more passionate and inciting about poetry than prose; a good poet with an evil mind, like Southey, could therefore write a powerful and yet untruthful poem. This point is one that none of Wooler's work-ing-class contemporaries expressed, and Wooler was the first working-class journalist to make a clear distinction between poetry and prose and to suggest that poetry could affect a reader in ways that prose could not.

In the review of *Wat Tyler* Wooler clearly drew historical parallels be-tween the fourteenth-century Peasants' Revolt (the nominal subject of the poem), the English war with the French Republic (which he main-tains was the true subject of the poem), and the turbulent political events of his own day (140). Of all the early popular journalists, Wooler was the first to understand the value of analogy in poetry, the first to un-derstand that poems about the past could be important to the working class of his day. Carlile never noticed *Wat Tyler*, but if he had, he very likely would have dismissed it as curtly as he dismissed *The Revolt of Islam* and *Macbeth*—as useless verse about the dead and buried. Wooler, on the other hand, liberates his nineteenth-century readers from the need for poetry to have a nineteenth-century setting to have any value; he gives the poem a close reading, explaining the relevance of each incident for a contemporary working-class audience. After one excerpt, for example, Wooler writes: "Here is a brave *Poet Laureate* for ye! here are truths for courts. Here is plain speaking with a vengeance. But Mr. Southey is not one of your *half-reformers*: he is not satisfied with *half*-advocating his opin-ions. *Annual Parliaments* and *universal suffrage*, you see are already *trifles* in his view:—he seems to wish that with the *Royal Pests* all *governments* should perish" (140).

Throughout the *Dwarf*, Wooler published several more of Southey's poems. Wooler particularly liked Southey's "inscriptions"—short poems to liberty that appeared in several places in the *Black Dwarf*, which would appear again in later working-class periodicals. Wooler carefully ex-plained the specific importance to a working-class audience of each one of these "specimen[s] of Robert Southey's Better Days" as they appeared (12 Mar. 1822: 372). About one of them, lines addressed to "the exiled patriots, MUIR, PALMER, AND MARGAROT," Wooler writes, "They would not now be inapplicably addressed to those who are now pining in English dungeons, for the maintenance of the same principles, and the demand of the same rights" (12 Mar. 1822: 372).

Obviously more aware than his fellows of the power of poetry, Wooler was the first popular journalist to regularly publish the verse of all classes and literary periods. In his periodical he combined poems about the Peterloo massacre with quotations from *King Lear* or *Paradise Lost*. In his "Blackneb" series, Wooler published poetry by Pope, Shakespeare, Milton, Cowper, Mark Akenside, Goldsmith, Burns, Coleridge, Byron, and many others. He was also the first working-class journalist to popularize many of the sonnets that appeared in Wordsworth's *Poems Dedicated to National Independence and Liberty* (1815), which appeared in later working-class periodicals far more frequently than anything else by that poet.[13]

The influence of Pope upon Wooler is important, and I cannot pass by a reference to Pope's work in *Black Dwarf* without mentioning it. Wooler uses as a headnote to almost every one of his issues a quotation from Pope's "The First Satire of the Second Book of Horace, Imitated," lines 69–72:

> Satire's my weapon, but I'm too discreet
> To run a muck and tilt at all I meet,
> I only wear it in a land of Hectors,
> Thieves, Supercargoes, Sharpers, and directors.

The quotation fitly sums up the tone of Wooler's prose attacks on the abuses of his day; indeed Pope's influence upon Wooler pervades his prose far more than it does the poetry he publishes or discusses. Of all the early journalists, Wooler is the most energetically and consistently satirical in his prose.

In his introduction to the "Blackneb" series, Wooler clearly makes a generic distinction between poetry and many kinds of prose: "Now and then we may relieve the severe gravity of the argumentative, by excursions into the fields of Anecdote and Poetry" (26 Jan. 1823: 89). Wooler was the first working-class journalist to take a Horatian approach to poetry: he felt that poetry must be both *utile et dulce*. He was the first working-class critic to notice and stress the idea of the pleasurable in poetry and the notion of its nonargumentative and emotional power. Of course, because poems were "pleasant" did not mean that Wooler did not have a political purpose in publishing them. The poetic excerpts in *Black Dwarf* aimed at reinforcing the ideological temper of his audience. Wooler simply believed that poetry and prose reinforced that ideology in different ways. In discussing the purpose and uses of poetry, and in trying to define a working-class canon, Wooler anticipated more than any of his contemporaries the uses to which later working-class journalists would put poetry.

Views of Poetry, 1830–36

Poetry and politics entwined inseparably in the working-class periodicals published during the "War of the Unstamped." Journalists during this period printed and lauded verse of the past and the present by writers of all classes, as long as they saw it as having a direct political relevance to their working-class audience. Their critical approach was strongly allegorical; to them, all true poetry of any age derived its primary meaning from the political state of the working class in the 1830s. Such a restricted focus indicates, perhaps, less the journalists' own narrowness, or that of their audience, than the limitations of time under which working-class readers suffered. Few could devote hours to reading for aesthetic pleasure alone. The aesthetic might have value, but it was secondary for these readers to the need for personal and social improvement. During the 1830s, certainly the decade of the nineteenth century that saw the greatest number and variety of British working-class movements, poetry was a tool used in the service of those movements; beauty ran a distant second to functionality. It is not surprising, then, that editors provided— and their readers welcomed—studies of *Coriolanus* rather than, say, *The Tempest*, preferred now-forgotten political poets to Tennyson or Browning, and that working-class journalists would generally limit their criticism to political readings tailored very specifically toward their audience and the events of the year, month, or day in which they wrote. These readings may seem alien—or even worse, quaint—today. It is well worth keeping in mind, however, that a limited though clear focus gave the poetry that working-class journalists published and discussed a highly charged relevance to their readers. These periodicals show that poetry could have greater energy for working-class readers of the time than it has for many readers today.

During this period working-class journalists quarried the works of many poets, including Shakespeare, Southey (mostly, of course, his *Wat Tyler*), Thomas Moore, and especially Burns, Byron, and Shelley, for headnotes or quotations to punctuate or counterpoint their own views, and often published works of established poets independently of their articles. Besides simply publishing a great deal of established poetry, though, the popular journalists of this time discussed poetry and its purposes much more frequently than did earlier working-class journalists.

A telling generic (and political) discussion appeared in the most popular working-class periodical of the time, Hetherington's *Poor Man's Guardian*, on 4 August 1832 (486–87). The discussion was sparked when a writer for that periodical noticed a poem, "The Weaver's Song," which was published in the SDUK's *Penny Magazine*. The poem, by the then-famous Barry Cornwall, romantically and unrealistically describes a weaver's happy condition:

> Weave, brothers, weave!—Swiftly throw
> > The shuttle athwart the loom,
> And show us how brightly your flowers grow
> > That have beauty but no perfume!
> Come, show us the rose, with a hundred dyes,
> > The lily, that hath no spot;
> The violet, deep as your true love's eyes,
> > and the little forget-me-not!
> Sing,—sing, brothers! weave and sing!
> > > Tis good both to sing and to weave:
> > Tis better to work than live idle:
> > > Tis better to sing than to grieve.
>
> Weave, brothers, weave!—Weave, and bid
> > The colours of sunset glow!
> Let grace in each gliding thread be hid!
> > Let beauty about ye blow!
> Let your skein be long, and your silk be fine,
> > And your hands both firm and sure,
> And time nor chance shall your work untwine
> > But all,—like a truth,—endure!
> > > So,—sing, brothers, &c.
>
> Weave, brothers, weave!—*Toil is ours*;
> > *But toil is the lot of men:*

> One gathers the fruit, one gathers the flowers,
>> One soweth the seed again.
> There is not a creature, *from England's King*,
>> To the peasant that delves the soil,
> That knows half the pleasures the seasons bring,
>> If he have not his share of toil!
>>> So, sing, brothers, &c. (486)[14]

The writer of the article is disgusted with *Penny Magazine* for reprinting the poem, disgusted with the collection of poems from which this verse is taken, Cornwall's *English Songs*—"more despicable, mean, grovelling, slavish un-English trash was scarcely put upon paper to insult the common sense of a reader" (486)—and especially disgusted with this particular poem. With a combination of close reading as well as political and social analysis, the writer of the article presents the poem not simply as bad but dangerous; its intent, he feels, is to blind the working class to the painful reality of their lives. He notes that Cornwall probably has not even visited a factory where weaving is done; for if he had, he would have witnessed only sadness and suffering. "He is not perhaps aware of the poor emaciated, worn down, half-starved creature who shows him how brightly the flowers grow 'that have beauty but no perfume,' into whose mouth he is pleased to put such charming verse. Nor perhaps does he know how deeply sunk into the aching head of the unhappy women employed are the eyes of the weavers' true loves, which he so prettily likens to violets" (487). The last four lines of Cornwall's poem, which equate the king's labor in degree with the peasant's, the writer sees as "pure and undisguised humbug," unless it is a great labor for "our *patriot* king . . . to sign his name," and "to eat and drink, and idle, and hold levees, and make knights of others, and mayhap a fool of himself" (487).

To this critic, the verses are a collection of complete lies—lies so obvious that they fool no one, least of all weavers themselves. Why, then, did Cornwall write the verses in the first place? The critic sees in them not mere ignorance but rather an attempt to support the ruling class; he believes that Cornwall "appears . . . to think that his verse will have the effect of making the wretched slave to the pampered pride of a master manufacturer, contented at his task by his inspiring lay. Vain Fool!" (487).

Terry Eagleton and others have argued that in the nineteenth century "literature" increasingly replaced religion as a discourse intended to gain ideological control over the working class (22–27). The critic in *Poor Man's Guardian* lashes out at a poem that he or she feels is written with that very intent. The poem might be "beautiful," but it attempts in its beauty to turn a factory into a garden and to present economic exploitation as a happy and fixed truth. The writer here will have no beauty that covers an ugly opinion. He or she sees beauty for the purposes of deception as nothing but a middle-class trick.

The article generated three responses: one in prose and two in verse. The prose response, by a writer identified as Justitia, who claimed to be a Spitalfields weaver, is a fascinating close technical reading of the poem. Justitia's occupational claim seems a valid one, for he or she shows in-depth knowledge of the mechanics of weaving. In discussing Cornwall's words "the rose, with a hundred dyes," for example, Justitia writes, "Why the most arrant fool in Spitalfields would laugh in his face to hear him say such a thing, for our roses have seldom more than two or three 'dyes,' very often only one" (*Poor Man's Guardian* 11 Aug 1832: 494).

Most of Justitia's letter compares Cornwall's romantic illusion to the hard material reality of the weaver's life. Justitia begins the letter with a definition of poetry: "If it be true, and I think it is, that '*Poetry be impassioned* TRUTH,' a man to be a poet must deal a little in that article" (494). Going through the poem almost line by line, Justitia shows that the verse does not deserve the name of poetry at all. After citing a line of "downright nonsense," "Let beauty about ye blow," Justitia writes, "This proves the whole 'song' to be merrily imaginative, and not to be '*impassioned* TRUTH,' so that it is not poetry, but fiction, written by folly" (495). To Justitia, then, true poetry is nonfiction; such nonsense as Cornwall's verse is not poetry at all.

The two responses in verse are in content, if not in meter, parodies of Cornwall's song. One poem, like Cornwall's, is entitled "The Weaver's Song," written "Not by Barry Cornwall." The second is called "The Weaver." Both attempt to describe accurately a weaver's degraded reality. The first decries the economic hardships of a weaver's life, in which almost all the produce of his labor profits another (3 Nov. 1832: 587). The second describes the physical and mental degradation imposed upon a weaver and bitterly exposes Cornwall's lies:

Toil, and still toil! I marvel that I bear
    To drudge so long; my little ones here too
Watching the loom with eyes of fear and care
    Lest some thread snap too swiftly for their view:
It is a harrowing sight—enough my arm
    To paralize, as it hath done my heart:
He lies who babbles to me of the charm
    Love lends to labour; 'tis that Love I start
To Think of, as dull habit goads me on
    To earn a pittance for its hapless fruit.
Nor is there refuge when the day is gone,
    I pause, but do not rest from my pursuit.
Night's a grim sentinel, forbidding sleep,
Lest morn should on it break, and find it all too deep.

That beauty's in the handywork of God
    The flow'rs I toil to imitate declare,
Tho' what their brightness on the earth's green sod
    Be, I know not;—I never saw them *there!*
My sky's my work-jail's roof; my clouds, the breath
    Of my pent fellows panting for the air,
Which brick close piled on brick, prohibiteth
    From entering with its heav'n-commissioned pass:
'Tis true I have my Sabbath—'tis a day
    God and not man allows me; but, alas,
The brute-like *six* have taken all away
    That should live on the *seventh*; not an ark
    Of peace my heart is, but a cavern dark:
I hear the church-bell ring, and sigh, but cannot pray.
                                (31 Aug. 1833: 283)

In confronting Cornwall's poem, this poem indicates a contrasting aesthetic: a successful poem must convey accurately a sense of the way things are, no matter how miserable that may be. This poem, one imagines, would be considered true poetry by Justitia and by Hetherington and Bronterre O'Brien, the editor and publisher of the *Poor Man's Guardian*. This kind of poetry was, to them, an antidote to Cornwall's fantasies.

The concept of "truth" carried strong class overtones in these periodicals, of course. In a world that these writers saw as full of oppressive class, economic, and literary lies, they—and other working-class journalists of the time—regarded themselves as among the few honest interpreters of what was and was not truthful. As poetry was, for them, by definition truth, they also necessarily saw themselves as the few honest interpreters of what was and was not poetry.

Because these critics were refining a poetic standard, almost every review—even the shortest—offers an important generic statement. While they did not believe that one had to be a member of the working class to be a true poet (though of course that never hurt), a true poet at least had to exhibit sympathy with that class. A poem, *A Voice from the Factories*, reviewed in 1836 in the full-feature, radical *Weekly True Sun*, was not by a laborer but by the Honorable Mrs. Norton.[15] The reviewer nonetheless holds the poem to be a good one because its subject—factory abuses—was fitting, "here urged with so much of force and of feeling, with such truth, beauty, grace, and earnestness, that any advocate, who could have been chosen from amongst our most illustrious living writers, would have done his fame no disservice by the avowal" (12 Dec. 1836: 1381). Norton's work, as poetry, is superior in the critic's mind to most of the prose written on factory reform. Indeed, he or she goes on to say more such poetry "would tend to purify the atmosphere of politics, and produce that elevated tone of thought and feeling which guide more surely to truth, than the blundering disquisitions of dogged economists, or the unprincipled logic of oratorical partizans" (1381). The great difference between Cornwall's poem and Norton's, of course, is that in Norton's, beauty does not mask truth; it promotes it. Beauty yoked to the service of truth raises this poem above much of the political prose of the day: "purity" and "elevation" allow a clearer sense of everyday working-class reality. The young Tennyson and Browning might not have been as completely ignored in the working-class periodicals of this time had they turned their minds to factory abuses, the Reform Bill, the new poor law, or the Tolpuddle Martyrs instead of to lotos-eaters or Paracelsus.

Two reviews of a poem by George Petrie, *Equality*, show working-class journalists applying distinctly working-class political views to their poetic criticism. One of the reviews, from John Cleave's very popular and strongly radical *Cleave's Weekly Police Gazette*, offers a hint as to why the working-class canon was necessarily limited at this time: "Mr. Petrie's poem, 'EQUALITY,' unites important truths and vigorous writing. It is genuine poetry consecrated to the service of mankind—a species of writing, of which, it must be admitted, there is a great dearth" (3 Sept. 1836: n.p.). A longer review of the same poem, from the *Poor Man's Guardian*, begins with a generic statement of the kind that could be (and was) made by critics of all classes and sympathies: "Poetry is the genuine expression of human thoughts, and of human feelings. Genuine poetry is that fine quality and power by which man, yielding to the impulses of his nature, sees, feels, and expresses the nobleness of his nature, and the vast and unbounded power of his thoughts. Ask what is poetry? *Poetry is the spirit of Nature!* A poem is the genuine thoughts of the mind traced out by the pen of the poet, and described in words. Poetry is Nature herself" (22 Sept. 1832: 542). Turning to the poem itself, the reviewer makes it clear that he or she does not define Nature as rocks, and stones, and trees, but as something far more social. "Here then is the true end of the poet kept in constant view. Not the idle chiming of a syren song, to lure mankind from the contemplation of truth—but the bold and manly vigour of a powerful mind is exercised, to brand with shame the upholders of that cruel system of rapine and injustice, which has rendered mankind miserable, and deluged the earth with the blood and tears of millions of our deluded brethren" (543). This critic radically binds nature, truth, and beauty to a sense of working-class reality. "Nature" is the cruel and oppressive social system; "truth" is the accurate perception of that system; "beauty" is the quality of presentation of that truth. The critic was obviously aware of attempts by critics of other classes to define and use those terms but refuses to accept their definitions without modifying them for his or her own class.

The journalists of this time applied the same rigid 1830s working-class standards to the poets of other ages and expected long-dead poets to live up to those standards. The *Literary Test*, the periodical that offered many class readings of fiction in its five weeks of publication, did not ignore poetry. In fact, on 14 January 1832 it took on what might be considered the most ambitious literary project of any early nineteenth-century working-class periodical (Cobbett's assault on Shakespeare and Milton, perhaps, excepted): one critic, called H., tried in two pages to "test" all Shakespeare's works. As the *Test*'s critics did with fiction, H. applied the usual proletarian-tilted Golden Rule to the subject. Admitting "that *Shakspeare's* powers of language and delineation are stupendous, and his poetry exquisite," H. argued that such talents meant next to nothing; much more to the point was whether Shakespeare applied those gifts toward the general good, or whether, "instead of applying them to the furtherance of knowledge and increase of happiness, he has not somewhat preferred the advancement of his own individual interest, and tended to the perpetuation of ignorance and wretched inequality, by truckling to the vicious and distempered opinions of those who benefited by their continuance" (48). In other words, H. considers whether Shakespeare is guilty of Southey's kind of literary betrayal. As far as H. is concerned, Shakespeare fails this literary and human test miserably.

> He has drawn his scenes among kings and nobles, and taught mankind little more than that princes are but men, and prone to all the faults and weaknesses of mortality;—occasionally, however, contenting himself by saying a kind sentence or two in favor of the unfortunate—and those too so admirably and effectively that I can the less excuse his omission to say more. *Shakspeare* in fact only studied the amusement of the aristocracy of his day, who were yet more difficult to please than the 'society' of the present;—if, indeed, he was not of himself rather inclined to agree with his betters,—or else, how could a mind of his substantial superiority have delighted so much in the pageantry of kings 'and the pomp and circumstance of glorious war?' (48)

In two sentences, H. condemns almost every line of Shakespeare as being reactionary and worthless. It should be noted that this critic and Cobbett stand almost alone in their absolute antipathy to Shakespeare. But they were not alone in their refusal to follow fashion or in their willingness to follow through with their political and critical ideas, even if that meant rebelling against two centuries of orthodox opinion.

In John Bell's *Political Mirror* (1837), one critic, in a short-running series called "The Political Philosophies of Shakespeare's Plays," did not reject Shakespeare out of hand. On the contrary, he or she believed that Shakespeare could offer a good understanding of the politics of any age, since, to this critic, there is essentially no difference between the politics of the present and the past. In the introduction to the first installment, the critic states:

In the pages of Shakespeare, may be traced not only the operation of those social relations which have, from the earliest periods, connected, or disjoined human beings—but a most faithful picture of those political relations, also, which human beings have always borne and still bear, to each other. In history, there is nothing new. All is re-production. Names may change—but the political principles and passions which now agitate the world, have agitated the world since the commencement of time.

In England we are in the habit of dividing politicians into Tories, Whigs, Radicals, and pretended Radicals. All these varieties may be found in Shakespeare—although the specimens are not so ticketed and labelled. (19 Aug. 1837: 12)

For three weeks the same critic studied the character of Brutus from *Julius Caesar*, explaining scene by scene why he should be considered a "pretender to Radicalism" and a "weak, vain, obstinate creature" (19 Aug. 1837: 12; 26 Aug. 1837: 24). The analogy to contemporary pseudoradicals is strong; obviously, the critic's intent here is to warn readers to be on guard against such characters. But after introducing the possibility of analogy at the beginning of the study, the critic makes no direct correlation between Brutus and nineteenth-century sham radicals, or between Rome (or Elizabethan England) and the writer's present. Instead, the writer leaves the task of making direct connections up to the reader—an assumption of literary sophistication rare in earlier popular periodicals (19 Aug. 1837: 12–15; 26 Aug. 1837: 23–26; 2 Sept. 1837: 42–43).

This critic follows up his views about Brutus with a study of the political philosophy of Shakespeare's *Coriolanus*. This study is as much a critical response to Hazlitt's criticism of the play (from his *Characters of Shakespeare's Plays*, published in 1817) as it is to the play itself. Completely overlooking the fact that in his essay Hazlitt's sympathies are wholly with the plebeians, this writer takes issue with Hazlitt's embittered declaration that poetry is the property of those in power, or that "the language of poetry naturally falls in with the language of power." To this critic, the language of poetry cannot be denied to the weak. "Poetry has an equal affinity with all social conditions. The language of suffering, issuing from a cotton-factory, may be quite as poetical as the language of independence in the mouth of a Swiss, rejoicing on his mountains" (16 Sept.

1837: 70). More than this, poetry offers the poor a way to transcend their weakness and helplessness. To be poetic is to be powerful. Hazlitt, the critic believes, has put the cart before the horse. "Hazlitt's definition, in truth, is based on mere confusion of thought. Wherever poetry is, *there* is power—and poetry may be any where, every where. Poetry gives no preference to beauty or rank, above decay and lowliness" (70). The critic believes, as Hazlitt does not, that the speeches of Coriolanus, "a vulgar-minded, foul-mouthed, swaggerer," are "admirably rebuked by the language which Shakespeare puts into the mouths of his plebeian opponents" (68). To the critic, the poetical and political messages of *Coriolanus* are exactly the same.

If a work could not be read in a way that would empower a working-class audience of that time, if it could not excite that audience to proper thought and action, if, in short, it could not serve the exact purpose that almost every working-class periodical at this time held, then working-class journalists usually scorned or ignored it. In discussing Shakespeare both the *Political Mirror*'s critic and the *Literary Test*'s H. write with much more concern for the present than for Elizabethan England. Working-class journalists, in effect, translated for a working-class audience all the poetry they discussed, distilling the hard truth from a poem's character, tone, plot, and setting. In introducing *Wat Tyler*, for example, to which most of one issue of *Cosmopolite* is devoted, one writer is clearly much more concerned with the fortunes of the working class in the near future than with those of the peasants of 1381. "Let the people read, mark, learn, and inwardly digest Southey's drama of Wat Tyler. Let them see what is to be imitated and what avoided. Let them qualify themselves by sobriety, by industry, by study, and by well-spent time, to play a better part in the next subject of the next Poet Laureate, and so we bid them *God speed*" (7 Sept. 1833: 167). The lessons in the rest of the introduction are concerned with the foolishness either of parlaying with the present oppressors or of thinking they will give up one bit of the power they hold without a struggle. Richard II's and William Walworth's betrayal of the peasants is significant only as a reflection of the betrayal of the working class by the Reform Bill of Lord Russell and Earl Grey, an event mentioned in the review and one that teaches the very same lessons (166).

Poems and references to poems in working-class journals generally reveal as much—and often more—about the historical and social context of the journal's reader and the journalist citing or discussing the work as it does that of the poet or poem. In other words, poetry was chosen and evaluated at this time for very specific reasons; to understand those reasons is to gain some understanding of the relation between a particular periodical and its readers. A writer for the Owenite *Co-operative Magazine*, for example, after publishing Coleridge's "Sonnet: On the Prospect of Establishing a Pantisocracy in America," notes, "little did the writer of this sonnet then think, that on abandoning the scheme, such a Pantisocracy would be actually established in that country by Robert Owen, in about thirty years from that time" (Apr. 1826: 133). The "pantisocracy" to which the writer refers is New Harmony, Owen's Co-operative community in Indiana. The same periodical argues that Shelley's poems are important Co-operationist statements; they "abound in the most glowing descriptions of social perfection, and in the most persuasive appeals to the finest feelings of the heart in favour of social equality, and a just division of the rights, duties, and enjoyments of life" (Feb. 1830: 32). In much the same fashion a reviewer of Francis Macerone's *Defensive Instructions for the People* in *Poor Man's Guardian* prefaces his notice with an excerpt from *Henry VI* that exhorts the people to "get thee a sword, though made of lath" (11 Apr. 1831: 345).[16] The excerpt had a clear and ominous import for a working-class audience during the turbulent time just before the passing of the Reform Bill.

If a poem could not be stretched to fit the context of the present moment, there was another option open to working-class journalists: it could be changed to fit that context. Parody is not quite the right term for such poetry. Revision is more appropriate: the journalists' main intent was usually less to ridicule the original poem than to broaden the political perception of a working-class audience. Such poems impart a working-class viewpoint to a neutral or even hostile poem. As we have seen, Cornwall's "Weaver's Song" elicited two such responses from working-class poets. Both of those verses do ridicule Cornwall, but they are far more concerned with correctly delineating the horrors of factory work. Three "Commentaries on Dr. Watt's Hymns," by I. H., which first appeared in *Carpenter's Monthly Political Magazine* (1831–32), typify this form. The first takes the most famous (and, incidentally, most parodied) of Isaac Watt's verses for children, and converts that well-known bit of conservative propaganda into a bitter political and anticlerical statement:

How doth the little busy bee
Improve each shining hour
And gather honey all the day
From every opening Flower

And is not the mechanic's toil,
As constant and as true?
Yet what just praise have priests bestow'd,
My fellow-men, on you?

Not that the empty purse they give
Could ease us of our pain;
For tho' the bees have praise obtain'd,
To them their toil is vain? [*sic*]

What lazy priests have ever been
A friend to toil-worn man?
Have they not all, for ages past,
Upheld each tyrant's plan?

Then let their praises go for nought,
Instruction we would find;
And their dark words no longer shall
Deceive our waken'd mind. (Feb. 1832: 271)

G. S. R. Kitson Clark notes that 1830–50 was "the great age of the extension of hymn singing" (230); I. H. was one among many to make hymns serve working-class secular ends.

A variation on this kind of revised poem borrows a well-known meter or song and grafts upon it distinctly working-class lyrics. Appropriating tunes for the cause was a favorite recreation for working-class poets, one popular during this period and throughout the Chartist years. By appropriating in this way, working-class poets could relatively effortlessly impassion their truths with verse. Moreover, the simple regularity of meter was in itself compelling, and many working-class critics considered truth with a beat more memorable than truth without. A writer called J. F. justifies his original verse in sending it to the *Guardian* by saying the lines offer ideas for those "too apathetic to search for them in the argumentative field of prose (of which persons I fear there are too many) but whose minds will readily retain a truth contained in the jingle of a couplet" (28 Apr. 1832: 326).

Many working-class poets wrote new lyrics to Burns's well-known songs, especially "Scots, Wha' Hae wi' Wallace Bled," and even more so to "A Man's a Man for A' That," his "union of balladry with Tom Paine" (Woodring 59). Such revisions do not suggest that working-class composers saw any political impropriety in Burns's original verse (as they did, for example, with Cornwall's); rather, they suggested the popularity of the poet and his tunes. Applying new words to popular music allowed anyone to sing at any gathering without a music lesson. Newspapers such as the *Poor Man's Guardian* often reported the minutes of working-class meetings; those reports show that group singing was a common, even central, activity. Burns's songs, original and revised, were among the most frequently sung at these meetings.

Even more popular than appropriating Burns's songs was "revising" and "correcting" national songs. Working-class writers simply kept the memorable and impassioned music and chucked out the reprehensible lyrics. This kind of composition can be found before the thirties; in Thomas Davison's *Medusa*, for example, one poem, "The Watchword of Britons," is meant to be sung to "Rule Britannia." During the thirties especially, however, the form proliferated. *The Lancashire and Yorkshire Co-operator* also published new lyrics to "Rule Britannia," entitled "Each for All," which offered the following Co-operative sentiments in its first verse:

> The social brotherhood of man
> > Alone can bless the boon of birth,
> And nature in her generous plan
> > Has taught us how to use the earth.
> Proclaim the truth in bower, hut, and hall
> Britons EACH must live for ALL! (n.d. [Nov. 1832?] 45)

Many other periodicals carried revised lyrics for this tune, among them the *Poor Man's Guardian* (two different versions) and William Carpenter's short-lived *Political Unionist* (a version by Ebenezer Elliott called "The Triumph of Reform"). New lyrics for "God Save the King" were equally abundant: different versions of that song are found in *Carpenter's*

Monthly Political Magazine and *Political Letters and Pamphlets*, in the *Republican, or Voice of the People*, the Glasgow *Agitator*, the *Cosmopolite*, and *Poor Man's Guardian*.

Using selection, rejection, and appropriation, the journalists of this period were the first of the working class to codify a set of standards for judging poetry. They created the same tools that the Chartists used. The Chartists, however, generally had a broader perspective of poetry, and enlarged the working-class poetic canon considerably.

Chartist Views of Poetry

Chartist journalists appropriated or changed the works of other ages and classes to suit their own world view; they sought out and prized the politically "correct" in works of poetry and demanded that a poet speak in some way to the working class in order to be accepted by that class. All these things, of course, working-class journalists had done before. The extent of the Chartist appropriation of poetry, however, was greater than that of their predecessors; they considered much more British poetry worth the reading, and widened their net, seeing much in the poetry of other nations as appropriate for their audiences. Moreover, Chartist critics valued far more than just the obviously political in poetry—or, more accurately, their sense of what was political broadened considerably and their ideas of what was politically "correct" were generally more subtle than those of preceding journalists; they did not lose their taste for fiery radicalism and pungent satire, but they began to appreciate equally other poetic subgenres.

To argue the justice of their cause, the Chartists looked to many of the same poets as had their predecessors. Burns, Shelley, and Byron were still favorites, and appeared more frequently than ever before. *Wat Tyler*, too, had the same relevance for the Chartists that it had for the working class when it was first published in 1817. Parts of the work appeared in headnotes to several periodicals, and in 1839 the *London Democrat*, the organ of Harney's London Democratic Association, published the second and third acts of the closet drama in full (18 May: 46–48; 1 June: 62–64). Contemporary poems by non-Chartists, too—those with an obvious relevance for Chartist audiences—were published in Chartist journals. The *Northern Star*, for example, in 1843 plundered "The Song of the Shirt" from *Punch*'s Christmas issue for their own, republishing it before the public knew that Thomas Hood was its author. In 1844 the *Star* carried Hood's "The Lay of the Labourer," a poem that calls for fair compensation for labor.

Like their predecessors, Chartist editors often published revised lyrics to well-known songs in order to make popular music serve a political purpose. A writer in the late Chartist periodical *Northern Tribune* (1854–55), introducing one of that periodical's "Songs for the People," put into words the reason working-class poets had been doing this for years:

> No Idea can be said to have reached the *hearts* of a People, until they have given it utterance in Song. Yet how many of our noblest National Airs are still united to sickly and unmeaning doggerel; while the words of others are absolutely sensual and indecent? . . . What an invaluable auxiliary in the work of Popular Regeneration Song *might* become, were sentiments of freedom, heroism, fraternity, and love allied to 'sweet sounds'! By attaching fitting words to some of our Popular Melodies, we shall strive to inspire higher and healthier social feelings; and "destroy custom by custom." (Feb. 1854: 40)[17]

A glance through Y. V. Kovalev's *Anthology of Chartist Literature* or Peter Scheckner's *An Anthology of Chartist Poetry* demonstrates convincingly that many Chartist poets favored this sort of metrical and musical appropriation.[18] "God Save the King" (or, after 1837, of course, "God Save the Queen") was still a favorite choice for this kind of treatment. A variation of that anthem is one of the "Songs for the People" in *Northern Tribune* (Sept. 1844: 319). Other versions are in *McDouall's Chartist and Republican Journal* (1841; 19 June 1841: 96; rpt. in Weisser 96), *The English Chartist Circular* ('Temperance Anthem,' 9 Jan. 1842?: 8), *People: Their Rights and Liberties* (3 Feb. 1849: 292), and *People's Paper* (24 July 1852: 3; 12 Feb. 1853: 6). Robert Nicholl (a prolific working-class poet), Linton, Jones, and others all aimed to create a national Chartist anthem by revising the old one.

The "Marseillaise Hymn" became very popular at this time, either in its original form (translated by such writers as William Howitt or Jones) or in revisions. Ralph Waldo Emerson, in London in 1848, noted that "the 'Marseillaise' was sung [at working-class meetings] as songs are in our abolition meetings" (quoted in Schoyen 160). In the same year

Northern Star published three different translations of the song within seven weeks to celebrate the flight of Louis-Philippe from France (26 Feb.: 3; 1 Apr.: 3; 8 Apr.: 3).[19]

The Chartist journalists' serious interest in a French political song is one sign among many that they selected their poetry from a larger pool than had their predecessors. The presence of foreign poetry of any kind was a striking rarity in working-class periodicals before 1837. After that date foreign poems and references to them were very common. As they had with their politics, comrades, and choice of fiction, Chartists—especially the later ones—looked toward Europe and America. As would be expected, they generally chose the foreign poetry they published on ideological grounds. A list of the European poets the Chartists respected differs greatly from those a modern reader would consider canonical for the period; indeed it differs greatly from those the British middle class of the time would have considered leading European poets. Of those from France, Pierre-Jean de Beranger received high praise in several different issues of *Northern Star*. Called "the prince of political poets" (23 Sept. 1848: 3), he was the subject of a two-week appraisal in that periodical in 1848 (23 Sept.: 3; 30 Sept.: 3). That study inseparably connects the political and poetical, for Beranger, besides being a poet, was a recently retired member of the revolutionary National Assembly of 1848. The statement from the appraisal, "How nobly Beranger contrasts with those *things* Southey and Wordsworth!" is thus, of course, commentary both poetical and political. Of Beranger's poetry, the *Star*'s critic writes, "His songs defy censure, and we despair to do him justice in the way of praise" (23 Sept.: 3).

Germany's Ferdinand Freiligrath was even more regularly noticed and highly praised in the Chartist press. His work, or discussions of it, appeared in the *English Chartist Circular* (n.d. [Jan. 1843?]: 399), *Northern Star* (5 July 1845: 3; 11 Apr. 1846: 3; and elsewhere), *Notes to the People* (four poems [5 July 1851: 186, 197; 13 Sept. 1851: 394; 11 Apr. 1852: 978–79]), and *People's Paper* (4 Sept. 1852: 6). Apparently, both Harney and Jones discussed Freiligrath's poetry at some length. Harney, the editor of the literary page of *Northern Star* in 1845, was almost certainly the critic incensed when in that year both the *Athenaeum* and *Tait's Magazine* complained that Freiligrath had become political; Harney replied that Freiligrath had no choice but to be political:

When the great German people, divided and separated, are made the prey of contemptible [*sic*] beggarly princes, whose wretched tyrannies are only endured because propped up by the bayonets of the Austrian and Prussian despotisms; when those despotisms are allied with the bloody autocracy of Russia to stem the progress of free principles, making Germany the informer, gaoler, and executioner of Polish, Italian, and Swiss liberty; when kings have violated the solemn pledges, on the faith of which the millions poured out their blood like water to save those regal perjurers; when the wealth-producers are driven to insurrection by lack of bread, and cannon and chains are the only remedies prescribed for their sufferings; when the German mind is chained down by a tyrannical censorship, and all its aspirations for the right, the good, and the true, are choked by the strong red-hand of kingly tyranny; when, in short, the muzzle is on the mouth, the sword hews down the pen, patriots languish in prison, and poets sing the strains of their father-land in exile—surely these are days when the bard may not only be permitted to throw himself into the political arena to combat for the right; but more than that, he is surely enjoined to do so, if he would not be a traitor to his most holy trust—a renegade to the mission for which heaven has endowed him with a gift the most glorious humanity can know. (5 July 1845: 3)

The statement is both a personal description and a generic observation: Harney clearly posits Freiligrath as the archetype of every poet in an unfree society. Jones, writing six years later in his *Notes to the People*, also makes Freiligrath the epitome of a "good" poet, but in a different way:

In his life and in his writings he stands alike before us, the pure democrat—and while too many other poets have sought the sunshine of an easy celebrity or the gain of a wide circulation, by a mean pliancy to existing powers, or, at least, by pandering to the prejudices and ignorance of a rich middle-class, this great man has scorned so to degrade his talents and violate his mission—and has ever consistently proved the poet and champion of the working man. (5 July 1851: 186)

Harney sees Freiligrath as a product of his time and place: Prussia in 1845. According to Jones's description, on the other hand, Freiligrath could as easily have been Polish or Welsh as German; Jones, the Fraternal Democrat, the friend of political exiles of many nations, clearly holds not only that good poetry is class based, but that class interests, in poetry as well as politics, transcend national ones.

Jones, the great internationalist of Chartism, was also the great internationalist of poetry. All his periodicals show some interest in the works of foreign poets. In *People's Paper* and *Notes to the People* are reviews of, or poetry by, many Europeans. On the pages of his and O'Connor's *Labourer* he offers a series on the literature—almost exclusively poetry—of other nations. He does this, he explains, to present a model for his Chartist poets. "We would recommend our poet-friends to study some of the models of foreign composition, both in prose and verse, and not in an imitative spirit, but since new lights and new views, will open to them as they read—and since the intercourse of minds, like the confluence of streams, deepens the tide of thought, feeling, and imagination, and is more likely to produce the great, than isolated brooding over individual fancies" (Nov. 1847: 240). In this series, Jones assesses works by Poland's Zygmunt Krasinski as well as by Pushkin and Schiller. Clearly, to Jones, the class sympathies he sees in these poets render them far more valuable than many British poets to a Chartist audience.[20]

American poets were also well represented in Chartist periodicals. John Greenleaf Whittier, a Chartist sympathizer and friend of Harney (Vicinus 108), was called in the *Northern Star* "the chief of American poets" (3 July 1847: 3) and was published often in that periodical. Linton had "a lifelong interest in American verse"; indeed, he may have been the first English editor of any class to publish Longfellow (F. B. Smith 39).[21] In *Northern Star* and other Chartist periodicals are poems by and reviews of Longfellow, James Russell Lowell, William Cullen Bryant, and more.

Several of the *Chartist Circular*'s many "Literary Sketches" are devoted to American poets, and the writer of that series explained why American poetry so attracted him:

America is the only democratic land of liberty and equality on the face of the globe; and though her political freedom is only about half a century old, yet she has already produced some of the most splendid poets not only of modern times, but men whose effusions, for sublimity, patriotism, beauty, and manly vigour, are unparalleled by the poetical rhapsodies of the ancient bards of Greece and Rome, and they stand alone in the loveliness of glory and liberty, like their native democracy—amid the despotisms of Europe, and the horrid slavery of Asia and Africa. (8 Jan. 1842: 494)

Of course, America at this time practiced its own "horrid slavery," and even this critic wished "American bards would awaken their wildly sounding lyres for the emancipation of their negro slaves" (494). The Chartists treasured not only American songs about freedom but also their songs against enslavement. A writer in *Northern Star* maintained that "the only poets America has yet produced, whose effusions are destined to live, are those who have devoted themselves to the Anti-Slavery cause" (5 July 1845: 3). On 9 March 1844 the *Northern Star* published a poem by a writer identified as W. B., "To the Poets of America," that sums up the Chartist attitude toward this American paradox. The poem exhorts the "Bards of Freedom's boasted land" to use their power to destroy slavery, which keeps them from being completely free and therefore from being fully poetic—"For Poetry is Freedom's child!" (rpt. in Kovalev 63–64).

Though they looked to other cultures for universal truths, Chartist journalists rarely forgot that they were working within a particular society—that they were writing for the working class of Great Britain and that their task was to expand the canon of poetry for that audience by giving them a functioning set of literary values. As before, a primary criterion for admission to their canon was that a work contain some political value for their class; to them, those who did not promote ideological values directly relevant to a Chartist audience—those who did not approach the condition of a Chartist reader directly, analogically, or allegorically—had nothing at all to offer. For some, it seems, only laborers had any poetry to offer laborers; the only poets George W. M. Reynolds discusses in *Reynolds's Political Instructor*, for example, are two that he considers working-class—Cooper and Elliott (1 Dec. 1849: 25–26; 22 Dec. 1849: 49–50).[22] Many Chartist critics, on the other hand, quoted established poets out of context in order to squeeze their truths into a working-class mold. A writer for the *Chartist Circular*, in a series called "The Politics of Poets," endeavored to transform every poet he or she discussed into a die-hard radical with working-class sympathies. Not surprisingly, this critic thus represents Byron, Shelley, Burns, and Milton as class champions. More surprising is the writer's treatment of Coleridge and Wordsworth. The critic maintains that Coleridge's works "abound with the warmest aspirations after liberty, and the loudest warnings to this country on the tendency of its politics under Whig and Tory management" (13 Mar. 1841: 323). Wordsworth is considered even more a Chartist: his poems "are Radical—deeply, essentially, entirely Radical." The critic is amazed that "he came to be called a Tory at all" (1 Aug. 1840: 182). Considering that both these assessments were written in the early 1840s, long after Wordsworth's and Coleridge's revolutionary sentiments had cooled (and indeed after Coleridge had died), one would imagine that this critic had to select his excerpts carefully. This is indeed the case. Though he purports to assess the entirety of Wordsworth's work, for example, all the excerpts he presents are sonnets from Wordsworth's *Poems Dedicated to National Independence and Liberty* (1815), sonnets with sentiments such as "Advance! come forth from thy Tyrolean ground, / Dear Liberty!" and "Milton! thou shouldst been [*sic*] living at this hour" (quoted in *Chartist Circular* 1 Aug. 1840: 182). The critic never mentions that all the poems are carefully culled from the same narrow source.

The "Literary Sketches" in *Chartist Circular* mostly concerned Scottish literary figures. Almost certainly a different writer composed this series, for this writer is far less compelled than the author of "The Politics of Poets" to find a Chartist dwelling in the soul of every British poet. Nonetheless, in this series, too, Chartist sentiments crop up in surprising places. For example, of George Buchanan, the sixteenth-century Scottish political writer, poet, and tutor to James I, the writer states that "his political opinions are the Radical doctrines of modern Chartism" (8 May 1841: 359). This critic even pored over the works of the medieval poet Robert Henryson for republican sentiments, quickly passing over Henryson's *Testament of Cresseid* in order to present the second stanza of his obscure poem "In Praise of Age." That stanza is important to the critic because it "contains the bold sentiments of a Radical Reformer, and we may almost class his opinions, with political justice, among those of modern Chartists" (12 June 1841: 378). The stanza contains such sentiments as

> Justice is fled—the helm is held by guile—
>   Despotic tyrants have the righteous slain,
> And Freedom languisheth in iron chain.
>   (quoted in *Chartist Circular* 12 June 1841: 378)

Shakespeare, too, could be made into a Chartist. A series in the *Northern Star* in 1840, "Chartism from Shakespeare," tried to do just that. In that series quotations from *Henry IV*, Parts 1 and 2, *Coriolanus*, *Julius*

Caesar, King John, Richard III, and other plays express sentiments appropriate to Chartism. One excerpt from *Henry IV*, Part 2 is given the title, "Frost and Physical Force," which draws a direct parallel between Hotspur's rebellion and John Frost's rising in Newport the year before. The editor of this series made other connections between Shakespeare's political values and those of the Chartists with such titles as "The Chartist" and "True Guard of Royalty." In the fifth and last installment of the series, the title was expanded to "Chartism from the Poets," and its editor had James Thomson, Milton, and Charles Churchill join Shakespeare as Chartists.

In the *Labourer*, one critic, almost certainly Jones, in two separate articles tested contemporary poets for their worth to a Chartist audience. These articles contradict one another several times, but both argue that true poetry strives to state working-class ideals. In the first article, "Literary Review," Jones notes that Chartist poetry is "the freshest and most stirring of the age" (Aug. 1847: 98). Comparing the works of established poets with those of Chartist writers, he argues that all the former are lost in imaginative worlds of their own making and are not "devoting their great talents to the great cause of the age," as they should be (98). Of Tennyson and Browning he writes:

> What is Robert Browning doing? He, who could fire the soul of a Luria, and develope the characters of a Victor and a Charles,—he, who could depict nature's nobility in a Colombe,—has he nothing to say for popular rights? Let him eschew his kings, and queens,—let him quit the pageantry of courts—and *ascend* into the cottage of the poor.
>
> "Can Tennison [*sic*] do no more than troll a courtly lay? His oak could tell other tales besides a love story. (98)

He goes on to attack James Sheridan Knowles, Charles Mackay, Archer Gurney, Philip Bailey (the author of *Festus*), and others, all in the same vein (98).

In the second article, primarily an assessment of the working-class poet Ebenezer Jones, Ernest Jones has a change of heart. He now argues that "there is decidedly a democratic tendency beginning to pervade our literature." He feels that the established poets share in that tendency. Thus, of Tennyson and Browning he writes, "Even the court poet,

Tennyson, has chided the pride of 'Lady Clara Vere de Vere.' Browning himself has illustrated the dignity of man in his magnificent play of 'Colombe's Birthday'" (Oct. 1847: 235–36).

Jones—if indeed Jones wrote both articles—might offer a muddled criticism of individual works of poetry; yet he sums up the most common Chartist approach to poets: if a work has value, that value is to be found in its application to a working-class audience. In the work, a working-class reader should see some application to his political position. If a work has no such application, it has no value, and Chartists should reject it. One Chartist critic might revile Wordsworth or Southey, and another might argue that both are radicals, but their critical approach is largely the same. Whether a Chartist critic rejected or praised a certain poet often depended upon how diligently the critic wished to search that poet's work for appropriate sentiments. Generally, the Chartists far surpassed their predecessors in their willingness to make that diligent search.

That Jones can find "democracy" in the chiding of Tennyson's Lady Clara Vere de Vere indicates that Chartists believed poems were more than just stirring anthems, hymns to popular causes, and sonnets to working-class heroes, although Chartist journals carried all of these. Linton published in his *National: A Library for the People* his own overtly political "Hymns for the Unenfranchised," parts of Southey's *Wat Tyler*, and parts of Shelley's *Queen Mab* and *Mask of Anarchy*, as well as the whole of his "Song to the Men of England"; he also published the description of the prioress from Chaucer's General Prologue to the *Canterbury Tales*, Wordsworth's "Intimations of Immortality," Tennyson's "Mariana," and many other poems or parts of poems that, unlike verse in pre-Chartist journals, apparently had no direct political application for the working class. In his introduction to the *National*, Linton suggests how such works can be useful to the masses:

> We purpose [*sic*] that [the *National*] shall most fully justify its title; that it shall indeed be a Library for the People, a Magazine of popular information. We well know how to appreciate the struggles of the Unmonied in their pursuit of knowledge. Our design is—to assist them in their difficulties, to aid the inquirer, to encourage the learner, to cultivate moral and intellectual power . . . to disseminate and aid the fructification of Truth, to assist to the uttermost the progression of humanity. (5 Jan. 1839: 3)

Linton's purpose here is much the same as Charles Knight's in his *Penny Magazine*. But while Knight and the SDUK carefully excluded direct references to politics from their periodical and had no desire for the working class to be any more powerful as a class, Linton strove to fuel with political verse the class consciousness of his readers, while cultivating their moral and intellectual improvement with verse not overtly political. Linton, like many other Chartists, believed in the self-help that reading "improving" works could bring. But while Samuel Smiles believed that that sort of self-help could allow workers to escape from the miseries common—and apparently inevitable—to working-class life, Linton shows in his *National* his belief that the elevation of some workers should lead to the elevation of the whole class. Smiles counseled working within the existing class structure; Linton advocated individual improvement in order to change it. That improvement, then, had to be political, but it also had to be moral and intellectual. The lessons of Tennyson and Chaucer are therefore in their own ways as politically important as the more explicitly political lessons of Shelley or Elliott.

Another reason for the greater variety of poetry in Chartist journals is that Chartist editors had a different sense of audience than did their predecessors. Pre-Chartist periodicals were generally oriented to men in tone and direct address; it's easy to picture working men passing around a well-worn copy of the latest *Black Dwarf* or *Poor Man's Guardian* in the coffeehouse, beer shop, or reading room. It would be hard to imagine such a group listening to one of their own reciting Robert Herrick's "To Daffodils" (which appeared in Linton's *National*) or reading to each other some of the less overtly political poems found in the "Feast of the Poets," a series in *Northern Star* that contained the work of both working-class and established writers. Many Chartist journals, unlike those of preceding years, were geared in whole or in part toward the hearth and the entire family, and not just toward politically minded men. That, in turn, affected the sense of what was "valuable" in poetry to Chartist journalists. Certainly, a wider sense of audience led some to adopt a hypersensitivity to the blushing of maidens' cheeks, a concern similar to that of many middle-class periodicals of the day. Many working-class journalists, on the other hand, recognized the need for a greater variety of poems in their periodicals to serve their more heterogeneous audiences.

Many Chartist critics differed from their predecessors in their avowed concern with the impact of certain poems on women or children. The author of the "Literary Sketches" in the *Chartist Circular* is especially concerned with the proper education of children and with the role poetry plays in that education. He writes of Burns: "Every Chartist mother should repeat his patriotic songs, and sing his melting songs to her children, in the winter evenings, by the cottage hearth. His writings should be familiar to every young Chartist, and constitute part of his juvenile education" (20 Feb. 1841: 310). This critic argues that a proper Chartist mind is formed early, and formed equally by "melting" songs and patriotic ones. In his next literary sketch, on Allen Ramsay, this critic offers the opposite lesson: the influence of bad poetry on children. The critic at times praises Ramsay's *Gentle Shepherd*, but he attacks Ramsay's habit in that poem of adoring the titled and scorning the low. He then offers an anecdote about his own education to show the way in which dangerous political principles could be taught insidiously to children through poetry.

> When I was at school, the Gentle Shepherd, and the tragedy of Douglas, were read as schoolbooks, by the scholars. I did not then comprehend their political tendency, and the master never explained it. I admired Patie and Douglas, and thought them gallant and noble; the vassals I laughed at and despised.
>
> Thus was the intention of the teacher of Toryism fulfilled,—the minds of his pupils were poisoned with false political principles, and the seeds of Toryism were sown, which, like weeds in the garden, can never again be entirely eradicated from the soil.
>
> In Chartist schools let no such books be read, nor principles taught; but should they at any time fall into the hands of youth, let the teacher explain their pernicious doctrines, and prevent them from impeding the progress of liberty, the triumph of intellect, and the independence of the people. (13 Feb. 1841: 314)

Children, then, are Chartists as well, and, for this critic, the class war begins in the classroom. Working-class children were part of the audience many Chartist journalists tried to reach with their poetry before Knight, the SDUK, and teachers of Toryism could.

Accompanying the widening sense of audience on the part of Chartist journalists was a widening sense of what made for great poetry. Political propriety and didactic quality were no longer enough; beauty, too, qualified poetry for goodness and greatness. Shakespeare could be, and was, used by the Chartists to illustrate their tenets or to parallel Chartist events. But Shakespeare could do more than this. A review of the *Pictorial Penny Shakespeare* in *Northern Star*, which presented that periodical edition as the cheapest Shakespeare ever and therefore the first truly available to all classes, shows that some Chartists saw Shakespeare as more than a politician, and valued his aesthetic power:

> The Englishman who has not read SHAKESPEARE may doubt his nationality; he is, at best, but half an Englishman, when ignorant of the works of his greatest countryman: and yet, to how many millions has SHAKESPEARE been but little, if anything, more than a mere name. It is painful to reflect that thousands, nay, millions have lived and died, and never known him, who, 'though dead yet speaketh,' and speaketh those words which, of mightier import than the words of priests or prophets, never fail to elevate the minds and purify the hearts of those who willingly list to them. (29 Nov. 1845: 3)[23]

Harney was one critic who valued the beautiful in poetry, emphasizing this requirement in the title of a series he edited for *Northern Star*, "The Beauties of Byron." Though his many selections in that series are largely political, Harney never forgets that Byron "has sung of Beauty and of love with a seraph's tongue" (10 Jan. 1846: 3). Months earlier, in the first "Feast of the Poets" in the *Star*, when Harney had instructed his readers in the elements of good poetry, he did not exhort them to write anthems or satires. Instead, he approvingly restated Leigh Hunt's definition of poetry as a valid standard for the working-class poet:

> Poetry . . . is the utterance of a passion for truth, beauty, and power, embodying and illustrating its conceptions by imagination and fancy, and modulating its language on the principle of variety in uniformity. Its means are whatever the universe contains; and its ends, pleasure and exaltation. Poetry stands between nature and convention, keeping alive among us the enjoyment of the external and the spiritual world: it has constituted the most enduring fame of nations, and, next to Love and Beauty, which are its parents, is the greatest proof to man of the pleasure to be found in all things, and of the probable riches of infinitude. (19 Apr. 1845: 3)

Such a statement, which yokes beauty, truth, and power together as the necessary elements of a good poem, does not downplay the political in poetry, but rather politicizes all good poetry. Poems lacking any one of the three components are not really poems at all. Beautiful verses without truth, in particular, are the confections of false poets such as Barry Cornwall, poets who served interests antithetical to those of the working class.

In 1852 Harney further delineated his beliefs about the power of beauty to elevate the individual. In one of the last issues of *Northern Star* (then called *Star of Freedom*) there appeared a literary dialogue, "Critic and Poet," in which Harney, the paper's new owner, took on the role of Critic (Vicinus 104 n). (The then Chartist and working-class poet Gerald Massey took on the role of Poet.) Harney is delighted by the beauty of Tennyson and emphasizes the importance of that beauty for a working-class audience: "His poetry is a very world of wondrous beauty—purifying and ennobling beauty; and working men should be made acquainted with it that they may get beauty into their souls, and thence into their daily lives" (8 May 1852: 3). Harney does find a fault in Tennyson: he "lacks the fire of passion." However, he states, "I am thankful for what he has given us" (3). The review mentions nothing about Tennyson's political stance. In his *Notes for the People,* Jones pays the same sort of homage to beauty in a review of Browning ("His excellences are, beauty of imagery, facility of diction, and highness of feeling"), and in close readings of "Anabel Lee" and "The Raven," by Edgar Allen Poe, whom Jones called "the most musical bard of the great west." According to Jones, "The purest of morals, the highest of thoughts, are compassed in these two astonishing efforts" (18 Oct. 1851: 644; 25 Oct.: 668–69; 8 Nov.: 704–6).

Keats, the least overtly political of the Romantic poets, and not surprisingly a poet long neglected by working-class journalists, finally entered the working-class canon with the Chartists. The first line of his *Endymion* ("A thing of beauty is a joy forever") appeared in Linton's *National* (16 Feb. 1839: 100), as well as in *Northern Tribune* (Jan 1854: 3) and in *Red Republican* (5 July 1850: 19). In the last case, the line forms the first words of an essay, "Poetry to Be Lived." The essay is by Massey, who was at this time a young and fiery republican, writing under the pen name Bandiera.[24] The essay illustrates several enormous differences between views of poetry held by Chartist journalists and those held by their predecessors.

To Massey, as stated in "Poetry to Be Lived," "the world is full of poetry." The greatness of any written poem is only a dim reflection of humanity itself; the human mind and soul are the greater texts.

> The commonest nature has some divine touch of poetry in it—crushed and degraded as we are, worn down by suffering and sorrow, blighted by the dry-rot of slavery, and the branding stamp of tyranny, there are times when we walk on the angel-side of life, and feel that our lives do not all turn in darkness—and the generous aspiration *will* be stirring at the heart, the sweet tears *will* be starting to the eyes, and we know we might have been something better, and lived a nobler life, if the world had done justice by us. Those tears are as a telescope to the soul, through which it catches big glimpses of the infinite: and those aspirations realize unto us the highest kind of poetry—*the poetry to be lived.*

Massey exhorts his audience to become poets themselves, to make great the texts of their lives. He tells them to find the inspiration they need to make their own lives great in poetry, in nature, and in the lives of great men. Among the great men whose lives Massey endorses as models of greatness are Kossuth, Bandiera, Mazzini, and other patriots—but just as important as models are the great English poets. In Massey's eyes, these poets' varied lives offer far more than simply political ideals to follow.

> Witness . . . the life of the poet Milton; grandly magnificent as is the poetry of "Paradise Lost,"—there was a nobler, a truer poetry, in the life of the stern old republican. Of all the poets upon record, the life of Milton was the proudest, the completest, the manfullest. The life of Shakspere was a chequered youth, a green old age. Coleridge's was dreaming and weird-like. Byron's was the storm, the grandeur, and the gloom of the tempest, his poetry was like fruit on the side of Etna! Shelley's was like a drama, wherein Christ, Rousseau, and Ophelia should play their parts! and Keats—dear Keats!—his life was like the song of the nightingale, heard in the rich, still summer night, pouring her soul out on the balmy air, in passionate cadences, singing you into tears, as though the old fable were true that she sang with the thorn in her bleeding bosom.

Though Milton and his republicanism may gain Massey's highest respect, the other poets hold places of esteem, most of them not for overtly political reasons. Massey's impression of Keats's nightingale life seems a far cry from his impression of Milton's republican life, but both are presented as appropriate exemplars of poetical greatness for the working class.

This new emphasis on Beauty—in life and in poetry—did not signal a softening on the part of the working-class thinkers of this time. Harney read Tennyson, Jones read Poe, and Massey read Keats, all with the question, "How does this writer speak to members of my class?" And the fact that each one recognized value in the writers they evaluated indicates that they all knew that the "political" in poetry is not just an incitement to riot, a mauling of Castlereagh, or a satire on the poor laws. To these three journalists, and others, all poetry was ideological; and all good poetry was ideologically sound and was a powerful tool with which to elevate the working class.

When Massey exclaims, later in his essay, "Brother Working-Men, let us endeavour to live this poetry in our lives!" he shows a respect for his audience as high as he has for any of the great poets. The essay, celebrating the boundless imaginative, intellectual, and political potential of the working class, puts into words the sentiments suggested by the many Chartist editors and critics who strove to bring a wider range of poetry than ever before to their working-class audience.

Shelley, Byron, and Burns

The Chartists of Sheffield adorned the walls of their public rooms with the names of those who they believed to be the greatest modern thinkers, politicians, and men of letters. Among such names as John Hampden, Washington, Jefferson, Paine, William Wallace, Algernon Sidney, Robert Emmet, and O'Connor, they listed three poets: Byron, Burns, and Shelley. Those walls serve as an emblem of a Chartist philosophy of ideas—indeed of a philosophy of ideas for the working-class for this period and before. Working-class thinkers respected these three poets as much as they did the greatest politicians; perhaps no higher compliment can be paid a poet by working-class writers. They had a deep respect for each of these poets as an individual—in life, in politics, and in poetic style. They recognized and celebrated the differences between the three. This ability—indeed, this need—to distinguish between the three and to respect the variety of work of each poet affirms that working-class critics were very much aware that they were forming and defining a working-class poetic canon.

Three modern scholars have studied the influence that individual poets had upon the working class, particularly upon the Chartists. Philip Collins discusses Byron's influence in his *Thomas Cooper, the Chartist: Byron and the "Poets of the Poor"*; Bouthaina Shaaban discusses Shelley's influence in "Shelley in the Chartist Press"; and Albert K. Stevens investigates the link between "Milton and Chartism." Each study offers pertinent insight into working-class literary values of this period; but each is unfortunately limited in several ways. For one thing, because each of these critics focuses upon only one poet, in none of their works do we get a strong sense of the amazing variety in the poetry in Chartist journals and the amazing variety of poetic influences on the Chartists. Such an exclusive focus implies in each case a far duller working-class culture than that which actually existed. All the critics, for example, argue that Cooper was strongly influenced by the particular poet they are concerned with. But not one makes the far more important point: Cooper read widely and with discrimination, and was sophisticated enough in his reading to note the beauty and the power in the works of all these poets and others. Much can be said for the Chartist intelligentsia as a whole. And much can be said of many of the working-class intellectuals of the entire period.

Another limitation of the three modern studies, one that is perhaps necessary, considering the sheer volume of information each has to deal with, is that they focus exclusively on the Chartists. But Chartist views on poetry, as we have seen, did not develop in a vacuum. Setting the Chartist views of these poets in the context of previous working-class views demonstrates far more clearly the strong affection many Chartists felt for these three poets.

In this section I shall focus upon working-class views of Shelley, Byron, and Burns, the poets by far the most widely discussed and excerpted in the working-class press; or, to put it another way, the three established poets who formed the core of a working-class poetic canon. I will look not at their poetic abilities but rather at the critical abilities of the working-class journalists who discussed and published them. These writers and editors applied distinctly working-class critical standards to each poet and understood and respected each for his life as well as his work. Choosing and promoting specific works particularly relevant to their audience from the corpus of each poet, working-class journalists endeavored to develop a canon of poetry, differentiating it from the dominant middle-class canon. They did not accept the poets wholesale; they judged and reevaluated them for a new audience. The many astute critical observations of working-class thinkers, I believe, indicate that they had a far greater literary sophistication than they have heretofore been accorded.

I do not wish, by focusing on these three very influential poets, to minimize the importance of other poets and their works. Southey, as we have seen, had a deep impact on working-class movements from 1817 on, particularly with *Wat Tyler* but also with the negative example he set through his political and poetical apostasy. Shakespeare was very important to working-class journalists during the entire period, of course; as I have tried to show, critics often tested their class-based literary ideas upon his plays. Indeed, in one case, a Chartist produced one of Shakespeare's plays. In 1843, to help cover his legal expenses, Cooper persuaded a group of Leicester Chartists to hire a hall in order to put on *Hamlet*, with himself in the title role. Cooper had, years before, committed the entire play to memory (Cooper 68). The show ran two nights (Cooper 228–29).

Milton, too, was certainly important to working-class thinkers. Samuel Bamford, for one, declared his affection for Milton several times in his *Passages from the Life of a Radical* (1: 165–66, 176, 199).[25] Cooper was deeply influenced by Milton as well; he stated that he knew the first four books of *Paradise Lost* by heart (Cooper 68). In most working-class periodicals, however, Milton's poetry was less important than his prose. Stevens notes in his study of Milton's influence on the Chartists that thirty-four cheap editions of Milton's prose appeared in the first half of the nineteenth century (378). Cobbett, as we have seen, disliked *Paradise Lost*; Carlile called Milton "a gloomy fanatic" (*Republican* 19 Nov. 1819: 201). Wooler published some of Milton's poetry, but much more of his prose, in his "Blackneb" series. Working-class periodicals of the thirties published little Milton; a review of Carpenter's *Life and Times of John Milton* in the *Weekly True Sun* makes no mention at all of his poetry (6 June 1836: 1157). Linton, in the *National*, reviewed the same work and suggested that Milton's prose is more dangerous than his poetry to the ruling class, and therefore more valuable to the working class (23 Feb. 1839: 113). Harney makes much the same point about Milton's prose in his *Democratic Review* (1849–50; July 1849: 75–80).[26] In his *English Republic*, Linton argues that Milton's life, and apparently his prose, are more important than his greatest work of poetry, holding that there are "some men who honor the memory of Milton (I say it reverently) for something more than one of his poems called 'Paradise Lost'" (Jan. 1851: 3). Massey, writing as Bandiera in *Red Republican*, shows that he is one of these men (5 July 1815: 19–20).

Goldsmith (with his often-excerpted attack on enclosure, "The Deserted Village"), Thomson (with *The Seasons*), Pope, Wordsworth, Coleridge, Moore, Tennyson, and others were important influences upon the working class as well. By focusing upon the poets—Shelley, Byron, and Burns—that working-class journalists most commonly cited and discussed, and by showing the ways in which the journalists actively appropriated the poets for their own class, I hope to suggest that they applied their critical thinking as conscientiously to many other established poets. These three poets may have been at the core of a nineteenth-century working-class canon, but they were far from being the only poets in that canon.

Arguing that Shelley was more "important" than Byron to working-class journalists during this period, or vice versa, would be sheer folly. Some journalists obviously favored Byron, others Shelley. Carlile, for example, though he pirated the works of both, clearly preferred Shelley's poetry. He called some cantos of *Don Juan* "*mere slip slop*," and maintained that *Cain*, a work Carlile himself published, "*is a Mystery*" (*Republican* 11 Feb. 1825: 164), its only good qualities stolen from Shelley's *Queen Mab* and, of *Cain* and *Queen Mab*, "as a poem, as a work of sentiment and merit, the former is much inferior to the latter, and not worthy of resting on the same shelf in the library" (*Republican* 15 Feb. 1822: 192). Carlile was capable of changing his tastes to suit a given situation; some of his comments are in response to a correspondent, Zephyrus, who audaciously suggested that Byron had had greater political influence than Carlile. Carlile's rebuttal consists in equal parts of belittling Byron's political importance and of making himself out to be the most important political figure alive: "I am, in my own judgment at the very acme of that which is right, best, and of the most importance, in a political point of view" (11 Feb. 1825: 164–68). Elsewhere, Carlile could be kinder to Byron, as when he called him "our great, persecuted, injured Byron" (19 Nov. 1819: 201). Never, however, did Carlile hold Byron to be as great a poet and thinker as Shelley (or Carlile).

Wooler, on the other hand, implicitly believed Byron to be more worthy of publication and study than Shelley; he published next to nothing by Shelley in his *Black Dwarf*, but published Byron's "Sonnet on Chillon," parts of *Don Juan*, *The Giaour*, and *Childe Harold's Pilgrimage*, and all or part of several other works by Byron. Cobbett published little by either, though he did argue that England's Byron was far better than Scotland's best writer, Scott, in an article contrasting the merits of the men of letters of each country (*Political Register* 5 Feb. 1825: 343).[27]

This individual preference, which cannot be construed as one of class or of any particular movement, continued in later periodicals. The periodicals of the early and mid-thirties published both Byron and Shelley, again some preferring one over the other. *The Poor Man's Advocate*, for example, clearly favored Byron. John Doherty, the editor of that periodical, was obviously an avid reader of Byron; among other items by and on the poet, Doherty published his "The Irish Avatar," which he claimed "has never before been published entire in England" (28 Apr. 1832: 118).[28]

Chartist journalists printed more poetry by Byron and Shelley than had any working-class journalists before them and showed the same preferences, as well as the same aversions. Linton, in his *National*, we have seen, published a great deal of poetry by Shelley. He published nothing at all by Byron. *Northern Star* published far more Byron than Shelley, especially in the days when Harney controlled the literary page. Collins points out that Harney "in his staider old age became an expert on minutiae of [Byron's] biography, in *Notes and Queries*" (19; see also Schoyen 274). Margaret Hambrick notes that Harney owned many works by and about Byron; her catalogue of the books in the Harney family library offers strong evidence of this (12). Harney's preference for Byron, and Linton's for Shelley, were, however, entirely personal.

Working-class journalists, rather than arguing which of the two poets was the better, or choosing one and rejecting the other, generally saw both as fighters on their side in the class struggle. To working-class writers, both were aristocrats who turned their backs on class privilege and embraced the causes of the working-class. Carlile wrote: "Shelley, we know, from a boy, was both republican and Atheist; that as a heir to a great fortune and some prospect of a peerage, he sacrificed every thing, fortune, and family, and lived in poverty, dependent on friends in principle, for the purpose of preserving and exhibiting pure and uncontaminated those important principles which in his youth he had adopted. The aristocracy of England has not turned out a second man of Shelley's stamp" (11 Feb. 1825: 168). Seven years later the *Chartist Circular* made a similar point about Shelley (19 Oct. 1839: 16) and said much the same thing of Byron:

> Of all the poets who have directed their minds to the study of the social condition of man, none has sympathised more deeply with the sufferers, none shown a more determined spirit of resistance and retaliation to the oppressor than Byron: his noble and dignified soul scorned the idea of fattening on the ruins of his country; nor could he quietly submit, and not raise his far-heard voice against the wretches who made their own gain and their country's ruin their study and practice. (22 Aug. 1840: 198)

Both Shelley and Byron were, in a sense, honorary members of the working class. The task for many working-class writers was less to choose one over the other than to promote the individual merits of the works of each for a working-class audience. T. Frost tried to do just that in his article "Scott, Byron, and Shelley" in the *Northern Star* of 2 January 1847 (3). Although Frost saw a bit of good in Scott, he criticized him for worshipping a feudal and aristocratic past. Byron was the poet of the present: "His sympathies were ever with those who sought the elevation of their fellow-men, and he launched the most brilliant efforts of his muse, fraught with the keenest irony, against the abuses of the day." Shelley, on the other hand, was the harbinger of the future: "not the futurity-idea inculcated by our clerical instructors, dim and shadowy as Ossian's hall of Loda, but the moral summer of the world, the realisation of Arcadian fable and Hebraic myth." Frost's article puts into words sentiments common to many working-class journalists. We have seen earlier several examples of the working-class rejection of Scott's feudal values. In one of his "Beauties of Byron" essays, Harney anticipated Frost's sentiments about Byron and

Shelley, holding that he views society much as Byron did, but "as respects the future, we cling to the belief in man's progress, and trust and believe with SHELLEY that 'A bright morn awaits the human day'" (*Northern Star* 10 Jan 1846: 3). Wooler, reviewing Byron's *The Age of Bronze* in *Black Dwarf* on 2 April 1823, is disappointed because that poem, unlike his others, deals for the most part with the recent past and not with the present (465–70). Cooper, in his *Plain Speaker*, notes Shelley's "prescience" (10 Mar. 1849: 58). In the hundreds of quotations and headnotes by the two poets, journalists generally used each to serve different purposes: most often Byron offered social commentary, Shelley expressed social ideals. Although some working-class thinkers preferred one over the other, most saw a different but important value in each.

Friedrich Engels described the deep respect the working-class had for Shelley and Byron in his *Condition of the Working Class in England in 1844*: "Shelley, the genius, the prophet, Shelley, and Byron, with his glowing sensuality and his bitter satire upon our existing society, find most of their readers in the proletariat; the bourgeoisie owns only castrated editions, family editions, cut down in accordance with the hypocritical morality of to-day" (240). His remark about the completeness of working-class publications of Shelley and Byron—at least as far as the working-class press is concerned—is not completely accurate. The poetry by Shelley and Byron most often published and excerpted in these journals was carefully selected, often cut down, and even at times cited out of context to display a working-class sensibility and sympathy.

In Shelley's case, "Song to the Men of England" was a favorite selection, one that appeared frequently in many periodicals, from Carlile's to the Chartists'. The free-thinking and utopian *Queen Mab* was another favorite, often excerpted, reviewed, and mentioned. Another popular work was *The Revolt of Islam*, written, according to Shelley, "in the view of kindling within the bosoms of my readers a virtuous enthusiasm for those doctrines of liberty and justice, that faith and hope for something good, which neither violence nor misrepresentation nor prejudice can ever totally extinguish among mankind" (2: 100). Also popular, after it was published in 1832, was *The Mask of Anarchy*. Almost all Shelley's poetry published or discussed by working-class journalists was explicitly political.[29] Although most of these journalists treasured the "beauties" of Shelley, they clearly respected him for his politics first and the beauty of his poetry second. Such works as "Mont Blanc," "Ode to the West Wind," or "Adonais" were strangers to the pages of working-class periodicals. If members of the British working class had more than the slightest acquaintance with poems by Shelley that were not primarily political, they gained that acquaintance elsewhere.

Most of the poems by Byron published in working-class periodicals were excerpts: parts of *Don Juan, Childe Harold's Pilgrimage,* or other works. This did not mean that working-class audiences did not have access to complete poems by Byron; Louis James has noted twenty-five editions of Byron's various poems, exclusive of reprints, in the bibliography of his *Fiction for the Working Man, 1830–1850* (235). The excerpts in working-class periodicals were generally presented not to provide the flavor of the whole work, but rather to stand on their own as points not needing the context of a larger work, or specific quotations to emphasize a journalist's argument. Thus, Byron was presented as a poet of quick satirical jabs and short political observations. He was a favorite for short illustrative quotations and for headnotes. A writer in the *Radical Reformer's Gazette* (1832–33), for example, quotes from *Childe Harold,* "Hereditary bondsmen know ye not / Who would be free, themselves must strike the blow" (canto 2, 720–21; quoted 26 Jan. 1833: 170), and quotes that passage not in the context that Byron gave it—a description of the Turkish enslavement of Greece—but rather as the headnote to an article describing the miserable condition of the poor in Birmingham. Byron was used similarly in *Black Dwarf,* Cobbett's *Political Register, Republican, or Voice of the People,* the *Herald to the Trades' Advocate, and Co-Operative Journal,* the *Poor Man's Advocate,* and many other papers, including, as might be expected, two influenced by Harney: the *Northern Star* and the *Democratic Review.*[30]

The poetry written by members of the working-class published in working-class periodicals shows that many of these writers were influenced by the poetry of Byron and Shelley. For one thing, working-class poems honoring those poets were common.[31] Moreover, several critics have noted thematic and semantic parallels as well as connections of imagery between these two Romantics and working-class poets. James, for instance, notes that "the popularity of Romantic poetry influenced the verse of radical poets, for writers like Shelley had provided imagery to express the overthrow of evil by the powers of good" (86). Kovalev states that "during its first few years Chartist poetry was chiefly imitative. Its models were usually popular working-class songs . . . as well as certain works by Shelley, Byron, and other democratic poets of the first three decades of the nineteenth century" ("The Literature of Chartism" 124). Certainly, many of the verses Kovalev published in his *Anthology of Chartist Literature* reflect the influence of both poets—and especially of Shelley. The following verses from E. C. H.'s "Address to the Charter," for example, originally from *Northern Star*, seem clearly derivative of that poet:

> The slave, oppress'd with canker'd chains,
>   O'erworn with grief and care,
> He knows, he feels, there still remains
>   A hope, though distant far.
>
> The instrument of slavery's form
>   Can flourish but an hour;
> Crush'd, like the moth, before the storm,
>   How transient is their power!
>
> A happier year, a brighter ray,
>   Shall usher a glorious morn;
> How happy the poor, on that free-born day,
>   Who have triumph'd o'er proud man's scorn.
>   (6 June 1840: 7)

The assumption that working-class poets borrowed wholesale from Shelley and Byron can be taken too far, however, and can cause one to mistake working-class creativity for mere derivation. The imagery of enslavement, chains, and rising up after slumber could suggest the influence of Shelley's "Song to the Men of England." More probably, such imagery reflects working-class poets' awareness of their own position; for what images are more appropriate to radical working-class poetry in the first half of the nineteenth century than chains, enslavement, and uprising? Several poems in the working-class press of 1819 and 1820, reacting to the Peterloo massacre, bear similarities to Shelley's poetic response to that event, *The Mask of Anarchy*. There seem obvious connections between Shelley's poem and the following verses from "Stanzas Occasioned by the Manchester Massacre," by Hibernicus:

Oh, weep not for those who are freed
From bondage so frightful as ours!
Let *tyranny* mourn for the deed,
And howl o'er the prey she devours!

The mask for a century worn,
Has fallen from her visage at last;
Of all its sham attributes shorn,
Her reign of delusion is past.

In native deformity now
Behold her, how shatter'd and weak!
With *murder* impress'd on her brow,
And *cowardice* blanching on her cheek!
(*Black Dwarf* 27 Aug. 1819: 564)

These verses were published a few days after the massacre. *The Mask of Anarchy* was not actually published until thirteen years later, in 1832. Hibernicus could not have read Shelley's *Mask,* and Shelley, in Italy at that time, almost certainly did not see this poem before writing his own. Neither poet influenced the other. Any connection between the two poems, and without question many of the similarities between Shelley's work and that of working-class poets, signifies not imitation but rather parallel class sympathies and political philosophies.

Byron had his imitators among working-class writers as he did among other classes. The third issue of the *Political Penny Magazine* (1836), for example, carried a poem: "The Devil's Visit to England," by a poet signed Harold, that bears a resemblance to Byron's poetry in more than its name (17 Sept. 1836: 24). Showing a similar influence are several poems by J. H. M. in Bronterre O'Brien's *National Reformer, and Manx Weekly Review of Home and Foreign Affairs* (1846–47).[32] Modern critics as well as those of the contemporary working-class noted the influence of Byron upon Cooper's *Purgatory of Suicides.*[33] But imitators of Byron—from any class—generally did not fare well at the hands of working-class reviewers; usually, when discussing an imitation, reviewers commented directly or indirectly on the originality of Byron—"the unattainable pattern of so many" and the lack of originality of his imitator (*Notes to the People* 3 Oct. 1851: 454).[34] Byron and Shelley may have provided models for working-class political verse, but a good working-class poet also had to be in touch with his own cultural reality to write good verse.

Burns was not as often quoted in the working-class press as Byron and Shelley, but this, I think, was a sign not that his poetry was any less popular, but rather that his best-loved lyrics were already familiar to a large section of the working class and did not need to be introduced to them, as Byron's and Shelley's poetry did. I have already noted that working-class writers appropriated the music to Burns's songs, especially of "Scots, Wha' Hae wi' Wallace Bled" and "A Man's a Man for A' That," more than they borrowed the music of any other writer. Harney, who notes that "Scots, Wha' Hae wi' Wallace Bled" was sung at every Chartist festival in England (*Northern Star* 25 Oct. 1845: 3), sees no reason to familiarize his audience with the "beauties" of Burns as he does those of Byron. In the *Northern Star*'s "Christmas Garland" for 1843 Harney almost apologizes for publishing the universally known "A Man's a Man for A' That," stating, "We think we hear some grumbling critic, growling: 'Why, man, these are all old songs, everybody knows about "A man's a man for a' that."'" He argues, however, that there is a great difference between familiarity with the poem and true knowledge of it: "O that the righteous principles contained in the above lyrics were really *known* to everybody; what a different world would this be to what it is!" (23 Dec. 1843: 3).

Despite the heavy dialect and the regionalism of most of Burns's poems, working-class writers saw his poetry as transcending nation. It is true that Scots working-class periodicals mentioned and published Burns more often than did their southern counterparts; the *Chartist Circular*, for example, repeatedly cited Burns as the standard for a good poet.[35] English periodicals, however, also sometimes cited Burns as a poetic standard. A critic in the new series of *Northern Star*, for example, accords the French poet Pierre Dupont the highest praise in calling him "the Burns of France" (5 June 1852: 3). But while English working-class journalists were well aware of Burns's country of origin, not one considers Burns any less important for the English. Harney comments repeatedly on Burns's internationalism.[36] A writer in *Northern Tribune* writes that Burns's simplicity allows him to transcend the regional: he "exhibits a striking example of the force, beauty, and true poetry of imagery and words the humblest and most unlettered can appreciate, admire, and adore" (Nov. 1854: 169).

While working-class writers generally held Burns's national origins to be unimportant, they did value his class origins highly. Burns, unlike Shelley or Byron, did not have to earn membership in the working class; he was always a member. Moreover, working-class journalists believed that Burns had always shared the interests of that class and never turned away from them. The reactionary *Bristol Job Nott, or, Labouring Man's Friend* (1831–33), a weekly periodical created in response to a then exploding working-class press, in publishing "The Cottar's Saturday Night," might "lament that [Burns's] pen was employed far more unworthily" (22 Dec. 1831: 8), but it was those "unworthy," class-conscious productions that endeared him to his class. It was his loyalty to his class, however, not simply his birth within it that earned him respect. Other poets born into the working class were far less respected. No working-class writer ever promoted George Crabbe, for example, as a working-class hero, in spite of his origins.[37]

Because of Burns's class consciousness and class fidelity as well as his origins, working-class journalists often saw him as the first true working-class poet. A writer in one of the final issues of *Northern Star*, reviewing a volume of poems by William Whitmore entitled *Firstlings*, emphatically accords Burns that place.

> Giant-hearted Robert Burns, was the first in a kingly line, and the founder of a glorious dynasty of the people's poets. With his lamp, which was lit with fire from Heaven, he descended into the lowliest human heart, read the inscription which God had written on its narrow, dark chamber walls, and proclaimed to the world that the signs of beauty and gleams of light still illumined its darkness. He it was who sang "a man's a man for a' that"; and at the words the poor crushed masses felt the spirit of manhood stirring within them, and the spirit of freedom effervescing at the heart of them. The Serf was made noble in Robert Burns. He hoped our hopes, wept our tears, despaired our despairs, and his heart was pulsed by all our living impulses. The people lived in the large brave heart of Robert Burns, and we have taken him to live for ever and aye in the heart of the people. (7 Aug. 1852: 3)

Critics often traced the poetic ancestry of every working-class poet to Burns. The above reviewer, for example, goes on to say, "since Glorious Burns we have had many a true singer in the ranks of the Working Classes who have seen that their mission has been that of hand and heart workers in the strife. We point with pride to John Clare, the peasant; Robert Nichol, the Scottish herd boy; Thomas Cooper, the Milton of Chartism; Prince, and Thom, and many another people's poet of the lineage of Burns" (3). A reviewer of Massey's *Voices of Freedom and Lyrics of Love* in *Northern Star* makes a similar observation about Massey's debt to Burns (12 Apr. 1851: 3).

Other working-class critics maintained that Burns had predecessors and was the outstanding working-class poet in a long line of them. Many critics maintained that Shakespeare, curiously enough, was an early working-class poet.[38] In the *Chartist Circular*, for example, Shakespeare is called "one of the enslaved and despised people, a poacher and a 'vagabond' player" (10 Oct. 1840: 216). In another article in that periodical, "The Genius of Working Men," one writer holds that not only Shakespeare, but also Homer, Aesop, Socrates, Milton, Johnson, Defoe, and others "sprang from humble origins." This writer believes that "genius is almost exclusive to working men" (16 May 1840: 135–36). But it is Burns more than any other figure who was believed to have revolutionized poetry with his working-class sensibility. In the poetic "march of the intellect," Burns marched in the vanguard.

Most working-class writers unquestionably felt that while Byron and Shelley were sometimes teachers and other times comrades, Burns alone was a brother. From Cobbett's *Political Register* to *Northern Star*, we find working-class writers visiting Burns's dwellings and haunts, as well as his gravesite, as if they were those of a close relative. In 1832 Cobbett visited Dumfries, the town in which Burns had died; in reporting that visit in his *Register*, he expressed concern for Burns's widow (16 Nov. 1832: 415). The *Poor Man's Guardian* noted her death not long afterward (10 May 1834: 71). The *Northern Star* showed a similar concern for Burns's daughter (7 Sept. 1844: 3; 5 Oct. 1844: 3). A writer in the *Chartist Circular*, with the style of the novelist of sentiment, described an emotional visit he made to Burns's birthplace, Alloway: "When I wandered among these streets, musing on the Bard,—rehearsing his poems—chanting his songs . . . my bosom glowed with a patriot's ardour—my heart melted with poetical tenderness, and tears involuntarily trickled down my cheeks. It was an hour of mental ecstasy, spent in rapture on the soft green oasis of the barren desert of human existence" (20 Feb. 1841: 309–10). Harney, following in the footsteps of Cobbett, paid two visits to Dumfries. During the first, in 1840, he dined with Burns's son, and during the second, in 1843, he made, "as a matter of course," an emotional visit to the grave of the poet, "this man of men . . . my hero, saint and sage" (20 Sept. 1843: 8). Although Byron was clearly Harney's favorite poet, he never recorded any desire to visit that poet's mausoleum. By the same token, it is difficult to imagine any working-class journalist showing a heartfelt concern for the welfare of Mary Shelley. Burns clearly occupied a far more familiar and familial place in the working-class canon.

While quoted, mentioned, and promoted less than Byron or Shelley, Burns's place in the working-class canon was as secure as theirs. But the three were not interchangeable: each was specifically evaluated by working-class thinkers; each was promoted for very different reasons, reasons of value particularly to the working class. In other words, there existed in the first half of the nineteenth century a definite working-class critical framework within which to view each writer, one quite different in emphases and standards from that of the middle class. That alternative critical framework has been forgotten, by and large, and the loss is a great one for the modern reader. For just as each of these three poets had unique value for the working-class of the early nineteenth century, so should the working-class critical framework in use between 1816 and 1858, in giving us a fresh way to evaluate these poets, ultimately make them more valuable to us.

5

The Drama and the Dramatic

AS HE DID with both fiction and poetry, Carlile offered some of the strongest condemnations of performance drama of any working-class writer. In an 1826 article in the *Republican*, "The Theatre," he described his visits to four theaters, concluding "I am heartily sick of them, and shall go no more. The solitude of a Gaol has charms for me; but the theatre has none" (13 Jan. 1826: 55). Carlile simply could not understand why a sane society would endure plays in the first place and drew some despairing conclusions about a society that does need theaters: "A play-going people must be in some measure a depraved or unhappy people. It must be a flight from domestic misery, or a depraved taste for an amusement which a well-formed mind cannot enjoy, and which is not needed by they who seek mental and moral improvement. It is a waste of time; in addition to which a great expence is incurred and nothing good is gained for the health of the body or the mind" (56). But as far as the state of the British theater was concerned, Carlile was not a curious, solitary iconoclast from whom later working-class critics differed greatly in their views, as he was in the case of both fiction and poetry. On the contrary, Carlile set the tone for subsequent criticism of the theater. Although later critics had a sense that the theater could serve positive ends, from 1816 to 1858 working-class critics distrusted performance drama, seeing it in its present state as useless or even dangerous.

I make a careful distinction here between drama as a whole and "performance" drama, or drama as presented in the theaters of the day. From the start, most working-class journalists approved of drama as a printed literary form. Both Cobbett and Wooler wrote dramatic scenes for their own periodicals. And, as we have seen, *Wat Tyler*, *Cain*, and Shakespeare's dramatic works were continuing and important parts of the working-class literary canon. But neither Wooler's *Dialogue between the Ghosts of Mr. Pitt and Lord Castlereagh* nor Cobbett's *Big O and Sir Glory; or "Leisure to Laugh"* were ever meant to be performed. Neither were *Wat Tyler* or *Cain*. Many working-class critics thought that Shakespeare's works as well were better read than seen. A critic in the *Northern Star*, for example, wrote of *Hamlet*: "the drama is more suitable for the closet than for the stage" (30 Dec. 1848: 3). Almost all the generic comments I have found about the great poetic dramatists appear not in reviews of performances but in essays about printed texts.

Working-class journalists did not ignore the theater. Indeed, several working-class periodicals are stuffed with reviews. But rarely does any statement appear in those reviews about the play as a work of literature. Reviews generally focused almost exclusively on the depiction of a work and very little on the inherent value of the play itself. Thus Wooler, for example, when he reviews a revival of Philip Massenger's *A New Way to Pay Old Debts*, tells us next to nothing of his opinion of the play as literature but a lot about the actors: "Mr. Booth has appeared as Sir Giles. Some of our co-temporaries [*sic*] will have it that he *does not copy* Mr. Kean; although every action, tone, and attitude come as nearly to the original, as the force of imitation can make it" (12 Mar. 1817: 110).

This type of review was the norm in working-class periodicals. The *Northern Star* carried hundreds of reviews in its fourteen-year run, but though it ran many reviews of Shakespeare's plays, for example, we learn very little in any of them about Shakespeare's *Hamlet* or *Macbeth*, but a great deal about Mr. Kirkland's or Mr. Barry Sullivan's *Hamlet*, or Mr. J. W. Wallack's or Mr. Macready's *Macbeth*. Apparently, few writers saw the theater as anything more than a means to a night's entertainment.[1]

There are a couple of reasons for the low value that working-class critics placed on performance drama as a useful genre. For one thing, presenting a work on stage involved at least one intermediary between the writer and his audience: the manager or director, whose views of what plays were worth producing and the way a work should be produced often did not accord completely with the views of working-class critics. Subsequently, productions often reflected a distorted sense of reality to these critics. As Wooler in *Black Dwarf* writes of the theaters, "they are in-stitutions . . . intended to reflect the face of nature; but nature never had such features as stage managers often mask her in" (6 Aug. 1823: 206). Jones, writing in 1847 in the *Labourer*, notes the same distortion, with a stronger sense of the class interests involved:

> Can no new fire be infused into what is called the "expiring drama?"—
> expiring, because it has been the pander to wealth and fashion, instead
> of the vindicator of manhood and industry. . . . We have had the misfor-
> tunes of younger sons, the mishaps of injured daughters of noble
> houses, but when has the Bastile victim, when has the lost child of
> labour, when has the hapless operative, (the martyrs of the nineteenth
> century,) when have these been brought before the public eye in the
> drama, or when will they? while a dramatic monopoly is kept up, in
> keeping with all others, that, while a censorship of the press is declared
> contrary to the constitution, establishes a censorship of the drama in
> direct violation of its recognised principle? (Aug. 1847: 94)[2]

A similar sense that there was nothing in the contemporary theater of any social relevance whatsoever led a writer in the *London Phalanx* (1841–43), a periodical promoting the ideas of Charles Fourier, to com-plain that, "we are almost ashamed to say a word about the Drama, for, at present, there is none in London" (18 Apr. 1841: 45). It is a "dramatic monopoly" that John Watkins complains about in *Northern Star*. Watkins was the writer of a play, *John Frost*, that he called "an attempt to illustrate Chartism itself," which he could not get anyone to produce. He notes bit-terly the difference between what the theaters actually were like and what they could have been: "I chose the dramatic form, because I agree with my friend Elliott, that the theatre (yet what theatre will bring this piece forward while the present censorship exists?) might be made the 'most powerful of state organs'" (2 Apr. 1841: 7). Interestingly, Watkins's complaint about "censorship" preceded by two years the Theatre Regula-tion Act of 1843, which removed the monopoly over serious drama held by the patent theaters—Drury Lane and Covent Garden. That monopoly over drama, however, had been eroding for decades (Rowell 10–13); by 1841 it alone would not have presented much of an obstacle to the production of a play such as *John Frost*. Moreover, working-class views about performance drama did not change noticeably after 1843. Censorship, therefore, was more that of the marketplace and theater managers than of the government.

Carlile, despite his disdain for performance drama in 1826, showed that the monopoly could be defied. If the hostile middleman, the manager (or director), could be removed or replaced, he reasoned, then performance drama might indeed serve the working class. In early 1830 Carlile leased a building, the Rotunda, that featured frequent dramatic performances. The Rotunda, with its two large halls, library, and several smaller meeting rooms, was the center of London radicalism in 1830 and 1831, and its many activities—lectures by a variety of speakers and meetings, as well as shows—reflected the eclecticism of working-class radicalism during those years. On Sunday evenings Carlile and Rev. Robert Taylor staged "elaborate theatrical performances"—radical, freethought sermons (of which more in a moment)—and plays (Wiener, *Radicalism* 164–65). One of these plays was *Swing, or Who Are the Incendiaries?*, written in "consciously Shakespearean" blank verse by Taylor (McCalman, "Irreligion" 57). *Swing* concerned the agricultural disturbances occurring at that time in the southern counties of England. In a "review" of the play he produced, Carlile shows a change of heart about drama—or at least about the drama that he had control over: "On Friday evening, 'SWING' was performed before a large and respectable audience, and gave high satisfaction. This is the most popular bit of public political proceeding and entertainment that has ever been provided. It is an entire novelty; in which, without fear or disguise, the whole question of popular grievance and desired reform is dramatised" (*Prompter* 19 Feb. 1831: 254). But putting on a serious play either written or produced by members of the working class was difficult, as Watkins discovered, and as Cooper realized when he and a group of Leicester Chartists put on two performances of *Hamlet*. Though the hall was packed on both nights, "the income," Cooper noted in his autobiography, "hardly covered expenses" (228–29).

There was another reason why working-class critics placed little value on the performance drama of the day. It was a reason working-class journalists cited infrequently, but it may go further toward explaining why pro-working-class dramas not only played badly at Drury Lane but also bombed at the local "penny gaff"—those "shops which have been turned into a kind of temporary theatre (admission one penny)," in which the stage, "instead of being the means for illustrating a moral precept, is turned into a platform to teach the cruelest debauchery," according to Henry Mayhew in his *London Labour and the London Poor* (36–37). Audiences—including working-class audiences—and their collective taste were largely to blame for the state of the drama in the eyes of working-class journalists. Managers, after all, were only catering to popular interest. A writer in *Northern Star* points out how questionable taste is preventing serious drama from being performed:

> Opera, burlesque, and melodrama may be safely said to have been obtaining for some years, to the prejudice of tragedy and comedy; and though it is beyond our limits analytically to discuss the why and the wherefore of this, it must be evident to the most commonplace understandings, that those who are the convenient scape-goats for all theatrical grievances—managers, are not in this instance the individuals who have brought about this change. A few general observations are sufficient to show that lessees are blameless in this matter, and that the *vox populi* has decreed, at all events for a time, the suspension of any representation of the poetic drama;—whether a reaction in its favour may take place, is quite another question. (26 June 1847: 3)

Many working-class intellectuals would argue that indeed a reaction in favor of "good" drama would come in time, believing that with the advancement of the working class would come the elevation of dramatic taste, and therefore of the theater. For the time being, though, the stage was corrupt. Drama that served the working class had to be found elsewhere, either through published works of literature—poetry, fiction, or plays that could target the individual working man or woman who sought a greater political and social consciousness and that could therefore indirectly serve the whole class by appealing to some—or, as we shall see, through the drama of working-class activity itself. The theater of the day, in trying to appeal to everyone, could serve class interests little.

Although few working-class journalists throughout this period defended the stage as a place where the laborer could have any sort of valuable literary experience, it is not quite accurate to say that there was no change at all in attitudes toward performance drama. Such drama was dead or dying, but a few later journalists showed a heightened belief that it could revive at some point in the future to serve a rising working class. Jones was one of these journalists. His confidence in the future of the theater is as great as his confidence in the class he serves. In the *Labourer* he writes "let our dramatic talent be on the look out. Chartism is marching into the fields of literature with rapid strides; the precincts of the drama it has not yet passed" (Aug. 1847: 95). Clearly, Jones believed that a successful invasion of the drama by the working class was inevitable. He, and others, struggled toward making fiction and poetry a power for the working class. But for performance drama, they could only offer hope.

Focusing exclusively upon attitudes toward the established theaters and inseparably connecting the theater with the dramatic suggests little or no sense of the utility of or fulfillment gained by drama and the dramatic for the working class and working-class journalists. Actually, from first to last, working-class periodicals bear witness to a powerful and thriving dramatic aesthetic on the part of that class. Most of the evidence in these periodicals, however, is not to be found on the literary page, but on every page—in the leaders and editorials, in the records of working-class "holidays" such as the anniversary of Peterloo or Paine's birthday, in transcripts of speeches, or reports of meetings, debates, trials, and elections. All of these clearly suggest an awareness of theater in the broadest sense—of performance to an audience for a purpose.

Bamford, in his autobiography, describes the procession of more than three thousand people from his town, Middleton, to St. Peter's Fields on 16 August 1819.

> First were selected twelve of the most comely and decent looking youths, who were placed in two rows of six each, with each a branch of laurel held presented in his hand, as a token of amity and peace; then followed the men of several districts in fives; then the band of music, an excellent one; then the colours: a blue one of silk, with inscriptions in golden letters, 'Unity and Strength,' 'Liberty and Fraternity'; a green one of silk, with golden letters, 'Parliaments Annual,' 'Suffrage

Universal'; and betwixt them, on a staff, a handsome cap of crimson velvet with a tuft of laurel, and the cap tastefully braided, with the word "*Libertas*" in front. Next were placed the remainder of the men of the districts in fives.

Every hundred men had a leader, who was distinguished by a sprig of laurel in his hat; others similarly distinguished were appointed over these, and the whole were to obey the directions of a principal conductor, who took his place at the head of the column, with a bugleman to sound his orders.

He continues, describing the merging of his group with other groups from other towns, the singing and dancing along the way, and the coming upon "that chasm of human beings" at Peterloo (2: 150–54).

Obviously, such a procession called for a great deal of forethought and organization. But what was the purpose of all this work? Who was watching? Who was this procession intended to impress—to cheer or dismay?

Bamford notes that on the morning of the sixteenth, the whole town was "on the alert"—including those who would watch, but not join in, the procession (150). The procession was, first of all, for these bystanders, those who could not (or would not) go to Peterloo. This ceremony allowed these Middletonians to feel a part of the excitement of the meeting; cumulatively, such processions served to include many more individuals within the gathering than the estimated 30,000 to 200,000 actually attending at St. Peter's Fields (Belchem 106), involving the entire region in the events of the day. But more than this, the procession was a performance intended for the edification of the marchers themselves, for every marcher was both participant and observer. The experience of marching among first 3,000 others, then 10,000, then even more, everyone with a common goal—reaching St. Peter's Fields in the short term, achieving working-class autonomy in the long term—and marching in careful order toward that goal, must certainly have promoted within each individual an awareness of the awakening power of the working class and a strong sense of the role of the individual in contributing to that power. Eric Hobsbawm's point about later processions surely applies to this one as well: "The major form of public ritual in modern mass societies, increasingly tended to be a sort of public drama, in which the distinction between participants and spectators, actors and spear-carriers, was attenuated, and where the mass itself acted as its own symbol" (81). To support this point, Hobsbawm cites plans to create ramps during a mass march in Vienna, so that every individual in the procession could have an opportunity to see the procession as a whole. The impulse behind that idea and the march to Peterloo is the same: the contribution to the education of the participant is as important as the lesson in power given to the bystander.

In a speech to the Middleton marchers, Bamford noted a third audience for his procession: he told them "I hoped their conduct would be marked by a steadiness and seriousness befitting the occasion, and such as would cast shame upon their enemies, who had always represented the reformers as a mob-like rabble; but they would see they were not so that day" (150). In other words, this march, characteristic more of a drilling army than a rioting horde, was intended as a display of the humanity, control, and conscious solidarity of the class they represented. The power of the mob might be great but it is always short-lived; the marchers of Middleton wanted their enemies to understand that their power was of a different sort, and of longer life. This was not a swinish multitude. The march to Peterloo demonstrated, as E. P. Thompson puts it, "the translation of the rabble into a disciplined *class*" (*Making* 748). Those people Bamford termed "enemies" can hardly consist only of the few antiradical citizens of Middleton: the marchers were playing their allotted roles to catch the attention of Sidmouth, Castlereagh, and anyone else who refused to acknowledge the political legitimacy of the working class.

The marchers knew that their actions would be textually transmitted to observers miles away from Middleton or Manchester, and therefore they were well aware of the most important audience for this procession and others like it. Through the medium of the press, the ordered, converging phalanxes depicted for the working class as a whole an idealized image of that class. The marchers' actual power and highly disciplined organization tangibly represented the potential discipline and power of the entire class. Their transformation, from relatively powerless individuals to a powerful body, encouraged class transformation, and, in turn, the transformation of society. In this sense, the march itself was a victory, a "public self-presentation of a class, an assertion of power, indeed in its invasion of the establishment's social space, a symbolic conquest"

(Hobsbawm 76).[3] By writing and publishing detailed (and, to be sure, dramatic) accounts of such events, working-class journalists played the parts of textual "theater managers," middlemen between performance and audience.

The history of the working class in the first half of the nineteenth century is a history of dramatic events—of public theater played out again and again, in which participants of all classes took on a variety of recognizable roles: hero, leader, martyr, traitor, villain. Class ritual and class theater were not new; E. P. Thompson, in his *Customs in Common*, ably delineates the many forms of public drama in the eighteenth century, noting "the sense in which rulers and crowd needed each other, watched each other, performed theatre and countertheatre to each other's auditorium, moderated each other's political behaviour"(57). What was new, from 1816 on, was the establishment of a sympathetic means to project those dramatic acts to a mass audience—textual playhouses, if you will—a medium whereby journalists as participants, became producers. Carlile became just such a producer: he was present at Peterloo, and published his eyewitness description in the last issue of *Sherwin's Weekly Political Register* (20 Aug. 1819) and the first issue of his own *Republican* (27 Aug. 1819).

Processions were one form of public theater among many that were transcribed into working-class periodicals. A quick glance at the *Poor Man's Guardian* or *Northern Star*, or any number of working-class periodicals, is enough to see that they were filled with "scripts"—reports of debates or meetings of local or national working-class organizations. *Poor Man's Guardian*, for example, faithfully summarized the meetings of the National Union of the Working Classes, with which the periodical was closely allied. And one of the primary reasons for the existence of *Northern Star* was to act as a clearing house for reports of meetings of National Chartist Association and Working Men's Association branches, as well as those from national Chartist conventions.

Also often presented, in script-form, summary, or commentary, were the many trials of both leaders and the rank and file, recurrent dramas that, in the working-class press, pitted the worthy individual against the terrible power of the state. Occasionally these trials ended with acquittal and celebration (as was the case with William Hone and Wooler in 1817); more often they were passion plays demonstrating moral force and truth crushed by the power of the government (as, for example, many of the persecutions of Carlile and the trials of the Tolpuddle Martyrs in 1834 or John Frost in 1840). Publication of the transcripts in periodicals and in books offered each reader a model of individual courage against a great and hostile power; courage that was a triumph in itself, whatever the trial's verdict. Typical is Wooler's assessment of Hone's defense of himself on charges of seditious libel: "Before the firmness of Mr. Hone, the Attorney-General shrunk into himself, and felt how contemptible is judicial chicanery, when met by the firm collected reason of courageous innocence" (*Black Dwarf* 24 Dec. 1817: 783).[4] Courtroom dramas were a common feature of working-class radicalism.

No survey of the appetite for the dramatic within working-class culture would be complete without a look at two figures who owe much of their success to their ability to satisfy that appetite: Henry "Orator" Hunt and O'Connor, who, between them, were the most popular speakers to the working class for four decades, and whose presence alone virtually guaranteed a huge draw at any mass gathering. The popularity of both men relied less upon what they said than upon how they said it. Both were demagogues. O'Connor embraced the designation, writing in *Northern Star*, "I say, I am a Demagogue, the word is derived from the Greek words, 'demos, populos', the people; and 'ago, duco', to lead; and means a leader of the people" (17 Feb. 1838: 7; rpt. in Epstein 90). Both cultured a dramatic oratorical style, combining rhetoric and action for powerful effect. John Belchem, Hunt's biographer, offers a superb analysis of several of Hunt's rhetorical devices: his assertions of his relentless efforts on behalf of the people, his "consistency by contrast"—contrasting his fidelity with his rivals' perfidity, his pride in his origins as an "independent country gentleman," his ridicule of the government's stance on any issue, his often-professed willingness to die for the cause—the last "one of his favourite rhetorical devices" (Belchem 63, 68–69). Besides effective scripting and delivery, Hunt buttressed his image with props—his distinctive white hat, for example, which became a symbol of radicalism—and with gestures, perhaps most notably his showing the scars he received at Peterloo, "like Mark Antony, exhibiting the mantle of Caesar," at a meeting several weeks afterward (Belcham 113 n, 119–20).[5]

O'Connor often called himself a Huntite and used the same rhetorical devices Hunt employed: complete devotion to the working class, "consistency by contrast" (O'Connor's term), and powerful ridicule of the oppressor. He combined these with a striking stage presence: "a charismatic vitality which placed him outside the ranks of ordinary speakers and which charged any meeting with a sense of expectancy and excitement."[6]

Hunt and O'Connor, despite their privileged origins, shared the ability to embody the aspirations of the crowd and to symbolically depict class struggle on the platform. As James Epstein writes of O'Connor, "As a personification of the working-class movement he regularly engaged the class enemy in a form of mock battle from the platform in which the people's oppressors were vanquished in a theatrical prefigurement of their eventual defeat in society at large" (112). Their histrionics and emotionalism had an appeal for audiences that was feared, at times, by allies and enemies alike. G. S. R. Kitson Clark, writing of O'Connor and his "physical-force" allies Joseph Rayner Stephens, Peter Murray McDouall, and Harney, notes that they "provide interesting examples of romantic oratory" (234). In this way they, and their audiences, are a part of, and not an exception to, the romanticism of the time, at least insofar as "romanticism" suggests the importance of the emotional. Hunt's and O'Connor's popularity testifies to a deep need for emotional excitement on the part of the British working-class—in spite of the many attacks on romances and the romantic in the teens, twenties, and thirties. That apparent contradiction does not necessarily suggest that working-class journalists were out of touch with the needs of their audiences, or that members of those audiences were confused about the value of emotions. The romantic "histories" of Scott, to journalists and many readers alike, were completely detached from nineteenth-century working-class reality, and in their eyes, at times, his ideas were hostile to their class. O'Connor and Hunt before him—and, it might be added, Cobbett and Carlile, both noted attackers of "romance"—all used the emotional in their speaking and writing in the service of the working class. Unlike Scott, their romanticism was securely grounded in hard working-class reality—a romantic realism if you will—in contrast to Scott's romantic "lies." When certain novels began to ground themselves in this reality, working-class critics began to allow that fiction, too, could be both romantic and valuable.

The speeches of all of the orators mentioned above, reprinted in working-class periodicals, are best read aloud—and they were read aloud, at working-class meetings, small and large, throughout the country. Of course there were other extremely popular orators throughout the period: John "Major" Cartwright, Henry Hetherington, William Lovett, Henry Vincent, Jones, and hundreds of other regional and national speakers, many of whose scripts were published in the working-class press and read—and recited aloud—by thousands. One speech could form the text for a hundred performances.

Most of these orators were also leading working-class journalists, and therefore it is not surprising that the same oratorical style can be easily discerned in the written articles in the working-class press. Many of the articles, too, were composed as if they would naturally be read aloud. Here, for example, is a sample from Cobbett, in his "Address to the Journeymen and Labourers":

> You have been represented by the *Times* newspaper, by the *Courier*, by the *Morning Post*, by the *Morning Herald*, and others, as the *Scum* of Society. They say, that you have *no business at public Meetings*; that you are *rabble*, and that you *pay no taxes*. These insolent hirelings, who wallow in wealth, would not be able to put their abuse of you in print were it not for *your labour*. You create all that is an object of taxation; for even the *land* itself would be good for nothing without your labour. But are you *not taxed?* Do you pay *no taxes?* (2 Nov. 1816: 448–49)

Cobbett's heavy emphasis, through capitalization and italicization, upon key terms, his repetition and alliteration for effect, his use of rhetorical questions that beg a resounding response, all point to a public, group reading of the text; Cobbett has all but inserted the stage directions. Moreover, his comfortable use of "you" in reference to his audience serves to deny the barrier of print and distance, and to put him, sympathetically if not physically, amid his audience.

Cobbett's style—like Paine's before him—served as a model for hundreds. The leader to the *Poor Man's Guardian*, written during the heat of the crisis over the passing of the first Reform Bill, exhibits many of the same devices and also was clearly intended for public readings:

> "The Bill," as has been shown to you over and over again in the pages of the *Guardian*, will not benefit the degraded mob. It is a partial, and must be an unjust measure, and therefore it cannot be beneficial to the

whole of the people. It may perhaps benefit a few, but it will still be at the expense of the many. It will benefit none but the proud and arrogant "shopocracy." My friends, you know what use they make of their power. Will adding to the power they already possess to oppress you, benefit you? You are not ignorant enough to think so. We have then our battle still to gain. And will you, with the effects of *Union* displayed before your eyes for the past three weeks, relax for one moment in your peaceful efforts to obtain your Rights? No—no!—you will not— you cannot do so. You must go forward!—you must vindicate yourselves as men!—and continue your exertions till success shall crown your efforts with the same triumphant victory which the "Bill" men have achieved. (26 May 1832: 401)

Working-class journalists, by and large, knew how to appeal to and rouse the emotions of the audiences they spoke before; much of their most powerful periodical writing conveys that oratorical knowledge and energy.

Others clearly realized the working-class thirst for drama: performers who combined showmanship with politicking so thoroughly that it is hard to tell whether they were popular for their performances or their messages. Rev. Taylor is the most striking example of such a performer. According to Iain McCalman, Taylor enacted "a form of collective ritual that allowed his congregation to discharge powerful emotional yearnings" ("Irreligion" 62). His performances at the Rotunda (and elsewhere) were high drama, with elaborate costumes and sets, combining comedy, blasphemy, and radicalism, and inverting church and government ritual for dramatic effect. McCalman describes one of these shows, "Raising the Devil," which Taylor performed a number of times in the winter of 1830. The show

customarily began with a reading of the lesson, after which Taylor was summoned onstage under the titles of "The devil's chaplain, Archbishop of Pandemonium and Primate of All Hell." Dressed in full canonicals, he swept into the darkened theatre, pledging solemnly to raise the Devil and put him down again without endangering his audience. Hell, he promised, would be turned into heaven, and every step of this cosmic inversion would follow true scientific principles. Satan himself was introduced by means of a dramatic materialization. After muttering the Lord's Prayer backward in accordance with English folk superstition, Taylor would incant the words, "Satan, Beelzebub! Baal, Peor! Belial, Lucifer, Abaddon, Apollyon, thou King of the Bottomless Pit, thou King of Scorpions, having stings in their tails to whom it is given to hurt the earth for five months—Appear!—Appear!" Instantly, the large glove lit up to reveal a hideous caricature of the Devil. Then, with a flick of his wrist—"Behold Satan himself is transformed into an angel of light." Both devil and angel, he later explained, had originally been zodiacal representations of the seasons formulated as a teaching device by ancient scientists, teachers, and poets. Gradually the physical allegory had been obfuscated by the Christian priesthood in order to exploit and enslave the common people. ("Irreligion" 55–56)

Such shows were incredibly popular; according to McCalman Taylor regularly drew crowds of a thousand people twice a week to the large theater in the Rotunda (56)—three or four times as many as Carlile was able to attract to his lectures (Wiener, *Radicalism* 167). No one can deny Taylor's serious intent in presenting such a performance. Nonetheless, it must largely have been the elements of burlesque and the special effects that attracted so many to the Rotunda. That Taylor's performances were theatrical, and not simply extravagant lectures, is made clear by the unsuccessful attempts to continue them after he was jailed, with different "actors" playing his role (Wiener, *Radicalism* 181). Another speaker at the Rotunda, Elizabeth Sharples, attempted to tap into the same dramatic vein with her lectures, given during the first part of 1832. Under the name Isis, Sharples "wore a 'showy' dress for the occasions and stood on a floor strewn with white thorn and laurel" (180–81). Both performers' lectures were reprinted in periodicals—Taylor's in the *Devil's Pulpit*, Sharples's in *Isis*.

As McCalman details in his *Radical Underworld*, Taylor and Sharples were not alone among radical/free-thought performers. Especially interesting as a precursor of Taylor is Robert Wedderburn, Spencean and son of a slave, whose 1819 "sermons" at his London "chapel" aimed to shock with blasphemy and profanity and "whether consciously or not . . . echoed styles, themes and motifs fashionable in contemporary English and French melodrama" (149). Wedderburn was assisted in his improvisations by another Spencean, Samuel Waddington, who played pantomime to Wedderburn's melodrama. His small stature (he was a midget) allowed him to take on the pantomime role of "imp of mischief"—and at times, he brought to life Wooler's black dwarf (43, 148–49).

If the radical press could not recreate such performances as Taylor's (even though periodicals printed transcripts and accounts of them), what evidence we have gives us a sense of every-day working-class theater and countertheater. In what they read and heard, and in their political rituals—in other words, in their daily lives exclusive of the theaters—the working class had a number of sources to feed their appetite for the dramatic. They looked less to Drury Lane for drama and more to their leaders and writers, and to themselves.

Conclusion

IN 1987 E. D. Hirsch Jr. published his solution to what he saw as a decline in literacy in the United States. That work, *Cultural Literacy: What Every American Needs to Know*, became a huge best-seller and, in a way, became in itself a part of American "cultural literacy," so that many who have not read the work are familiar with its basic premise: that the knowledge of a number of facts and concepts generally known to other Americans is essential to becoming literate, to educational growth, to communicating clearly with others across class, regional, and occupational lines, and therefore essential to success in life. As an aid to teaching or learning this cultural literacy, Hirsch, along with Joseph Kett and James Trefil, supplies an enormous appendix listing facts and concepts, a "preliminary" attempt at a guide to cultural literacy, with entries from "Hank Aaron" to "Zurich," including "Thomas Malthus," "kleptomania," and "April showers bring May flowers."

The readers of *Poor Man's Guardian* or *Northern Star* were familiar with such benevolent attempts to lift the apparently illiterate out of their sad ignorance and bring them into the light of reason. To them, however, cultural literacy went by the name useful knowledge, Hirsch's nineteenth-century British counterparts were Henry Brougham and Charles Knight, and the nineteenth-century guide to cultural literacy was *Penny Magazine*.

Brougham and Knight had similar political objectives in their work as Hirsch does in his. Hirsch, like his predecessors, takes great pains to deny any political slant to his sense of cultural literacy, but he does believe that an individual with a greater knowledge of cultural concepts is better able to think politically. He maintains that "the civic importance of cultural literacy lies in the fact that true enfranchisement depends upon knowledge, knowledge upon literacy, and literacy upon cultural literacy" (12). Exchange the twentieth-century American jargon for that of nineteenth-century Britain, and the words could easily have been those of Brougham, or Knight, or any other middle-class liberal who held that working-class "enlightenment" must precede working-class suffrage.

Working-class journalists were well aware of the value of "useful knowledge" (or "cultural literacy"), and saw themselves as the purveyors of such information. They knew that their readers needed knowledge that transcended class or region in order to read, say, Byron's *The Vision of Judgment*—and they attempted to provide their readers with that knowledge. They also were well aware that distinguishing useful from nonuseful knowledge is necessarily an exercise in ideology. And, in the end, they did something with their periodicals that Brougham or Knight, George Canning or Southey, or even Dickens could not do with theirs: cumulatively, working-class journalists provided their readership with a sense of the works that could serve their class and those that could not. They established, largely from scratch, a working-class canon. And in evaluating works, they considered the importance of their readers, seeing them not as aspirants to middle-class knowledge and values but as part of a group with its own power, sensibilities, and sense of the uses and values of literature. These journalists worked toward, and in some measure achieved, the literary and intellectual elevation of their class. In other words, they offered a workable solution to the kind of problem that Hirsch grapples with.

For that reason, I believe that the largely ignored literary writings of these mostly forgotten periodicals should be neither ignored nor forgotten; their subjects may be dated but their implications about literacy and canon are not. It might be worthwhile for the resurrectors of the belief in useful knowledge, and for anyone concerned with the way that literacy grows, to consider a few of their implications.

It is clear from this model of canon formation, first of all, that need precedes literacy, or, to be more specific, need precedes the "second literacy" I discuss in chapter 2—the pursuit of literate knowledge that follows simply learning to read a text. In early nineteenth-century Britain there was a huge potential readership among the working class, which showed itself periodically, by turning Paine's *Rights of Man* into a bestseller, and by ballooning the circulations of periodicals such as Cobbett's *Political Register* and *Northern Star* in times of political crisis. The same potential readership surely existed for fiction, nonfiction, and poetry, waiting only for a good reason to read a particular work. Working-class journalists attempted to provide a rationale for reading some works and shunning others. In essay after essay, for example, Carlile promoted the pantheon of himself, Paine, and Shelley—with the demigod Byron knocking at the door—while disqualifying just about every other writer, living or dead, from serious consideration. Clearly, he perceived literature as consisting of a very few pearls in a sea of mud. At the other extreme, Jones offered a hugely inclusive sense of the valuable in his criticism, challenging his readers to read a large number of writers, particularly foreign, politically aware ones such as Pierre-Jean de Beranger and Ferdinand Freiligrath. Despite Carlile's and Jones's greatly different senses of the valuable, both were insiders, with one eye upon the interests of the class for which they were writing and the other upon those works that best served those interests. Canon cannot be imposed from outside; what is valuable cannot be understood without some conception of the values and beliefs of the readership. It is difficult to conceive that any working-class reader would be inspired to literary creation by studying issue after issue of *Penny Magazine*; on the other hand, the many submissions of poetry by members of the working class to *Northern Star* and *People's Paper* suggest strongly that working-class periodicals provided, at least partially, the inspiration for many to create. Moreover, some of the earliest reactionary responses to the working-class press, pseudo-working-class periodicals such as *Shadgett's Weekly Review* or the *White Dwarf*, are laughable and must have been laughable to working-class readers of the time, because they are so patently at odds with working-class values, literary and otherwise.

The success of Carlile and Jones and many others as literary journalists, and their obvious influence over the thinking of their readers, suggests that canon is manipulable: that they were able to impose their sense of values, and of valuable writers, upon their readership. This is true, but only in a limited way. Carlile, both as publisher and promoter, most certainly introduced Shelley to many working-class readers, and therefore did much from the beginning to establish the poet's place in the working-class pantheon. But Carlile, in both publishing and promoting Shelley, was working to serve a need of his audience—even if they were unaware that the poet could serve that need. Had Carlile enthusiastically promoted Tom Moore instead of Shelley, or Dr. Johnson instead of Tom Paine, his exhortations would likely have fallen upon deaf ears—as did those of his reactionary contemporaries in the pseudo-working-class periodicals of Carlile's day. Jones, too, was working to satisfy specific needs by promoting class-conscious foreigners in the late forties and early fifties: He was well aware that his audience was deeply concerned with the international events of and around 1848, and that it was beginning to perceive that class-interests transcended national ones. He was also aware, in promoting writers like Tennyson and Browning, that his audience was more sophisticated than Carlile's, combining overtly political and aesthetic values in their views of literature.

The persistent attempts by working-class journalists to establish a working-class canon in opposition—or at least in contrast—to that of the middle class, suggests that there is no such a thing as a "national" canon. "National" canon could be defined in two ways, both of them problematic. A national canon might be considered a combined canon—consisting of all the works contained in each subcanon (or, rather, alternative canon) of each subculture within a nation. The result would be insubstantial indeed, a canon which involves little to no consensus about works or how to evaluate them. Or, national canon might be defined as one containing the tiny core of works within the overlap of individual alternate canons. Even this small body of works could hardly be said to derive from any consensus about value: we have seen, for example, that the working-class evaluations of Byron differed completely from those of the middle class, although Byron was a fixture of both canons. E. D. Hirsch notes that "literate culture is the most democratic culture in our land: it excludes nobody; it cuts across generations and social groups and classes; it is not usually one's first culture, but it should be everyone's second, existing as it does beyond the narrow spheres of family, neighborhood, and region" (21). The writings in these periodicals emphasize the dangers of ignoring the importance of that first culture and the significance of literature within it. If a sense of canon is to serve the individual reader, then it must take into account what is important to that reader; in other words, canon must serve primarily one's first culture. The purpose of any canon should be to enlighten, not to homogenize.

One way to create the illusion of a dominant, established national canon, of course, is to confuse the dominant class with the literate one and to marginalize all others either as having no literature and literary values to speak of, or as aspirants to the same literature and literary values as the dominant class. In the specific case of Great Britain in the nineteenth century, one could easily create such an illusion by seeing in the middle class and their quarterlies the alpha and omega of literary criticism. But such partial blindness is, for the literary historian, equivalent to the blindness of the historian who views history as exclusively the study of those in power. Because of the relative fame of the great nineteenth-century middle-class literary critics, and the relative obscurity of the great working-class critics, such blindness is not surprising—but we have the resources to correct that blindness, and should do so.

Any attempt to isolate a particular canon is more complicated than listing the works valuable to a particular group. Every canon is, by necessity, ever changing—so fluid as to suggest that there is never really any such thing as a canon. Canon must depend upon the values and beliefs of the readers of a group, who are themselves affected by and dependent upon cultural and moral shifts. For example, the violent agitation of the months leading up to the passing of the First Reform Bill in 1832 led to the periodical publication and promotion of Francis Macerone's *Defensive Instructions for the People,* a primer on urban guerrilla warfare. That work must be considered an important part of the working-class canon of the time, however short-lived its placement there. The condition and needs of any readership are never static and neither is its canon. Working-class critics were aware of this, and were generally more concerned with what should be in their canon rather than what already was. Therefore, the early history of the development of a British working-class canon is characterized at least as much by debate as it is by consensus. Debates were conducted either directly—that between Carlile and his correspondents over fiction being perhaps the most striking example— or indirectly, as critics offered differing arguments for the value of one writer over another. The many different assessments of Shelley's and

Byron's place in the working-class literary pantheon is a good example of this. Canon, by definition, is consensus, but since absolute consensus is impossible, so is any sense of a fully developed, fully definable canon. Canon never *is*, but always is coming into being. In the perpetual formation of any canon, debate about value and the sense that many values must change, is the sign of health, not weakness.

A refreshing aspect of working-class criticism (and something that modern critics would be wise to consider) is the clear recognition of the connection between what is read and what is happening, and, in consequence, an openness to testing all works for value and wariness of relying without question upon established notions of value. We might smile at the propensity of these critics at first to regard some apparent literary drivel on the same level as "Tintern Abbey" or *Coriolanus*, but such openness doesn't cheapen any work; rather, it is the best way to establish the immediate, living—although, by necessity, temporary—greatness of a work. We should smile, rather, at modern attempts to codify great works and at modern whinings that the American mind is closing because students today don't have the same values their fathers and mothers did. Values change; the need to evaluate does not.

I believe that the working-class critics and their audience can remind us what reading should be. In particular, they remind us that reading is a dialogue between writer and reader, and if a reader engages in that dialogue without some sense of his or her own value, what might be useful knowledge loses its utility. No Carlile or Jones, Hirsch or English professor can give a reader that sense of personal value; the best they can do is recognize it and promote particular works that serve it. The greatness of the working-class critics lies in their recognition of the greatness of their audience.

Notes

Introduction

1. Brougham delivered the speech on 29 Jan. 1828 (quoted in Stewart 183). The term "schoolmaster abroad" was taken up by the working class; it appears frequently in the writings and titles of working-class periodicals.

2. This self-creation of political values by the working class is the central thesis of E. P. Thompson's *The Making of the English Working Class*.

3. The best of these are Vicinus's *The Industrial Muse*, and James's *Fiction for the Working Man, 1830–1850*.

4. *Chartist Circular* 13 Mar. 1841: 321–22; *National: A Library for the People* 9 Feb. 1839: 44.

5. No one study looks with complete comprehension at working-class journalism between 1816 and 1858. At the beginning of each section of chapter 3, however, I provide information on a number of works that deal with different aspects of the working-class journalism of this period.

Chapter 1

1. For information on working-class literacy in the first half of the nineteenth century, see Webb, "Working-Class Readers" 349, and *British Working Class Reader* 21–22; Altick 170; E. P. Thompson, *Making of the English Working Class* 783; Stone, "Literacy and Education in England, 1640–1900" 69–139.

2. England did not begin to establish a national system of education until 1870. For literacy and education in Scotland, see Stone 80, and Webb, "Literacy among the Working Classes" 100–14. A recent study of literacy in Scotland, however, suggests that "we should be rash to claim that Scotland's experience [of literacy] was 'dramatically different' from that of her southern neighbour" (Houston 57).

3. See also Webb's "Working Class Readers" 349.

4. For a study of these working-class educational options, see Laqueur, "Working-Class Demand" 192–205.

5. *Rights of Man* continued to be a best-seller throughout the first half of the nineteenth century; it appeared regularly on the lists of radical publishers.

6. In his "Literacy and Social Mobility," Sanderson notes that, at least in parts of the industrial north of England, literacy declined between 1780 and 1820—but there, and elsewhere, the literacy rate gradually rose thereafter (75–81).

7. This claim, originally spoken to George Bernard Shaw, is quoted in Shaaban 41.

8. The views of this "Lancashire Weaver" appear in Carlile's *Republican* 6 Feb. 1824: 185–87. See chapter 3, "Early Views."

9. See Vincent's *Bread, Knowledge, and Freedom* 116–20, for more on the many sources of working-class reading.

10. See chapter 3, "Later Views."

11. See also James 23–24.

12. Although individual numbers of this periodical were not dated, Wiener, in his *Finding List*, notes that the first issue of *Half-Penny Magazine* came out sometime in 1832 (20).

13. The two *Halfpenny* magazines mentioned above are exceptional for their kind in that they both lasted more than a few weeks. The London *Halfpenny Magazine* lasted for at least nineteen issues; the Edinburgh *Half-Penny Magazine* for a full fifty weeks.

14. It is worth pointing out that the first issue of *Chambers'* predated the *Penny Magazine* and was not modeled upon it. Indeed, there are several differences between the two periodicals, an important one being that *Chambers'* published fiction and *Penny Magazine* did not. It would be more accurate to say that many periodicals from this time and after modeled themselves on both *Penny Magazine* and *Chambers'*.

15. The *London Democrat* (13 Apr.–8 June 1839) was the short-lived organ of the militant Chartist London Democratic Association (LDA). Harney was intimately connected with this periodical, but the introduction was written and signed by J. C. C. and C. R.—certainly J. C. Coombe, and perhaps the "Chartist" Ryder who was a member of the LDA at this time (Hovell 126).

16. Except for a fragment from the first issue that now exists in the Place newspaper collection at the British Library, the first seven issues of *Northern Star* no longer exist (Harrison and Thompson 107–8).

17. See chapter 5.

18. MacFarlane also wrote for the *Democratic Review of British and Foreign*

Politics, History, and Literature, also edited by Harney. Schwarzkopf 90 n, 104 n, 192 n, 193 n, 197 and n, 198 and n.

19. See chapter 4, "Shelley, Byron, and Burns."

Chapter 2

1. Wiener notes in his sketch of Sherwin's life (Baylen and Gossman 1: 445–46) that Sherwin's *Memoirs of the Late Thomas Paine* was "the first sympathetic treatment of Paine to appear since his death." This is not exactly true, as the *Medusa*'s praising memoir precedes Sherwin's by two or three months. It is the first sympathetic memoir in book form, however.

2. See, for example, *Northern Star* 13 Jan. 1844: 1, for an announcement of one such dinner.

3. Williams, in his *Cobbett,* notes a lively assault by Cobbett upon Paine in 1796: "How Tom gets a living now, or what brothel he inhabits, I know not, nor does it much signify to any body here or anywhere else. He has done all the mischief he can in the world, and whether his carcass is at last to be suffered to rot on the earth, or to be dried in the air, is of very little consequence. Whenever or wherever he breathes his last, he will excite neither sorrow nor compassion; no friendly hand will close his eyes, not a groan will be uttered, not a tear will be shed. Like *Judas* he will be remembered by posterity; men will learn to express all that is base, malignant, treacherous, unnatural and blasphemous, by the single monosyllable, Paine" (20). This attack takes on a stronger contrast, of course, when one considers Cobbett's curious relationship with Paine's "carcass," described below. For more attacks on Paine by the young Cobbett, see Williams 8–9.

4. The first of these attacks is addressed "To Mr. William Cobbett . . . Romancing Historian"—a particularly dirty insult, considering the views of both men toward romance, views I discuss in the following chapters.

5. See Williams 21 and Spater 2: 388 for examples of verses, including Byron's, ridiculing this act; Byron's poem, beginning "In digging up your bones, Tom Paine," can be found in Byron 235. See Spater 2: 386 for an illustration of Cobbett leaving Liverpool with Paine's coffin strapped to his back, and 2: 389 for an illustration of Cobbett as a "Hampshire Hog" dragging the skeleton of Paine behind him. Cobbett intended to collect funds and build a fitting memorial to Paine. He never collected enough, the memorial was never built, and the present whereabouts of Paine's bones is a mystery.

6. For a thorough discussion of Paine's style, see Olivia Smith 35–64.

7. Cobbett's *Rural Rides* first appeared in book form in 1830, but originally it appeared in essay form in his *Political Register* between 1822 and 1826.

8. This section and the two that follow are intended to give short sketches of the journalists and periodicals of this time, and some sense of their literary backgrounds and literary values. I cannot hope to provide a comprehensive history of working-class journalism for this period. Fortunately, such studies do already exist; here, and at the start of the following two sections, I will provide information on some texts that allow a reader a fuller sense of the nonliterary history of working-class journalism and the nonliterary values of working-class journalists.

For the period 1816–29 there is, unfortunately, no comprehensive study that takes into account recent scholarship. One older study, however, is helpful: Wickwar's *Freedom of the Press.* E. P. Thompson's *Making of the English Working Class* is helpful too, especially 739–44, 780–887.

9. For more on Cobbett's stylistic debt to Pope, Swift, and Dryden, see Birell 214–17; for his particular debt to Swift, see Bromwich 88–89. Incidentally, Cobbett quotes all three writers in his *Register.*

10. See chapter 3, "Early Views," and chapter 4, "Views of Poetry in the Early Working-Class Periodicals."

11. *Gorgon* was "an explicit attempt to effect a junction between Benthamism and working-class experience" (E. P. Thompson, *Making* 845). I should say that *Gorgon* was edited by Place and Gast, as well as by Wade. But, as Thompson notes, "John Wade set the tone and emphases of the periodical" (846). Indeed, I would guess that it is Wade himself who buries Latin and Greek here as truly dead languages.

12. There are exceptions, of course, none more exceptional, perhaps, than the flamboyant Rev. Taylor, whose free-thought lectures and essays in Carlile's *Lion* show the marks of his preparation for and attendence at Cambridge University. He punctuated his articles (and his speeches) with quotes from Demosthenes, Cicero, Juvenal, Seneca, Horace, Virgil, and others, and often ended by quoting, untranslated, Cato's rousing "Delenda est Carthago" (as, for example, in two articles in the *Lion* 13 Mar. 1829). Many of Taylor's working-class listeners and readers must have been as confused by these quotes as they were by the "baroque clerical attire" that he wore when he lectured (Wiener, *Radicalism* 131). Nonetheless, he clearly appealed to many; see chapter 5.

13. See chapter 4, "Views of Poetry in the Early Working-Class Periodicals."

14. Biographical details on Wooler are taken from Stuart Stumpf's short sketch in Baylen and Gossman 1: 557–58, and from Edward Irving Carlyle's entry on Wooler in *Dictionary of National Biography* (1917), 21: 899. No full-length

biography of Wooler exists. It is worth noting that, while publishing the *Dwarf* for a wide audience, Wooler also catered to a more exclusive audience with the 8 ½d. *Wooler's British Gazette* (1819–23).

15. For a discussion of Wooler's use of satirical humor and the influence of Pope see Hendrix, "Popular Humor and 'The Black Dwarf.'"

16. *Black Dwarf* 26 Jan. 1823: 89, 93–104; 10 Dec. 1817: 258; 20 May 1818: 318–19. The authors of "The Reformer's House that Jack Built"—Wooler mentions that there are two—are unknown.

17. "BLACKNEB is a term of ridicule and scorn, applied, in the bravery of their wit, by old supporters of passive obedience, to the bolder writers in the maintenance of the good old cause" (*Black Dwarf* 26 Jan. 1823: 89).

18. The poem, not yet the national anthem of the United States, was taken from Leigh Hunt's *Examiner* and described as a work unfamiliar to the *Dwarf's* (or the *Examiner's*) audience.

Several notes appended to later "Blackneb" selections are signed N, which suggests that Wooler might not have been the editor of that section, as Wooler didn't use that signature anywhere else in *Black Dwarf*. As publisher and general editor of the *Dwarf*, however, Wooler deserves much of the credit for bringing these writers to a working-class audience.

19. Davison, poor and with little formal education (Baylen and Gossman 1: 114), emerged from obscurity in 1819 to publish *Medusa, or Penny Politician*, the *London Alfred*, and the *Deist's Magazine, or Theological Enquirer*. The *Medusa* was by far the most popular of these. *Cap of Liberty* was "edited by an obscure Deist," John Griffin, according to Wickwar (65), or James Griffin, according to Hollis (96). Wickwar states that the periodical was published by Davison (65).

20. *Hone's Reformists' Register* 9 Aug. 1817: 78–82; *Medusa* 21 Aug. 1819: 215; *Spirit of the Union* 8 Jan. 1820: 83. Hone, more famous as the author of radical pamphlets, tried his hand at popular journalism with *Hone's Reformists' Register*, a periodical that ran from January to October of 1817, which Prothero states was an attempt for the Westminster "Rump" to regain a working-class audience after Cobbett's flight to the United States in 1817 (94).

21. See chapter 4, "Views of Poetry in the Early Working-Class Periodicals," for more on Hone's assessment and for Wooler's, which appeared soon after Hone's.

22. For a fuller discussion of these periodicals, see Webb, *British Working Class Reader* 53–59.

23. For Cobbett's and Wooler's 1817 reaction to Owen, see E.P. Thompson, *Making* 861; for Owen and his influence on the working class in general, including the working-class politicization of Owen, see 857–77.

24. Two excellent recent studies of this period exist: Hollis's *The Pauper Press*,

and Wiener's *War of the Unstamped.* Himmelfarb's chapter on the *Poor Man's Guardian* in *The Idea of Poverty* is helpful as well (230–52). Also important for making sense of the hundreds of unstamped periodicals published during this time is Wiener's *Descriptive Finding List.* I am extremely indebted to this book for many of the bibliographical notes to this section.

25. The *Trades Newspaper* later became an Owenite periodical, the *Weekly Free Press* (1828–31).

26. Doherty's other trade union periodicals are the *Conciliator,* the *United Trades' Co-operative Journal,* and the *Herald of the Rights of Industry.*

27. See also Wiener, *War* 147, and *William Lovett* 31, which imply that Lovett also collaborated with this group. The *Guardian*'s editor, O'Brien, was a formidable working-class thinker who later became one of the primary theorists of the Chartist movement.

28. Wiener's *Finding List* supplies all the first names here but Hancock's, which comes from Hollis 46. Wiener also notes one more contributor; Somerville was the periodical's last editor (*Finding List* 12). Both Wiener and Hollis estimate the circulation of the paper at its highest at 5,000 (Wiener, *Finding List* 12; Hollis 118).

29. See, for example, the poem "The Dorchester Job," *Pioneer* 10 May 1834: 295.

30. *Berthold's Political Handkerchief* is just that: a periodical printed on linen in a clever, albeit unsuccessful, attempt to avoid prosecution by the Stamp Office.

31. *The Truth!* lasted for only two issues, just long enough to give a hint as to what gave a work of literature value in its producers' eyes: "The softer arts in life, namely, Poetry and Painting, which, when *properly,* that is *usefully* cultivated, civilize and adorn the rugged nature of man, will not be forgotten." The tone of *The Truth!*'s two issues shows that its utilitarian view of literature and art is strongly class based.

32. For a review of Cole, see *New Political Register* 14 Nov. 1834: 53.

33. More commonly referred to today as Edward Bulwer-Lytton, I use the name Edward Bulwer because this is the name by which he was known in the periodicals of the time. He did not add Lytton to his name until 1844.

34. For more on the review in *Literary Test,* see chapter 3, "Later Views." *Cobbett's Magazine* was conducted by Cobbett's son, John.

35. Dorothy Thompson takes this quote from an unspecified number of *Northern Star* (40). See also Wiener, *War* 267–72.

36. No full-length history of the Chartist press yet exists. Dorothy Thompson does devote a chapter to the subject in *The Chartists.* Some of the best discussions of Chartist periodicals and Chartist journalists can be found in individual biographies of Chartist leaders; works, for example, such as Cooper's

autobiography, *The Life of Thomas Cooper*, Schoyen's *The Chartist Challenge*, Saville's introduction to *Ernest Jones, Chartist*, F. B. Smith's *Radical Artisan*, Plummer's *Bronterre: A Political Biography* and two biographies of O'Connor, *Feargus O'Connor*, by Read and Glasgow, and Epstein's *The Lion of Freedom*. For discussions of some non-Chartist—or, at best, peripherally Chartist—periodicals of importance during this period, see Driver's *Tory Radical*, and Grugel's *George Jacob Holyoake*.

37. Hovell's hatred of O'Connor, and of everything connected with O'Connor—including the *Northern Star*—is apparent throughout his *Chartist Movement* (1918). He calls the *Star* "truly the worst . . . of the Radical papers, a melancholy tribute to the low level of intelligence of its readers" (96). A glance at one copy of *Northern Star* belies the gross absurdity of this remark.

38. See chapter 4, "Chartist Views of Poetry."

39. All of them published their imaginative work, except perhaps O'Connor, who wrote a novel, *The White Boy*, and several plays in the 1820s, and who apparently wrote another novel while in prison in 1840 (Cole, *Chartist Portraits* 309, 319).

Chapter 3

1. Indeed, in all the working-class periodicals I have looked at, I have not found one reference, good or bad, to Austen or her works.

2. For discussions of the view that fiction is a time waster, see Taylor 108–10; Watt 39; and Stang 5.

3. *Political Register* 28 Jan. 1826: 280; 17 Mar. 1826: 750–51; 26 Jan. 1828: 108; 18 June 1831: 718.

4. Olivia Smith, in the sixth chapter of *Politics of Language* (202–51), dicusses Cobbett's ideas about grammar, power, and class.

5. Green sickness: "An anaemic disease which mostly affects young women about the age of puberty and gives a pale or greenish tinge to the complexion; chlorosis" (OED 1933).

6. For an 1832 view of a "silver-fork" novel, see chapter 3, "Later Views."

7. Bentham described the literary department of the periodical as dealing with "literary insignificances" (Nesbitt 96).

8. The quotation is by A. A. in the *Christian Observer*.

9. Carlile's formal schooling consisted of lessons at Sunday school and attendance "at two local free schools up to the age of twelve" (Wiener, *Radicalism* 4–5).

10. This is a mistake on Webb's part, as Godwin never wrote a novel by this

name. Webb is probably thinking of a work by Godwin's friend, Thomas Holcroft, called *Anna St. Ives* (1792).

11. *Tremaine, or the Man of Refinement* was written by Robert Plumer Ward (1825); *The Mummy, A Tale of the Twenty-Second Century*, by Jane Webb, afterward Loudon (1827). Whether or not Jane and R. T. Webb were somehow related is impossible to tell.

12. James notes that the useful-knowledge *Chambers' Edinburgh Journal*, originally directed toward the working class, concurred with Carlile's opponents' views of fiction: "Fiction was only admitted [to *Chambers'*] to attract those who would not take the solid food without sugar" (17).

13. Macconnell's lectures, if they ever existed as a published work, no longer do; their absence in the *British Library Catalogue* (which implies an absence of British copyright) and the *National Union Catalogue* suggest that this excerpt might be from an unpublished record of a series of lectures given by Macconnell. Incidentally, A. B. C.'s remarks, though they differ in places, are so close to Macconnell's that one is forced to assume that the same writer is reworking his own essay, or that one of these writers is a plagiarist, at least in the modern sense of the term. The differences between the two, however, allow both a place in this study.

14. To be fair, this writer has nothing but praise for Scott and applies his criticisms to Scott's many imitators, "as plenty as mantua makers," and their "nauseous undigested stuff" (*Artizan's Miscellany* 25 June 1831: 39). The writer, however, only offers vague hints as to what separates Scott from his successors; there is no clear idea here what makes for good fiction.

15. Of the many working-class periodicals from the 1830s and before I have looked at, only four praise Scott. All are from Scotland. Besides the *Schoolmaster*, the Edinburgh *Artizan's Miscellany*, as we have seen, is ambiguous in its praise; the Glasgow *Herald to the Trades Advocate* copies a speech given "from the Heteroclitical Club—communicated by S. Clyde, as delivered on the Anniversary of Burns," which is abundant in its praise of Scott (29 Jan. 1831: 317–18); and the *Radical Reformers' Gazette*, also from Glasgow, praises Scott's fiction while noting that he "contributed to retard the cause of Reform, and perpetuate the slavery of the people" (7 Nov. 1832: 14–15). English working-class appraisals of Scott are consistently negative. There is clearly a strong regional bias at work here.

16. This questioning about the class standing of Scott's heroes and the class basis of his novels, first raised, so far as I can tell, in the working-class press, is one that is still important today. Lukács's viewpoint about Scott's heroes contrasts strongly with both these critics. To him, Scott's heroes are intentionally mediocre, "unsurpassed in their portrayal of the decent and attractive as well as

narrow-minded features of the English 'middle-class'" (35). Eagleton and Pierce largely concur with this view (20–22). Cazamian, on the other hand, sides more closely with the Chartist critic: he believes that Scott "pointed out the charm and merit of the ancient heirarchical society which had been destroyed by the bourgeoisie's individualist energy" (40).

17. O'Brien was already beginning to disseminate in the *Poor Man's Guardian* the political philosophy that later earned him the title the "Schoolmaster of Chartism," and while it is interesting to see that this early in his career he showed no fear of even the worst fiction, it should be noted that his later work in Chartist periodicals reveals that he, unlike many of his contemporaries, had very little use for the genre; as an editor, he avoided publishing reviews or fiction.

18. See also Wiener's *War of the Unstamped* 171–73, for general comments on this type of periodical.

19. A good contrast to this review is to be found in *Carpenter's London Journal*, which offers a glowing review of Bulwer's *Paul Clifford*. To that reviewer, Bulwer has rendered the novel "the vehicle for inculcating sound principle and high moral truths," and he is a hero for the working class, "working out for many a deliverance from their thralldom" (13 Feb. 1836: 4–5). See also the *Destructive* 13 Mar. 1833, which excludes by name only Bulwer from a general condemnation of "men of letters."

20. The critic is probably Jones; the periodical from which the quote is taken was a Chartist miscellany edited by Jones and O'Connor in 1847 and 1848.

21. Schoyen, in his biography of Harney, identifies him as the author of these articles (126).

22. Webb, in *Harriet Martineau*, identifies Martineau's critic here as Doherty himself. Webb also notes that both the Manchester and Salford Association for the Spread of Co-operative Knowledge and the *Poor Man's Guardian* approved of Martineau's *Illustrations of Political Economy*, of which *A Manchester Strike* formed a part.

23. One example of this month-to-month testing appeared in early numbers of the *Northern Star*, which charted the progress of *Nicholas Nickleby*. A critic there holds the first number "amply to sustain the credit of the author"; thereafter, the critic notes the monthly deterioration of the work, with a few recoveries and relapses: of number 7 the critic writes "Nicholas mends"; of number 9, "Nicholas lags again" (13 Oct. 1838: 7; 15 Dec. 1838: 7).

24. Dickens made this assertion in a letter to John Forster, 8 Oct. 1844; rpt. in Forster 1: 334.

25. "Doctrines" in this review refer largely to those of "the desciples of

Malthus who would quell every feeling of humanity to carry out his heartless theory" (*Northern Star* 4 Jan. 1845: 3). Malthus and his followers were hated by almost every working-class writer from Cobbett on.

Much of this review of these two Christmas books is reprinted in Collins, *Dickens* 157–58. Also, Peyrouton discusses Chartist attitudes toward Dickens and *The Chimes* in "Dickens and the Chartists." That article is limited by its almost complete focus on only two Chartist critics, Harney and Reynolds, and by its strong implication that Chartist attacks on Dickens's fiction had much to do with Dickens's political and personal actions and little to do with the works of fiction themselves. Such may indeed have been the case with Reynolds, but certainly was not the case with Harney or other critics. Peyrouton, like others, has difficulty seeing these working-class figures as literary as well as political animals.

26. An approving Chartist review of *The Revolt of the Bees* is in the *Northern Star* 2 Feb. 1839: 7.

27. Other periodicals of the early thirties that contain fables are *The Voice of the Country, and General Provincial Politician* (July 1832: 17) and *The Pioneer; or, Trades Union Magazine* (throughout).

28. Among poets, Cooper and Elliott also earn places. Incidentally (and suprisingly), I have found very few references to Reynolds's fiction in the late Chartist working-class press. This paucity could be due, at least partially, to the fragmentation of Chartism and to rivalry between the remaining Chartists after 1848. As Dorothy Thompson notes in *The Chartists*, "By the early fifties the old Chartist journalists . . . had divided into small groups, publishing journals based on their own particular viewpoints, which had little sense of speaking for or to a movement" (45).

29. The "Manifesto of the German Communist Party" was published 9 Nov. 1850 in Harney's *Red Republican*, which is the same periodical in all but name as *Friend of the People*. Harney changed the name because he feared it unnecessarily intimidated much of his audience.

30. My intent here in discussing fiction written by the working class is not to enter into a detailed analysis of Chartist fiction itself; I defer to Vicinus's excellent study in *Industrial Muse* 113–35 for this. Rather my intent is to fit the late appearance of working-class fiction in the journals into the evolving view of fiction taken by these journalists—that their publishing such fiction both affirms the genre and offers an alternative to fiction by middle-class writers.

31. Vicinus discusses both Jones's *DeBrassier* and Wheeler's *Sunshine and Shadow* in her *Industrial Muse* 125–35. Mitchell, in "Aesthetic Problems," discusses Wheeler's novel.

32. The article reviews Bulwer's *The Caxtons,* Dinah Mary Mulock's *The Ogilvies,* A. Ballie Cochrane's *Ernest Vane,* and Charlotte Brontë's *Shirley,* all published in 1849.

Chapter 4

1. Carlile was not the first working-class journalist to publish a discussion of *Queen Mab.* On 11 March 1821 Benbow, in *John Bull's British Journal,* pirated a letter by F praising the poem (22). That letter had appeared in the Spencean *Theological Inquirer, or Polemical Magazine* six years before, in March 1815 (34–39). Although this may be the first review of Shelley in a working-class journal, the article, probably written, according to White in *Unextinguished Hearth,* by the liberal General Sir Ronald Crawford Ferguson, M.P., was certainly not written by a member of the working class. Both the original review and the piracy (where it differs from the original) appear in White 46–48, 52 and in Barcus's *Shelley* 63–66, 70–71.

2. The article from which this quote is taken has been republished both in White 95–97 and Barcus 84–87.

3. *Republican* 15 Feb. 1822: 192; 25 Feb. 1825: 168.

4. *Republican* 11 Feb. 1825: 164; 1 Feb. 1822: 145, 147.

5. Not all Utilitarians were as adverse to poetry as Bentham; see, for example, Webb's comments on John Bowring's love of poetry in his "John Bowring and Unitarianism" 49–51.

6. Rufus Lyon, the dissenting Minister in George Eliot's *Felix Holt,* also holds that reading Shakespeare is antithetical to his religion.

7. This article was published a year before Cobbett lowered the price of *Political Register* and therefore was prohibitively expensive for many working-class readers. The article raises a number of points Cobbett refers to in later, less-expensive issues, and when he does discuss the subject later he assumes his readers are familiar with his thoughts on the subject.

Cobbett's curious views about potatoes were well known. In *Felix Holt* (1866), Eliot characterizes the general lack of political knowledge on the part of the citizens of Treby Magna by maintaining that they "saw little in Mr. Cobbett's *Weekly Register* except that he held eccentric views about potatoes" (128).

8. See also 20 Jan. 1816: 82; 17 Oct. 1829: 472–78, 505–6.

9. See chapter 1, "1816–29."

10. The extracts from Cowper appear on 28 June 1817: 733–36 and 4 Oct. 1817: 336. Defoe is found in 4 Oct. 1817: 337–41. The excerpt by Hazlitt (9 Aug.

1817: 78–82) is taken from his *Characters of Shakespeare's Plays* and is given, curiously for this periodical, without a word of introduction or commentary. The essay was memorable enough to earn careful appraisal in the pre-Chartist *Political Mirror;* see this chapter, "Views of Poetry, 1830–36."

11. Hone's comments on the poem are reprinted in Madden's *Robert Southey* 232. This was not Hone's only personal attack on Southey; on 17 June 1817 he published a poem by Edward Rushton that also condemned Southey's apostasy (638–40).

12. Madden publishes a part of Wooler's review that includes this quote in *Robert Southey* 239–40. Madden maintains that the review is anonymous, though there seems little question that Wooler, who wrote most of *Black Dwarf,* wrote this as well.

13. See chapter 2, "1816–29," for a fuller discussion of the "Blackneb" series, which contained both poetry and prose. For a discussion of Wooler's use of humor and the influence of Pope, see Hendrix, "Popular Humor and 'The Black Dwarf.'"

14. Barry Cornwall was the pen name of Brian Waller Proctor, a poet active since 1815. His *English Songs,* in which this poem originally appeared, was published in 1832 (Drabble 230–31).

15. The Honorable Mrs. Norton, a.k.a. Lady Stirling-Maxwell, is now best remembered as the original for Meredith's Diana in *Diana of the Crossways.* According to Saintsbury in *The Cambridge History of English Literature,* she "wrote much that has not worn well" (730).

16. For more on Macerone's work, see chapter 2, "1830–36."

17. The poem to which this is a preface is called "Small Service," intended to be sung to the now-forgotten air "Had I a Heart for Falsehood Framed." It was written by Linton, who wrote all six of the "Poems for the People" in the *Tribune* and could very likely have written this preface as well.

18. It should be noted that the poetry section of Kovalev's collection is heavily weighted toward poems originally in *Northern Star.* What is typical of the *Star* in this case, however, is typical of other Chartist periodicals as well.

19. The Chartists weren't the first to discover the song, of course. The song appeared in Carlile's *Republican* in two versions: one undoctored translated, according to Carlile, either by Sheridan or Holcroft, and one parody, beginning "Peruvians wake to glory!" (23 Aug. 1822: 387–88; 15 Dec. 1820: 576). Certainly many members of the working class were familiar with the republican French national anthem well before 1820.

20. As the *Labourer* was written and edited by both Jones and O'Connor and the articles are unsigned, there is some question as to who wrote these studies.

Considering Jones's passionate interest in foreign political movements and poetry, and that O'Connor had little interest in either, an attribution to Jones seems a safe one. See Weisser 150–54, on O'Connor's relative lack of interest in foreign movements.

21. The periodical in which this Longfellow poem appeared, however—the *Odd Fellow*—was not Chartist but was, F.B. Smith notes, a penny weekly newsletter "with a tiny circulation among independent friendly society lodges in London" (39).

22. I think it worthwhile to note again that calling Elliot, better known as "The Corn-Law Rhymer," a "working-class poet" is really a mistake. He was, after all, a factory owner. Reynolds, however, in this study clearly presents Elliott as a working-class hero.

23. Contrary to this critic's assertion, the *Pictorial Penny Shakespeare* was not the first "penny Shakespeare." An apparently short-lived *Penny Shakespeare* appeared on 8 Sept. 1832.

24. Bandiera is not identified as Massey in this article, but evidence elsewhere makes this attribution all but certain. Bandiera composed several poems for *Red Republican*, including one called "Song of the Red Republican," which is also signed G. M. A reviewer of Massey's verse in a later issue of this periodical notes that Massey is indeed the writer of that song.

25. Bamford also quotes Milton's "L'Allegro" twice in volume 2 of *Passages* (120, 324).

26. Carpenter's *Life and Times of John Milton* was also reviewed in *Northern Star* (2 June 1838: 7). Both Harney and Linton had a suspicion that the ruling class had an interest in supressing Milton's prose. As Linton writes: Milton's "prose writings have been most carefully kept out of sight, by his orthodox *admirers*" (*National* 23 Feb. 1839: 113).

27. Cobbett ignored Burns here, apparently to make his argument that much stronger: he hated Scott, of course, while elsewhere in the *Political Register* he praised Burns highly.

28. Doherty's claim is mistaken. Most versions of "The Irish Avatar" were indeed expurgated, including two versions in Leigh Hunt's *Examiner* (21 Apr. 1822: 252–53; 28 July: 473–74), but when Doherty published the poem two complete versions had already been published. The first appearance was in a twenty-copy private printing in 1821, by Moore on behalf of Byron; the second was published in John Murray's 1831 edition of Byron's collected works (Wise 2: 27–28; Beaty 166 n).

29. The only work by Shelley that is not overtly political that I have found in any working-class periodical is a landscape, "A Night Scene," in *Carpenter's Monthly Political Magazine* (Feb. 1832: 233).

30. *Black Dwarf* 28 Jan. 1824: 113; *Political Register* 23 Dec. 1826: 775; *Herald to the Trades' Advocate* 23 Oct. 1830: 79; *Republican* 26 Mar. 1831: 7; 25 Dec.: 209; *Poor Man's Advocate* 3 Mar. 1832: 56; *Democratic Review* July 1849: 42. The headnotes and quotes by Byron in *Northern Star* are far too numerous to list.

31. See, for example, an "Ode to the Memory of Lord Byron," by Imray, and "An Ode to the Memory of Percy Bysshe Shelley," by D.M., both in Carlile's *Lion* (10 Oct. 1828: 463–64; 13 Mar. 1829: 346–49), as well as "Byron Defended," by W. L. Warren and a "Sonnet to Byron," by George Tweddell, both in *Northern Star* (24 Jan. 1846: 3; 6 Oct. 1849: 3).

32. See, for example, J. H. M.'s "A Poem for the People" (*National Reformer* 6 Mar. 1847: 11) and "The Age We Live In" (27 Mar. 1847: 10–11).

33. Note, for example, the review, probably by Harney, in *Northern Star* 6 Sept. 1846: 3. Collins also notes this influence (13).

34. See also the lashings at imitators of Byron in the *Literary Beacon* (25 June 1832: 26; 2 July: 39, 43–45) and *Northern Star* (21 Oct. 1843: 3).

35. See *Chartist Circular* 20 Feb. 1841: 309–10; 27 Feb.: 314; 27 June: 397; 25 July: 413–14; 8 Aug.: 422.

36. *Northern Star* 24 Aug. 1844: 3; 5 July 1845: 3; 25 Oct.: 3.

37. That working-class journalists did not see Crabbe as a champion of their class does not mean that they did not publish and discuss his works. In fact there are discussions of him throughout this time, most of them positive. One critic in the *Schoolmaster* praises Crabbe's ability to depict the poor (13 Oct. 1832: 163–65). Jones especially liked Crabbe and quoted him often in *Notes to the People* as well as making him the first poet in the "Poets of England" series in that periodical. In publishing Crabbe, however, Jones noted that Crabbe had long been "much unknown" to most in his audience (19 Sept. 1851: 411).

38. *Literary Beacon* 2 July 1831: 33–36 (rpt. in *Poor Man's Guardian* 27 Aug. 1831: 60); *Northern Star* 24 Aug. 1844: 3; 5 Dec. 1846: 3; 22 May 1853: 3.

Chapter 5

1. 6 July 1850: 3; 2 Nov.: 3; 8 Mar. 1851: 3; 28 Feb. 1852: 7.

2. By "Bastile victim," Jones means an inhabitant of the poorhouse.

3. Again, Hobsbawm is describing a later ritual—international May Day, which dates to 1889—but his words apply equally to this procession.

4. For a few examples (among thousands) of reports of legal proceedings directed against members of the working class, see *Black Dwarf* 11 June 1817 (on Wooler's two trials); *Gauntlet* 26 May 1833; and *Poor Man's Guardian* 25 May 1833 (*Gauntlet* and *Guardian* providing partial transcripts of the inquest on a

policeman who had been stabbed while breaking up a working-class meeting at Cold Bath Fields); *Poor Man's Guardian* 29 March 1834, on "The Horrible Sentence!" imposed upon the Tolpuddle Martyrs; and *Northern Star* throughout late 1839 and early 1840 on the trials of many Chartist leaders, including Frost. Transcripts published as books include *A Verbatim Report of the Two Trials of T. J. W[ooler], Editor of the Black Dwarf, for Alleged Libels* . . . (1817); *The Three Trials of William Hone, for Publishing Three Parodies* . . . (1818)—a work which went through at least twenty editions; and *The Trial of Feargus O'Connor and Fifty Eight Others at Lancaster on a Charge of Sedition* . . . (1843).

5. The last quote appeared originally in the *London Alfred*, both the 29 Sept. and 6 Oct. 1819 issues. Curiously enough, "Orator" Hunt's nickname may have been coined by Southey; the first reference to the term may be in Southey's "Parliamentary Reform," in *Quarterly Review* 16 (1816), 248 (Belchem 59 n).

6. Epstein 90–92, 111–13; Belchem 60, quoting O'Connor from *Northern Star* 31 Mar. 1849.

Bibliography

Primary Sources

(All periodicals are weeklies unless otherwise noted.)

The Advocate; or, Artizans' and Labourers' Friend. Including a Review of Arts, Sciences, and Literature. Ed. John Ambrose Williams for the Printers' Protection Society. London: 16 Feb.–20 Apr. 1833.

The Agitator. Pub. John Sharp. Glasgow: 9 Mar.–13 Apr. 1833.

The Anti-Cobbett. "Written by Canning, Gifford, and Southey" (Webb, *British Working Class Reader* 53). London: 15 Feb.–5 Apr. 1817.

The Artizan's Miscellany, or Journal of Politics and Literature. Produced by "several members of the Working Classes." Edinburgh: 28 May–30 July 1831.

Berthold's Political Handkerchief. Pub. and ed. Henry Berthold. London: 3 Sept.–5 Nov. 1831.

Black Dwarf. Ed. Thomas Jonathan Wooler. London: 28 Jan. 1817–5 Nov. 1823.

The Boys' and Girls' Penny Magazine. Pub. W. Howden. London: 12 Sept. 1832–31 Mar. 1833.

The Bristol Job Nott, or Labouring Man's Friend. Pub. J. and W. Richardson. Bristol: 15 Dec. 1831–26 Dec. 1833.

The British Labourer's Protector, and Factory Child's Friend. Ed. George Stringer Bull. Leeds: 21 Sept. 1832–19 Apr. 1833.

British Liberator. London: 13 Jan.–3. Nov. 1833.

Cap of Liberty. Ed. James or John Griffin. London: 8 Sept. 1819–4 Jan. 1820.

Carpenter's London Journal. Ed. William Carpenter. London: 13 Feb.–30 Apr.(?) 1836 (Wiener, *Finding List* 8).

Carpenter's Monthly Political Magazine, a.k.a. *The Political Magazine*. Ed. William Carpenter. London: Sept. 1831–July 1833.

Chambers' Edinburgh Journal. Eds. William and Robert Chambers. Edinburgh and London: 4 Feb. 1832–31 Dec. 1853. Continued under other titles.

Champion of What Is True and Right and for the Good of All. Ed. Richard Oastler. Manchester: 10 Nov. 1849–n.d. [1850].

The Chartist Circular. Ed. W. Thomson, for the Universal Suffrage Central Committee for Scotland. Glasgow: 28 Sept. 1839–9 July 1842.

Cleave's Weekly Police Gazette. Pub. and ed. John Cleave. London: 11 Jan. 1834(?)–24 Sept. 1836 (Wiener, *Finding List* 10).

Cobbett's Magazine. Ed. John Cobbett. London: Jan. 1833–1834. Monthly.

The Conciliator, or Cotton Spinners' Weekly Journal. Ed. John Doherty. Manchester: 22 Nov.–13 Dec. 1828.

Co-operative Magazine, then *London Co-operative Magazine.* Organ of the London Co-operative Society. Produced by James Watson and William Lovett. London: Jan. 1826–Apr. 1830. Monthly.

The Co-operator. Ed. William King. Brighton: 1 May 1828–1 Aug. 1830.

Cooper's Journal: or, Unfettered Thinker and Plain Speaker for Truth, Freedom and Progress. Ed. Thomas Cooper. London: 5 Jan.–26 Oct. 1850.

The Cosmopolite. Eds. George Pilgrim, Richard Carlile, and Alexander Somerville. London: 10 Mar. 1832–23 Nov. 1833. Merged with the *Man.*

The Crisis. Ed. Robert Owen, Robert Dale Owen, and James E. "Shepherd" Smith. London: 14 Apr. 1832–20 Apr. 1833.

Deist's Magazine, or Theological Inquirer. Ed. Thomas Davison. London: 1820.

The Democratic Review of British and Foreign Politics, History, and Literature. Ed. George Julian Harney. London: June 1849–Sept. 1850. Monthly.

The Destructive and Poor Man's Conservative, then *The People's Conservative and Trades Union Gazette.* Pub. Henry Hetherington. Ed. James "Bronterre" O'Brien. London: 2 Feb.–7 Dec. 1833.

The Devil's Pulpit. Pub. Richard Carlile. London: 4 Mar. 1831–20 Jan. 1832.

Edinburgh Review. Eds. Francis Jeffrey (1802–29), Macvey Napier (1829–47), William Empson (1847–52), George Cornewall Lewis (1852–55), Henry Reeve (1855–95), and others after. Edinburgh: 1802–1929.

The English Chartist Circular and Temperance Record for England and Wales. Ed. James Harris. London: 3 Jan. 1841–Jan. 1843.

The English Republic. Ed. William James Linton. London, Leeds, Brantwood: 1851–55. Irregularly issued.

Every Man's Library of Republican and Philosophical Knowledge. Pub. Henry Hetherington, then James H. B. Lorymer. London: ca. June–Dec. 1832. No copies are presently known to exist (Wiener, *Finding List* 16–17).

Figaro in London. Pub. William Strange, eds. Gilbert à Beckett and Henry Mayhew. London: 10 Dec. 1831–17 Aug. 1839.

Fleet Papers. Being Letters . . . from Richard Oastler, with Occasional Communications from Friends. Ed. Richard Oastler. London: 2 Jan. 1841–18 Nov. 1843.

The Friend of the People. See *Red Republican.*

The Gauntlet; a Sound Republican Weekly Newspaper. Ed. Richard Carlile. London: 10 Feb. 1833–30 Mar. 1834.

Green Man; or Periodical Expositor. London: 31 Oct. 1818–24 July 1819. Then *Green Man; and Independent Weekly Expositor.* London: 21 Aug.–11 Sept. 1819.

Gorgon. Ed. John Wade. London: 23 May 1818–24 Apr. 1819.

The Halfpenny Magazine. Pub. and ed. R. Seton. London: 5 May–8 Sept. 1832.

The Half-Penny Magazine, or, Cheap Repository of Amusement and Instruction. Pub. and ed. John Glass. Edinburgh: n.d.; Wiener suggests 1832–33 (*Finding List* 20).

Herald of the Rights of Industry, and General Trades Union Advocate. Ed. John Doherty. Manchester: 8 Feb.–24 May 1834.

Herald to the Trades Advocate, and Co-operative Journal. Ed. John Tait(?) for the Trades Committee in Glasgow (Wiener, *Finding List* 21). Glasgow: 25 Sept. 1830–28 May 1831.

Hetherington's Twopenny Dispatch, and People's Police Register. Pub. Henry Hetherington. Ed. Bronterre O'Brien. London: 14 June 1834?–10 Sept. 1836 (Wiener, *Finding List* 21).

Hone's Reformists' Register. Ed. William Hone. 25 Jan.–25 Oct. 1817.

Illustrated People's Paper. London: Apr.–June 1854.

The Isis. A London Weekly Publication, Edited by the Lady of the Rotunda. Ed. Eliza Sharples. 11 Feb.–15 Dec. 1832.

John Bull's British Journal. Ed. William Benbow. London: 25 Feb.–11 Mar. 1821.

Johnstone's Edinburgh Magazine. Ed. John Johnstone. Edinburgh: Aug. 1833–Apr. 1834. Monthly.

The Labourer. Eds. Ernest Jones and Feargus O'Connor. London: Jan. 1847–Dec. 1848. Monthly.

The Ladies' Penny Gazette; or, Mirror of Fashion, and Miscellany of Instruction and Amusement. London: 27 Oct. 1832–1 Nov. 1834? (Wiener, *Finding List* 23).

Lancashire and Yorkshire Co-operator. See *Lancashire Co-operator.*

Lancashire Co-operator, then *Lancashire and Yorkshire Co-operator and Useful Classes' Advocate.* Ed. E. T. Craig. Manchester: 11 June 1831–4 Feb. 1832.

The Lawyer. A Legal Penny Magazine. Pub. Robert Fenn. London: 26 Jan.–16 Mar. 1833.

The Lincoln Cabinet. Pub. Robert Ely Leary. Lincoln: 1 Feb.–18 Apr. 1832.

The Lion. Ed. Richard Carlile. London: 4 Jan. 1828–25 Dec. 1829.

The Literary Beacon; a Guide to Books, the Drama, and the Fine Arts. Pubs. T. Griffiths, then Thomas Richardson, then Benjamin Steill. London: 18 June–24 Sept. 1832.

The Literary Test; a Liberal, Moral, and Independent Weekly Review of Books, the Stage, and the Fine Arts. The Friend of All; the Rich Man's Adviser, and the Poor Man's Advocate. Pub. Benjamin Steill. London: 1–28 Jan. 1832.

The London Alfred. Ed. Thomas Davison. London: 25 Aug.–17 Nov. 1819.

The London Democrat. Eds. J. C. Coombe and George Julian Harney. London: 13 Apr.–8 June 1839.

The London Phalanx. Produced by Hugh Doherty. London: 3 Apr. 1841–May 1843. Weekly, then monthly.

The London Policeman. Pub. Charles Penny. London: 6 July–28 Dec. 1833.

The Magazine of Interest. London: 31 Aug. 1833.

The Man. A Rational Advocate. Pub. and ed. Richard E. Lee. London: 7 July 1833–10 Aug. 1834.

Materials for Thinking; or, Facts and Opinions, Relating to Man in his Individual and Social Capacity. Extracted from the Works of Ancient and Modern Authors. By an Investigator. Compiled by John Taylor. London: ca. 1832–34 (Wiener, *Finding List* 31). Rpt. in book form, London: Darton, 1852.

McDouall's Chartist and Republican Journal. Ed. Peter Murray McDouall. Manchester: 3 Apr.–2 Oct. 1841.

The Medusa, or Penny Politician. Ed. Thomas Davison. London: 20 Feb. 1819–7 Jan. 1820.

Monthly Political Magazine. See *Carpenter's Monthly Political Magazine.*

The Movement, Anti-Persecution Gazette, and Register of Progress. Ed. George Jacob Holyoake and M. Q. Ryall. London: 16 Dec. 1843–2 Apr. 1845.

The National: A Library for the People. Ed. William James Linton. London: 5 Jan.–25 June 1839.

The National Association Gazette. Ed. John Humffreys Parry (Harrison and Thompson 105). London: 1 Jan.–30 July 1842.

The National Reformer and Manx Weekly Review of Home and Foreign Affairs. Ed. J. Bronterre O'Brien. Douglas, Isle of Man: Nov. 1844–29 May 1847.

The New Political Register. Ed. John Bell. London: 17 Oct. 1835–?.

The Northern Star. Eds. William Hill (1837–43), Joshua Hobson (1843–44), George Julian Harney (1845–50), William Rider and G. A. Fleming (1850–52). Produced by Feargus O'Connor (1837–52) and Harney (1852). Leeds, then London: 18 Nov. 1837–Apr. 24, 1852; 1 May–27 Nov. 1852 as *Star of Freedom.*

The Northern Tribune: A Periodical for the People. Pub. William James Linton; eds. Joseph Cowen and George Julian Harney. Newcastle-upon-Tyne: Jan. 1854–Mar. 1855. Monthly.

Notes to the People. Ed. Ernest Jones. London: 3 May 1851–2 May 1852. Originally known as *Poems and Notes to the People.*

The Odd Fellow. Pub. Henry Hetherington. Eds. William James Linton et al. London: 5 Jan. 1839–10 Dec. 1842.

The Oracle of Reason. Eds. George Jacob Holyoake et al. London: 6 Nov. 1841–2 Dec. 1843.

The Parterre: A Journal of Fiction, Poetry, History, Literature, and the Fine Arts. Ed. Horace Guilford. London: n.d [Aug. 1834?]–25 Feb. 1837.

The Penny Lancet, a Medical Magazine. Pub. George Berger. London: 3–14 Oct. 1832.

The Penny Magazine of the Society for the Diffusion of Useful Knowledge. Produced by Charles Knight for the SDUK. London: 31 Mar. 1832–27 Dec. 1845.

A Penny Shakespeare, Complete with Life, Glossary, etc. From the Best Editions; Being No. 1 of British Poets and Dramatists. London: 8 Sept. 1832–?.

The People. London: 19 Apr.–26 July 1817.

The People's Paper: Champion of Political Justice and Universal Right. Ed. Ernest Jones. London: 8 May 1852–4 Sept. 1858.

The People's Police Gazette, and Tradesman's Advertiser. Pub. Charles Penny. London: Aug. 1833?–3 May 1834 (Wiener, *Finding List* 42).

The People's Review of Literature and Progress. Eds. "Friends of Order and Progress" (George Jacob Holyoake et al.). London: Feb.–Apr. 1850. Monthly.

The People: Their Rights and Liberties, Their Duties and Their Interests. Pubs. Joseph Barker and James Watson. Wortley, near Leeds: 27 May 1848–25 Sept. 1852.

The Pioneer; or, Trades' Union Magazine. Ed. James Morrison. Birmingham: 7 Sept. 1833–5 July 1834.

The Plain Speaker. Eds. Thomas Cooper and Thomas Jonathan Wooler. London: 20 Jan.–22 Dec. 1849.

Poems and Notes to the People. See *Notes to the People.*

Political Letters and Pamphlets, Published for the Avowed Purpose of Trying with the Government, the Question of Law—Whether All Publications Containing News or Intelligence, However Limited in Quantity or Irregularly Issued, Are Liable to the Imposition of Fourpence. Ed. William Carpenter. London: 9 Oct. 1830–14 May 1831. Irregularly titled and issued.

The Political Mirror. Ed. John Bell. London: n.d. [six issues in 1837].

The Political Penny Magazine. Pub. S. Whaley, then Edward Morris. London: 3 Sept.–29 Oct. 1836.

The Political Register. Ed. William Cobbett. London: 16 Jan. 1802–12 Sept. 1835.

The Political Soldier. A Paper for the Army and the People. Eds. Alexander Somerville, then Richard Carlile. London: 7 Dec. 1833–4 Jan. 1834.

The Political Unionist. Ed. William Carpenter. London: 30 June–7 July 1832.

The Poor Man's Advocate. Eds. John Doherty and James Turner. Manchester: 7

Jan. 1832–5 Jan. 1833, 11 Oct. 1833–6 Dec. 1834. The first two issues of this periodical were called the *Workman's Expositor.*

The Poor Man's Guardian. A Weekly Newspaper for the People, Established Contrary to "Law" to Try the Powers of "Might" against "Right." Pub. Henry Hetherington. Eds. Thomas Mayhew, James "Bronterre" O'Brien, and "possibly Julian Hibbert" (Weiner, *Finding List* 46). London: 9 July 1831–26 Dec. 1835.

The Prompter. Ed. Richard Carlile. London: 13 Nov. 1830–12 Nov. 1831.

Punchinello! or Sharps, Flats, and Naturals! A Family Gazette of Fun, Fashion, Literature, and the Drama. Pubs. Thomas Griffiths and Benjamin Steill. Ed. Thomas Hood? (Wiener, *Finding List* 48). London: 20–27 Jan. 1832.

Quarterly Review. Eds. William Gifford (1809–25), John Taylor Coleridge (1825–26), John Lockhart (1826–53), Whitwell Elwin (1853–60), and others after. Edinburgh: Feb. 1809–1967.

The Radical; later known as *Radical Reformer.* Ed. James H. B. Lorymer. London: 20 Aug. 1831–26 Jan. 1832.

The Radical Reformer's Gazette. Ed. A. Dallas. Glasgow: 17 Nov. 1832–16 Feb. 1833.

The Reasoner and Statistical Journal. Ed. Thomas Wooler. London: 2 Jan.–16 Apr. 1808.

The Reasoner, and Herald of Progress. Pub. James Watson. Ed. George Jacob Holyoake. London: 3 June 1846–30 June 1861.

Red Republican. Ed. George Julian Harney. London: 22 June–20 Nov. 1850. Then *Friend of the People.* London: 14 Dec. 1850–26 July 1851, 7 Feb.–24 Apr. 1852.

The Republican. Ed. William T. Sherwin. London: 23 Feb.–30 Mar. 1817. Then *Sherwin's Weekly Political Register.* Pub. Richard Carlile. Ed. William T. Sherwin. London: 5 Apr. 1817–20 Aug. 1819. Then *The Republican.* Pub. and ed. Richard Carlile. London: 27 Aug. 1819–29 Dec. 1826.

The Republican; or, Voice of the People. Pub. Henry Hetherington. Ed. James H. B. Lorymer. London: 26 Mar. 1831–27 Apr. 1834.

Reynolds's Political Instructor. Ed. George W. M. Reynolds. London: 10 Nov. 1849–11 May 1850.

The Schoolmaster, and Edinburgh Weekly Magazine. Ed. John Johnstone. Edinburgh: 4 Aug. 1832–29 June 1833. Succeeded by *Johnstone's Edinburgh Magazine.*

The Scottish Trades' Union Gazette. Ed. Alexander Campbell. Glasgow: 14 Sept.–14 Dec. 1833. Succeeded by the *Tradesman.*

Shadgett's Weekly Review of Cobbett, Wooler, Sherwin, and other Democratical and Infidel Writers. London: 1818–19.

Sherwin's Weekly Political Register. See *The Republican.*

A Slap at the Church. Ed. John Cleave and William Carpenter. Illus. by George Cruikshank. London: 21 Jan.–12 May 1832.

The Spirit of the Union. Glasgow: 30 Oct. 1819–8 Jan. 1820.

The Sunday Herald. Pub. G. Cowie. 15 July–Oct. ? 1832 (Wiener, *Finding List* 56).

The Ten Hour's Advocate, and Journal of Literature and Art. Pub. for Joseph Mulleneaux, secretary to the Lancashire Central Short Time Committee. Ed. Philip Grant. Manchester: 26 Sept. 1846–12 June 1847.

Theological Enquirer and Polemical Magazine. Pub. and ed. George Cannon. London: Mar.–Sept. 1815. Monthly.

The Trades Free Press. See *The Trades Newspaper.*

The Tradesman. Ed. Alexander Campbell. Glasgow: 28 Dec. 1833–31 May 1834. Successor to the *Scottish Trades' Union Gazette.*

The Trades Newspaper and Mechanics' Weekly Journal. Produced by John Gast. Ed. J. C. Robertson. "Governed by a committee of the [London] trades" (E. P. Thompson, 853 n, 854, 854 n). London: 17 July 1825–22 July 1827. Then *The Trades Free Press.* London: 29 July 1827–16 Aug. 1828. Then *Weekly Free Press.* Ed. William Carpenter. London: 23 Aug. 1828–19 Mar. 1831.

The True Sun. Eds. John Bell and William Carpenter. London: 14 Mar. 1832–25 July 1836.

The Truth! Pub. William Strange. London: 22–29 Aug. 1832.

Union. Pub. Richard Carlile. London: 26 Nov. 1831–28 Jan. 1832.

The United Trades' Co-operative Journal. Ed. John Doherty for the National Association for the Protection of Labour. Manchester: 6 Mar.–2 Oct. 1830.

The Voice of the Country, and General Provincial Politician. Ed. Thomas Noble. London: July 1832.

The Voice of the People. Ed. John Doherty. Manchester: 31 Dec. 1830–24 Sept. 1831.

The Voice of the West Riding. Pub. and ed. Joshua Hobson. Huddersfield: 1 June 1833–7 June 1834.

The Weekly Free Press. See *The Trades Newspaper.*

Weekly True Sun. Partially ed. William Carpenter (Wiener, *War* 141). London: 10 Feb. 1833–29 Dec. 1839.

Westminster Review. Eds. John Bowring and Henry Southern (1824–28), William Molesworth (1836–37), John Stuart Mill (editor in all but name, 1837–40), William E. Hickson (1840–51), John Chapman (1851–94), and others after. London: Jan. 1824–Jan. 1914.

The Whig-Dresser. Pub. G. Cowie. London: 5 Jan.–23 Mar. 1833.

White Dwarf. Ed. Gibbons Merle "on a subsidy from the Home Secretary," Sidmouth (Webb, *British Working Class Reader* 54). London: 29 Nov. 1817–28 Apr. 1818.

Wooler's British Gazette. Ed. Thomas Jonathan Wooler. Manchester: 3 Jan. 1819–14 Dec. 1823.

Workman's Expositor. See *Poor Man's Advocate.*

Secondary Sources

Altick, Richard. *The English Common Reader: A Social History of the Mass Reading Public, 1800–1900.* Chicago: University of Chicago Press, 1957.

Aspinall, Arthur. *Politics and the Press, ca. 1780–1850.* London: Home & Van Thal, 1949.

Bamford, Samuel. *Passages from the Life of a Radical.* 2 vols. London: T. Fisher Unwin, 1893.

Barcus, James E., ed. *Shelley: The Critical Heritage.* London and Boston: Routledge & Kegan Paul, 1975.

Baylen, Joseph O., and Norbert J. Gossman. *Biographical Dictionary of Modern British Radicals.* 2 vols. Sussex: Harvester Press, 1984.

Beaty, Frederick L. *Byron the Satirist.* Dekalb: Northern Illinois University Press, 1985.

Belchem, John. *"Orator" Hunt: Henry Hunt and Working-Class Radicalism.* Oxford: Clarendon, 1985.

Benbow, William. *Grand National Holiday, and Congress of the Productive Classes.* London: Benbow, 1831.

Birrell, T. A. *"The Political Register*: Cobbett and English Literature." *English Studies* 45 (1964): 214–19.

Bromwich, David. *A Choice of Inheritance: Self and Community from Edmund Burke to Robert Frost.* Cambridge, MA: Harvard University Press, 1989.

Bulwer, Edward George. *Eugene Aram.* London: Colburn & Bently, 1832.

Burnett, John. *Destiny Obscure.* Harmondsworth: Penguin, 1984.

Byron, George Gordon. *The Complete Poetical Works of Byron.* Boston: Houghton Mifflin, 1933.

Carlile, Richard. *The Life of Thomas Paine.* London: Carlile, 1819 [1820].

Cazamian, Louis Francis. *The Social Novel in England, 1830–1850: Dickens, Disraeli, Mrs. Gaskell, Kingsley.* London: Routledge & Kegan Paul, 1973.

Clare, John. *John Clare's Autobiographical Writings.* Ed. Eric Robinson. Oxford: Oxford University Press, 1983.

Cobbett, William. *A Grammar of the English Language.* 1819. London: A. Cobbett, 1838.

Cole, G. D. H. *Chartist Portraits.* London: Macmillan, 1965.

———. *The Life of Robert Owen.* 1925. London: Archon, 1966.

Collins, Philip. *Dickens: The Critical Heritage.* London: Routledge & Kegan Paul, 1971.

———. *Thomas Cooper, the Chartist: Byron and the "Poets of the Poor."* Nottingham Byron Lecture, 1969. Nottingham: Nottingham University Press, 1969.

Cooper, Thomas. *The Life of Thomas Cooper.* 1872. Leicester: Leicester University Press, 1971.

Dickens, Charles. *Hard Times.* 1854. Oxford: Oxford University Press, 1989.

Drabble, Margaret, ed. *The Oxford Companion to English Literature.* 5th ed. Oxford: Oxford University Press, 1985.

Driver, Cecil. *Tory Radical: The Life of Richard Oastler.* New York: Oxford University Press, 1946.

Eagleton, Mary, and David Pierce. *Attitudes to Class in the English Novel from Walter Scott to David Storey.* London: Thames & Hudson, 1979.

Eagleton, Terry. *Literary Theory: An Introduction.* Minneapolis: University of Minnesota Press, 1983.

Eliot, George. *Felix Holt, the Radical.* 1866. Harmondsworth: Penguin, 1972.

Engels, Friedrich. *The Condition of the Working Class in England in 1844.* London: George Allen & Unwin, 1892.

Epstein, James. *The Lion of Freedom: Feargus O'Connor and the Chartist Movement, 1832–42.* London and Canberra: Croom Helm, 1982.

Forster, John. *The Life of Charles Dickens.* 2 vols. London: J. M. Dent, 1927.

Frye, Northrop. *The Secular Scripture: A Study of the Structure of Romance.* Cambridge, MA: Harvard University Press, 1976.

Gallagher, Catherine. *The Industrial Reformation of English Literature.* Chicago and London: University of Chicago Press, 1985.

Grugel, Lee E. *George Jacob Holyoake: A Study in the Evolution of a Victorian Radical.* Philadelphia: Porcupine, 1976.

Gutteridge, Joseph. *The Autobiography of Joseph Gutteridge. Master and Artisan in Victorian England.* Ed. Valerie E. Chancellor. New York: Augustus M. Kelley, 1969.

Hambrick, Margaret. *A Chartist's Library.* London and New York: Mansell, 1986.

Harrison, J. F. C., and Dorothy Thompson. *Bibliography of the Chartist Movement.* Hassocks, England: Harvester, 1978.

Hawthorne, Nathaniel. *The House of the Seven Gables.* 1851. New York: Readers League of America, 1930.

Hendrix, Richard. "Popular Humor and *The Black Dwarf.*" *Journal of British Studies* 16 (1976–77): 108–28.

Himmelfarb, Gertrude. *The Idea of Poverty: England in the Early Industrial Age.* New York: Vintage, 1985.

Hobsbawm, Eric. *Workers: Worlds of Labour.* New York: Pantheon, 1984.

Hirsch, E. D. Jr. *Cultural Literacy: What Every American Needs to Know.* Updated and expanded ed. New York: Vintage, 1987.

Hollis, Patricia. *The Pauper Press: A Study in Working-Class Radicalism of the 1830s.* London: Oxford University Press, 1970.

Houston, R. A. *Scottish Literacy and the Scottish Identity: Illiteracy and Society in Scotland and Northern England, 1600–1800.* Cambridge: Cambridge University Press, 1985.

Hovell, Mark. *The Chartist Movement.* 1918. New York: Augustus M. Kelley, 1967.

James, Louis. *Fiction for the Working Man, 1830–1850.* Oxford: Oxford University Press, 1963.

Johnson, Edgar. *Sir Walter Scott: The Great Unknown.* New York: Macmillan, 1970.

Kirby, R. G., and A. E. Musson. *The Voice of the People: John Doherty, 1798–1854: Trade Unionist, Radical, and Factory Reformer.* Manchester: Manchester University Press, 1975.

Kitson Clark, G. S. R. "The Romantic Element, 1830–1850." *Studies in Social History: A Tribute to G. M. Trevelyan.* Ed. J. H. Plumb. London: Longmans, Green, 1955. 211–39.

Kovalev, Y. V., ed. *Anthology of Chartist Literature.* Moscow: n.p., 1956.

———. "The Literature of Chartism." Trans. J. C. Dumbreck and Michael Beresford. Translated introduction to *Anthology of Chartist Literature.* *Victorian Studies* 2 (1957): 117–38.

Laqueur, Thomas W. "Working-Class Demand and the Growth of English Elementary Education, 1750–1850." In Stone, *Schooling and Society* 192–205.

Lukács, Georg. *The Historical Novel.* London: Merlin, 1962.

McCalman, Iain. "Popular Irreligion in Early Victorian England: Infidel Preachers and Radical Theatricality in 1830s London." *Religion and Irreligion in Victorian Society.* Eds. R. W. Davis and R. J. Helmstadter. London: Routledge, 1992. 51–67.

———. *Radical Underworld: Prophets, Revolutionaries and Pornographers in London, 1795–1840.* Cambridge, England: Cambridge University Press, 1988.

Madden, Lionel. *Robert Southey: The Critical Heritage.* London and Boston: Routledge & Kegan Paul, 1972.

Manning, D. J. *The Mind of Jeremy Bentham.* London: Longmans, Green, 1968.

Martineau, Harriet. *A Manchester Strike.* London: C. Fox, 1832.

Marx, Karl, and Friedrich Engels. *Selected Correspondence: 1846–1895.* Marxist Library 29. New York: International Publishers, 1942.

Mayhew, Henry. *London Labour and the London Poor.* 1851–52. Harmondsworth: Penguin, 1985.

Mill, John Stuart. "Bentham." *Bentham and Coleridge.* By Mill. 1838. London: Chatto and Windus, 1950.

Mitchell, Jack. "Aesthetic Problems of the Development of the Proletarian-Revolutionary Novel." *Marxists on Literature.* Ed. David Craig. Harmondsworth: Penguin, 1975. 245–66.

Paine, Thomas. *The Age of Reason*, part one. 1794. *The Thomas Paine Reader.* Ed.

Michael Foot and Isaac Kramnick. Harmondsworth: Penguin, 1987. 399–451.

Peyrouton, N. C. "Dickens and the Chartists." *Dickensian* 60 (1964): 78–88, 152–61.

Place, Francis. *The Autobiography of Francis Place.* Ed. Mary Thale. Cambridge: Cambridge University Press, 1972.

Plummer, Alfred. *Bronterre: A Political Biography of Bronterre O'Brien, 1804–1864.* London: George Allen & Unwin, 1971.

Prothero, I. J. *Artisans and Politics in Early Nineteenth-Century London: John Gast and His Times.* Folkestone, England: Dawson, 1979.

Read, Donald, and Eric Glasgow. *Feargus O'Connor: Irishman and Chartist.* London: Edward Arnold, 1961.

Rogers, Frederick. *Labour, Life and Literature: Some Memories of Sixty Years.* Brighton, England: Harvester, 1973.

Rowell, George. *The Victorian Theatre: A Survey.* Oxford: Clarendon, 1956.

Saintsbury, George. "The Minor Poets." *The Cambridge History of English Literature.* Vol. 13. 1907. New York: Macmillan, 1932. 15 Vols.

Sanderson, Michael. "Literacy and Social Mobility in the Industrial Revolution in England." *Past and Present* Aug. 1972: 75–104.

Saville, John, ed. *Ernest Jones: Chartist.* London: Lawrence & Wishart, 1952.

Schoyen, A. R. *The Chartist Challenge: A Portrait of George Julian Harney.* New York: Macmillan, 1958.

Scheckner, Peter, ed. *An Anthology of Chartist Poetry.* Rutherford: Fairleigh Dickinson University Press, 1989.

Schwarzkopf, Jutta. *Women in the Chartist Movement.* New York: St. Martin's Press, 1991.

Scott, Walter. *The Black Dwarf, and A Legend of Montrose.* Originally pub. under the pseudonym "Jedediah Cleishbotham," as vol. 1 of *Tales of My Landlord.* Edinburgh: Blackwood; London: John Murray, 1816. London: J. M. Dent and Sons, 1906.

Shaaban, Bouthaina. "Shelley in the Chartist Press." *Keats–Shelley Memorial Bulletin* 34 (1984): 41–60.

Shelley, Percy Bysshe. *The Complete Poetical Works of Percy Bysshe Shelley.* Vol. 2. Oxford: Clarendon, 1975.

Sherwin, Thomas. *Memoirs of the Late Thomas Paine.* London: Carlile, 1819.

Smiles, Samuel. *Self Help.* 1858. London: Murray, 1958.

Smith, F. B. *Radical Artisan: William James Linton, 1812–97.* Manchester: Manchester University Press, 1973.

Smith, Olivia. *The Politics of Language, 1791–1819.* Oxford: Clarendon, 1984.

Somerville, Alexander. *The Autobiography of a Working Man, by "One Who Has Whistled at the Plough."* London: Charles Gilpin, 1848.

Spater, George. *William Cobbett: The Poor Man's Friend.* 2 vol. Cambridge: Cambridge University Press, 1982.

Spufford, Margaret. *Small Books and Pleasant Histories.* Athens, GA: University of Georgia Press, 1981.

Stang, Richard. *The Theory of the Novel in England, 1850–1870.* New York: Columbia University Press, 1959.

Stephen, Leslie. *The English Utilitarians.* New York: Peter Smith, 1950.

Stevens, Albert K. "Milton and Chartism." *Philological Quarterly* 12 (1933): 377–88.

Stewart, Robert MacKenzie. *Henry Brougham, 1778–1868: His Public Career.* London: Bodley Head, 1986.

Stone, Lawrence. "Literacy and Education in England 1640–1900." *Past and Present* Feb. 1969: 69–139.

———. *Schooling and Society: Studies in the History of Education.* Baltimore: Johns Hopkins University Press, 1976.

Taylor, John Tinnon. *Early Opposition to the English Novel: The Popular Reaction from 1760 to 1830.* New York: King's Crown Press, 1943.

Thompson, Dorothy. *The Chartists.* New York: Pantheon, 1984.

Thompson, E. P. *Customs in Common.* New York: New Press, 1991.

———. *The Making of the English Working Class.* 1963. Harmondsworth: Penguin, 1968.

Vicinus, Martha. *The Industrial Muse: A Study of Nineteenth-Century British Working-Class Literature.* London: Croom Helm, 1974.

Vincent, David. *Bread, Knowledge, and Freedom: A Study of Nineteenth-Century Working Class Autobiography.* London and New York: Methuen, 1982.

———, ed. *Testaments of Radicalism: Memoirs of Working Class Politicians, 1790–1885.* London: Europa, 1977.

Watt, Ian. *The Rise of the Novel: Studies in Defoe, Richardson, and Fielding.* Berkeley: University of California Press, 1957.

Webb, R. K. *The British Working Class Reader, 1790–1848: Literacy and Social Tension.* London: George Allen & Unwin, 1955.

———. "John Bowring and Unitarianism." *Utilitas* 4 (1992): 43–79.

———. "Working Class Readers in Victorian England." *English Historical Review* 65 (1950): 333–51.

Weisser, Henry. *British Working-Class Movements and Europe, 1815–1848.* Manchester: Manchester University Press, 1975.

White, Newman Ivey. *The Unextinguished Hearth: Shelley and His Contemporary Critics.* New York: Octagon, 1966.

Wickwar, William H. *The Struggle for the Freedom of the Press, 1819–1832.* London: George Allen & Unwin, 1928.

Wiener, Joel H. *A Descriptive Finding List of Unstamped British Periodicals, 1830–1836.* London: Bibliographical Society, 1970.

———. *Radicalism and Freethought in Nineteenth-Century Britain: The Life of Richard Carlile.* Westport, CT: Greenwood, 1983.

———. *The War of the Unstamped: The Movement to Repeal the British Newspaper Tax, 1830–1836.* Ithaca: Cornell University Press, 1969.

———. *William Lovett.* Manchester: Manchester University Press, 1989.

Williams, Raymond. *Cobbett.* Oxford: Oxford University Press, 1983.

Wise, Thomas James. *A Bibliography of the Writings in Verse and Prose of George Gordon Noel, Baron Byron.* London: Dawson's, 1963.

Wolff, Michael, John North, and Dorothy Deering. *The Waterloo Directory of Victorian Periodicals, 1824–1900.* n.p.: Wilfrid Laurier University Press, n.d.

Woodring, Carl. *Politics in English Romantic Poetry.* Cambridge, MA: Harvard University Press, 1970.

Index